LITERATURE
&RELIGION

LITERATURE
&RELIGION

◆

PASCAL GRYPHIUS LESSING HÖLDERLIN NOVALIS KIERKEGAARD DOSTOYEVSKY KAFKA

WALTER JENS HANS KÜNG

Translated by
Peter Heinegg

PARAGON HOUSE
New York

First American edition, 1991

Published in the United States by Paragon House

Paragon House
90 Fifth Avenue
New York, NY 10011

Copyright © 1991 by Paragon House

Originally published in German under the title *Dichtung
und Religion*. Copyright © 1985 by Kindler Verlag GmbH, Munchen

Designed by Jules Perlmutter/Off-Broadway Graphics

Library of Congress Cataloging-in-Publication Data

Jens, Walter, 1923–
    [Dichtung und Religion. English]
    Literature and religion : Pascal, Gryphius, Lessing, Hölderlin,
Novalis, Kierkegaard, Dostoyevsky, Kafka / Walter Jens, Hans Küng ;
translated by Peter Heinegg. — 1st American ed.
        p.   cm.
    Translation of: Dichtung und Religion.
    Includes bibliographical references.
    ISBN 1-55778-283-0 (pbk.)
    ISBN 1-55778-282-2
    1. Religion in literature. I. Küng, Hans, 1928–   . II. Title.
PN49.J4613   1990
809'.93382—dc20   90-33061
                                                                          CIP

Manufactured in the United States of America

CONTENTS

ACKNOWLEDGMENTS

I could venture to operate in a field that was at best half-familiar only because I was able to count on threefold help: first of all, from the scholarship mentioned in the Bibliography (especially Hans-Henrik Krummacher's articles on Gryphius, in particular the studies of the Perikope sonnets and the *Passionslieder*; Horst Rumpf's far too little-known dissertation on "The Meaning of the Figure of Christ in the later Hölderlin"; as well as the introductions by Hans-Joachim Mahl, Richard Samuel, and Gerhard Schulz in their edition of the Novalis).

Second, I want to thank my colleagues in Tübingen, who, whenever I needed it, were there for support: Wilfried Barner, Jochen Schmidt (for Hölderlin), and Ludolf Müller (who introduced me to Dostoyevsky's novels, with their Christian "ductus").

Third, I acknowledge the help that I got, in many cases a long time ago, from scholars who are no longer alive and whom I now thankfully remember: Romano Guardini, the analyst of Pascal, Hölderlin, and Dostoyevsky, whose private dispute with Walter F. Otto about God and the gods I was there to witness; Ewald Wasmuth in Tübingen, who shaped my reading of Pascal; Steffen Steffensen in Copenhagen, who commented with Danish wit and stupendous erudition on the art of Kierkegaardian paradox in his study; and finally Heinz Politzer in Berkeley, who gave me an informal lecture on Kafka's Jewish poetic theology.

Walter Jens

———————◆———————

Admittedly, this undertaking was full of risks for me on a number of counts. As a theologian, I had to betake myself to nontheological territory, and with each of the authors (about whom a small library had already been written) an immense abundance of pertinent literature had to be worked up. Nevertheless, I ventured to do the job because in our Institute for Ecumenical Research the area of theology and literature, which is all too often neglected in academe, has for some time now found a home.

My collaboration with Walter Jens began when he read through the manuscript of *On Being a Christian* with critical approval. We both encouraged our doctoral student Karl-Josef Kuschel, who is now in charge of research in this field at our institute. Kuschel has just now published twelve interviews with contemporary writers on the relation between literature and religion (*Because We Don't Feel Quite at Home Here on Earth*, 1985), which superbly complement our efforts with a view of present-day literature. All of us "went public" at the international symposium on "Theology and Literature: Possibilities and Limits of a Dialogue in the Twentieth Century," which was held in May 1984 at the University of Tübingen with roughly seventy writers, literary critics, and theologians taking part.

I myself was somewhat prepared for this study as a result of my books, *Does God Exist?* (in connection with Pascal and the seventeenth century) and *God Made Man* (in connection with Lessing and the Enlightenment, Hegel, Hölderlin, and Novalis). I was able to work my way intensively into the topic by means of the seminar I gave on Kierkegaard and Dostoyevsky with Karl-Josef Kuschel. I would like to express to him here my heartfelt thanks. The participation of our Tübingen colleague Ludolf Müller in the seminar enabled me to get a better understanding of Dostoyevsky.

For understanding the authors and putting them in historical context, I got important help from the most recent hermeneutical and theoretical discussions about paradigms and paradigm changes in the history of theology, as voiced in the international symposium on "A New Paradigm in Theology?" This was put on in 1983 by our institute in conjunction with the University of Chicago (see the volume *Whither Theology? On the Way to a New Paradigm*, 1984, edited by David Tracy and myself).

Hans Küng

PREFACE

Literature and Religion: "Ah, Louisa, stop . . . that's too broad a field," as Fontane's jovial skeptic, Herr von Briest, would have said, and, in his usual way, to Frau von Briest's distress, he would have worried about the "continual ambiguities" that have characterized the relations between poetry and faith since the beginning of the modern period.

Ambiguity, ambivalence, discordant unity, reciprocal illumination, dialectic, played out between heaven and earth (hell, too, sometimes puts in an appearance): a relationship as tense as it is fruitful; as beneficial to literature as it is to religion; sometimes edifying, sometimes provocative, indeed occasionally shocking. This is the subject to be elucidated in the sixteen pieces that follow. These essays aim to reconnoitre a territory still largely unexplored, to offer a bird's-eye view of the landscape. In the process, certain areas and epochs will be illustrated with the help of exemplary leading figures, who in turn will be clarified by descriptions of individual works. Macroanalysis will be complemented by microanalysis, historical overview by interpretation of details, and major themes by significant specifics. In general, the theologian will take the view from Olympus; the literature professor will take the (no less rewarding) worm's perspective. (Every now and then role switching will not only be allowed, but welcome.)

The goal of these essays, which are based on lectures and whose oral character has been preserved, is to point to the constants and variants in the great conversation that writers since the seventeenth century have been having about the possibility and limits of faith in an age of enlightenment. This conversation, in fact, has been more radical, consistent, and hence often more revealing than the one carried on by theologians and professors of literature.

What follows in *Literature and Religion* is designed to show how the monologues of the poets, those exemplary witnesses, have looked, and what sort of dialogues have gone on across the ages. Here we have the exchanges among Kierkegaard, Lessing, and Pascal, and those among Kafka, Kierkegaard, and Dostoyevsky. Our essays are meant literally as "tries." They have grown out of long years of conversation between colleagues. Our aim is to challenge readers to think afresh about literature and religion. At the same time, we wish to invite writers and theologians to look honestly at each other—and to learn. As the founder of the University of Tübingen said some five hundred years ago, *Attempto*: Let the attempt be risked.

Walter Jens / Hans Küng
Tübingen, March 1985

BLAISE PASCAL

◆

PENSÉES

HANS KÜNG

◆

Religion
at the
Dawn of Modernity

"**W**hat happened to religion in the modern period? What happened to modernity because of religion?" Thus we postmoderns wonder, heirs of the Enlightenment now grown insecure. *How could religion have come to this?* Once the queen, now the maid, the second-class citizen, begging for a patient hearing in the academy and the world; first neglected, then ignored, finally despised, cursed, and persecuted. And so we ask, doubting which way to take between banal unbelief and neoromantic piety, hesitating on all points between demythologizing and remythologizing. Perhaps something *has* gone awry in the history of modernity, which self-consciously equated itself with human progress. That progress was, in the first analysis, hypostatized into the Most High, the force praised, in word and above all in deed, as the Almighty.

It is neither accidental nor arbitrary that these lectures begin with Pascal and end with Kafka. We are dealing with a diagnosis of modernity in the strict sense—the modernity that, as far as intellectual history goes, begins with the crisis of the seventeenth century, with Descartes and Pascal, and ends with the crisis around the time of the First World War, with Nietzsche and Kafka. Between Pascal and Kafka, we shall study key works of great writers, thereby sketching out a survey of the complex, vital,

and contradictory history of religion in modern times. With
Gryphius—a contemporary of Pascal—we explore the Reformation thinking that was still deeply entrenched in the Germany
of the Thirty Years War. With Lessing, we meet the Enlightenment, which had no more brilliant representative in Germany,
but which by the end of the eighteenth century found itself under
increasingly violent attacks from classicism and romanticism. Romanticism will be represented here by Hölderlin and Novalis. The
actual crisis of modernity, of course, was yet to be. Kierkegaard
and Dostoyevsky alert us to it as early as the nineteenth century,
but only in the twentieth century would it fully take effect. If the
name of Pascal stands for the dawn of modernity, then the name
of Kafka stands for its breakdown.

Three hundred years ago, the world still seemed in perfect
order; the state was Christian, France was Catholic, and every
afternoon *le Roi de France* attended a solemn mass. Every Sunday, the whole court went to church. Around that time Blaise
Pascal (1623–1662) wrote in one of his countless jottings, fragments, or rough drafts later called *Pensées* (Thoughts): "People
despise religion, they hate it, and fear that it might be true"
(*Pensées*, Léon Brunschvicq, fragment #187—translations of Pascal taken from the E. P. Dutton edition, W. F. Trotter, trans.).
He had planned to turn those "Pensées"—around two dozen
packets or paper bags of them were found after his death—into
a large-scale apologia "on the truth of the Christian religion."

Around the middle of the seventeenth century, France still
greatly prized order, authority, and discipline, the church, hierarchy, and dogma. But critical minds, *les esprits forts*, had long
since noticed that, behind the glittering façade of establishment,
religion was unscrupulously exploited by absolute rulers and their
devoted princes of the church to advance their own power and
splendor. There was a threat of a sharp cooling off in religion;
indeed away on the horizon a general cultural and political revolutionary storm was brewing: a fundamental transformation of
convictions, values, and ways of behaving—what we nowadays
call a new paradigm, a *paradigm change*.

"Cleopatra's nose: had it been shorter, the whole face of the
earth would have been transformed" (#162). Pascal was right.

The course of world history is often shaped by trifles. And yet history is shaped not only by the unique "great moments of mankind" (Stefan Zweig), but by the great "whole constellations" (paradigms) and "world-shaking transitions" (Goethe) that are in no sense accidental.

In Pascal's day, for the first time in the history of Christianity there were impulses toward a new paradigm, toward a new basic model of the world, society, the church, and theology. These fresh impulses came not, in the first instance, from inside, from theology and the church, but from outside. They came from a society that was rapidly turning worldly, and hence seeking emancipation from the tutelage of the church and theology. This was a complex, all-embracing process of secularization and liberation that had roots going back to the High Middle Ages. It became visible in the Renaissance, which rejoiced in the here and now, and humanism, which rejected asceticism—but it did not forcefully break through until the seventeenth century.

This breakthrough of *epochal proportions* was no less of a historical divide than the Reformation period. Up till the seventeenth century, Western culture, whether Catholic or Protestant, had been essentially shaped and penetrated by Christianity. But now an intellectual life developed that was independent of the church—and since the church had adopted a fortress mentality—increasingly opposed to it. The adjective "Copernican" has come to suggest a simultaneous "scientific and philosophical revolution." The medieval unity of thought had begun to crumble. Man as an individual moved to the center of the stage, and at the same time the horizon of the human expanded nearly into infinity—geographically through the discoveries of new continents and physically through the telescope and the microscope. What would emerge from all this? Humanity's *grandeur*—or its *misère*?

In the brilliance of his genius, Blaise Pascal—together with René Descartes—represents this modern mode of intelligence in France's *grand siècle*. In his personality and his work, he embodies precisely those powers that would increasingly shape the next epoch of the world, and then, of course, lead to the crisis posed by science, technology, and industrialization.

The first great power in the coming modern world was *science*. By the age of sixteen, Pascal was already a leading mathematician of his day. He was one of the founders of the theory of probability, and did crucial foundational work in the study of integers and differential equations. Against the old myth that nature abhors a vacuum, he demonstrated the existence of empty space, and at the same time formulated the theory of hydrostatic equilibrium. As an experimenter, Pascal was far superior to his contemporary Descartes. He gave visual proof to his age of what the new inductive science, based on mathematics and experimentation, was capable of achieving. Knowledge *is* power, and modern science (according to the vision of Francis Bacon, the English politician and philosopher, writing in "The New Atlantis" a generation before Pascal) would allow the human race to satisfy all its needs without clash or collision. This constructive politics with the help of scientific and technical experts was leading to universal peace.

The second great power of modernity was *technology*. Pascal was nineteen when he invented the first operative calculating machine in France (Schickhard, a professor at Tübingen, invented his in 1623). With his invention of the hydraulic pump, Pascal put his theory of hydrostatic equilibrium to practical use. As the engineer and builder of one of the first computers, he could no doubt only surmise how empirical knowledge turned into technology would fundamentally alter the world, nature, and the human race.

Industrialization—begotten by science and technology—was the third great power of modernity. As mirrored in the person of Pascal, this meant the following: He built over fifty different models of the calculating machine—not for his own enjoyment but as a help for his father and private tutor, an extremely busy president of the Assize Court in the service of Richelieu. He immediately tried to patent it, and printed up prospectuses and plans for mass production of the machine, which failed only because of the lack of capital and trained mechanics. In his last, lonely years, he worked out plans for an omnibus service through greater Paris, founded an omnibus society (presumably the first corporation on the continent), whose operations would bring the "Archimedes of Paris" still more fame than the calculating machine.

All this means that in Pascal we see the prototype of the modern organizer and entrepreneur. Such men would be needed more than ever under the new minister of finance, Colbert, who was organizing the manufacturing economy along mercantilist lines.

One characteristic of this system was "industry," the "inventive diligence" that formed the prerequisite, in intellectual and social history, of the Industrial Revolution. The transition from agrarian to industrial society would constitute the greatest economic and social upheaval since the emergence of agriculture and the cities, and would finally turn the modern age into an industrial age.

But what was the mainspring, the driving force, that lent this moment in intellectual and social history its enormous thrust? For the medieval Roman Catholic paradigm, the key words were "ecclesia sive papa" (the church equals the pope); for the Reformation they were the "Word of God." And now, for modernity? The key word was "ratio," "raison," "reason." The unprecedented dynamic of modern times is based on a great trust in man's rational nature, on an altogether nonecclesiastical and certainly nonpapal "reason," as the case of Galileo showed in contrast to Luther. Reasoning was the highest activity of the human race. "Reason" and with it measure, restraint, balance, and proportion would make possible a humane *savoir faire* and *savoir vivre*.

In the Italian Renaissance and in humanism, to be sure, a new attitude toward life and the world, a new reflection of human dignity, had come to light, releasing men and women from the medieval order. Art in particular was no longer bound up in that medieval system, so totally oriented to transcendence; it became instead an end in itself. The aesthetic order acquired autonomous value, manifest in purely secular theories of art, histories of art, collections of art. But all this took place with a clear view backward, in looking back to antiquity; the magic word was Renaissance, or rebirth.

But now in the seventeenth century the intellectual elite of Europe began, in a self-conscious, open, independent, nonauthoritarian fashion, to think forward. In a *progressive* direction characteristic of modernity, it appealed not to the ancient world (Re-naissance) or to the Bible (Re-formation), but to humanity's autarkic reason. According to Voltaire, it was the principle of reason—as the absolute standard of human thinking and the motive force of human progress—that made the age of Louis XIV appear superior to the other three great cultural ages of European history, superior not only to the Athens of Pericles and Rome under Augustus but even to Medicean Florence. Now for the first time people invoked autonomous reason in a thoroughly central and not marginal way, and found in reason compensation for losing humanity's central place in the universe. In this experience of loss and gain lies the root of both man's weakness and his greatness: "L'homme n'est qu'un roseau . . . mais c'est un roseau pensant." "Man is no more than a reed, but he is a thinking reed" (#347).

Theology and Christian faith obviously remained dependent on authorities (Scripture, the Fathers). In physics, however, the spirit of *rational argument* was to prevail. Indeed, thanks to Descartes the spirit of mathematics advanced to become the spirit of the age. For Pascal, too, who could work like a man possessed, and with incorruptible objectivity, on mathematical or physical problems, the truth of physics rested on the evidence of ideas or facts. Physics would find truth in two ways—through mathematical deduction or experimentation—and Pascal's procedure here was much more empirical and experimental. His proof of empty space, for example, was an imposing victory for the new mathematical-empirical study of nature over a basic dogma of traditional Aristotelian-Thomistic physics and metaphysics (*horror vacui*), which Galileo and Descartes still took for granted. Like Descartes, Pascal was anything but a dogmatic thinker. Man should learn to make increasingly better use of his reason. In scientific enlightenment, he could scrutinize and explore, systematically and without prejudice, nature and its laws, but above all himself and finally social relations in all their various aspects.

And yet, unlike Descartes, Pascal aimed at a universal system. The history of modern times would have been very different if Westerners, in the spirit of Pascal, had rejected the *rationalistic absolutizing of rationality* for the sake of full human existence and genuine enlightenment. For as Pascal sees it, we have not only discursive reason but intuitive knowledge. We have not just the slow, analytic-synthetic construction by the understanding, but also simple, rapid feeling. Sensitive individuals have a greater need of *raisonnement*, while rational types need *sentiment*.

Did not modernity, so quicky rationalized by science, technology, and industrialization, lack above all what Pascal comprehensively called *le coeur* (heart)? "We know the truth not only with the reason, but also with the heart" (#282). Sentimentality, mawkishness, emotional self-indulgence? No, "heart" does not designate the irrational-emotional element as opposed to the rational-logical, but the spiritual-personal center of the individual, for which the bodily organ is only a symbol. The "heart" is a person's innermost active core, the point of departure for his or her dynamic-personal relations with others, the specific organ humans have for comprehending totality. "Heart" does mean the human mind, not insofar as it thinks and concludes in a purely theoretical way, but insofar as it is spontaneously present, as it intuitively senses, existentially recognizes, and holistically evaluates, insofar as it is in the broadest sense a loving (or hating) mind. And so we can understand Pascal's most famous, but scarcely translatable, play on words: "Le coeur a ses raisons, que la raison ne connaît point: on le sait en mille choses." "The heart has its reasons, which reason does not know; we see this in a thousand things" (#277). There is a logic of the heart, and the heart has its own rationality.

Today, in the transition to postmodernity, we read Pascal's remarks on the *esprit de finesse*, "delicacy" (flair, tact, sensitivity, second sense, "nose")—from the perspective of numerous alternative movements—and with a newly intensified awareness of the problem. Pascal said the *espirit de finesse* has to complement and complete the *esprit de géométrie*, the "mathematical mind." We are startled to acknowledge how much we have repressed, ignored, and torn apart. C. P. Snow talked about the "two cultures." According to Pascal, all "geometricians," all mathematicians, physicists, and technicians should also be intuitive-sensitive, should have a sense of interrelationships, atmosphere, the dynamics of the whole, while conversely all sensitive minds should also be "geometricians."

Sensitive minds, accustomed to judge things in a purely spontaneous way, feel dumbstruck when they are confronted with rationality, with definitions and principles of exact science. But the exact scientists should not make themselves ridiculous by trying to deal geometrically with matters requiring *finesse*. With this in view, we can readily understand what Pascal means when in his great work he writes an extremely critical chapter against the most important representatives of the *esprit de géométrie*, as indicated by an ominous note: "Write against the people who press all too deeply into science: Descartes!" (#76).

Just as Pascal was no rationalist, neither was he an irrationalist; if he was not a dogmatic thinker, neither was he a skeptic or a cryptofreethinker. Though his approach was altogether different, he was like Descartes in his concern for the truth, for *objective and inner certainty*—and this, it goes without saying, within the framework of Catholic spirituality. In opposition to the prejudices that are still widespread today, the American historian of science Benjamin Nelson, in his book on the "Origins of Modernity" (1977), which discusses the most recent literature on the subject, observes:

> Copernicus, Galileo, Descartes, Pascal and many others in the first rank of innovators of the early modern revolution of science and philosophy received their intellectual formation in Catholic "culture areas." . . . To destroy the pieties of the unlearned was no part of the plan of the pioneers, nor were they cryptolibertines or skeptics. Rather, their animus was directed against a complex of views which had the endorsement of their own teachers and which prevailed among the leaders of the religious establishments of their own day, including Cardinal Bellarmine and Pope Urban VIII, the prime antagonists of Galileo. (Benjamin Nelson, *On the Roads to Modernity* [Totowa, NJ, 1981], 123–24)

But among all these "first-rank innovators" of the modern paradigm, Pascal is undoubtedly the one who had the sharpest view of the heavy human consequences, offering a nearly incomparable, clear-sighted analysis of humanity's *fundamental ambivalence*. He describes the conflicting features of human nature—a psychological unmasker long before Kierkegaard, Dostoyevsky, Freud, and Kafka—mercilessly piercing through all possible situations, habits, coincidences—a thinker in terms of *véritées opposées*. In other words, he was a dialectician par excellence.

Above all, Pascal senses the existential meaning that the *cosmological* discoveries of scientists like Copernicus, Kepler, and Galileo had for the men and women of his day—the feeling of being lost in the infinite, impenetrable universe, where the voice of the Creator could no longer be heard. "The eternal silence of these infinite spaces terrifies me" (#206), he notes. In the face of this infinite space, what is the individual? Compared with the universe, he is nothing. But, looking at it the other way around, what is man in the face of the microcosm, of infinity *in parvo*? In the face of the void, is not man a universe? This creates the disproportion, the basic incongruity, the misery *and* greatness of man in the world: "A Nothing in comparison with the Infinite, an All in comparison with the Nothing, a mean between nothing and everything. Since he is infinitely removed from comprehending the extremes, the end of things and their beginning are hopelessly hidden from him in an impenetrable secret" (#72).

The fact that man knows about this problematic, highly endangered hybrid position constitutes his dignity: "If the universe were to crush him, man would still be more noble than that which killed him, because he knows that he dies and he knows the advantage which the universe has over him. The universe knows nothing of this" (#347).

Meanwhile, Pascal is a sensitive analyst not only of man's cosmological, but also of his *psychological*, ambivalence. He is one of the great early "discoverers of the ego," according to Richard Friedenthal. In ever-new forms, he describes the double-bottomed quality of everyday human existence. What is hidden behind all the official social business, the love affairs, behind hunting and dancing, games and sports? What do we discover, what do we see, behind all the masks? Don't we find everywhere man's fear of being alone? Doesn't that lead to a feeling of abandonment, powerlessness, emptiness? Pascal notes, "There will immediately arise from the depth of his heart weariness, gloom, sadness, fretfulness, vexation, despair" (#131).

In this way, we could interpret fragment after fragment so as to find the human situation sketched out by Pascal in all its nuances. I wish to focus on just one of these, a thought that is especially close to us and practically expresses the mood of today's no-future generation: "I know not who put me into the world, nor what the world is, nor what I myself am. I am in terrible ignorance of everything. I know not what my body is, nor my senses, nor my soul, not even that part of me which thinks what I say, which reflects on all and on itself, and knows itself no more than the rest. I see those frightful places of the universe which surround me, and I find myself tied to one corner of this vast expanse, without knowing why I am put in this place rather than in another, nor why the short time which is given me to live is assigned to me at this point rather than at another of the whole eternity which was before me or which shall come after me. I see nothing but infinites on all sides, which surround me as an atom, and as a shadow which endures only for an instant and returns no more" (#194).

And Pascal ends with a prospect of being-unto-death: "All I know is that I must soon die, but what I know least is this very death which I cannot escape. As I know not whence I come, so I know not whither I go. I know only that in leaving this world, I fall forever either into annihilation or into the hands of an angry God, without knowing to which of these two states I shall be forever assigned. Such is my state, full of weakness and uncertainty" (#194).

What matters, then, for this man? Unlike Descartes, Pascal is concerned not only with the uncertainty of human knowledge but also with the *radical insecurity of human existence*. Kierkegaard, Dostoyevsky, and Kafka, Heidegger, Jaspers, and Sartre will later analyze this in greater detail, but they will find no more dramatic words than Pascal, who ends by exclaiming: "What a chimaera then is man! What a novelty! What a monster, what a chaos, what a contradiction, what a prodigy! Judge of all things, imbecile worm of the earth; depositary of truth, a sink of uncertainty and error; the pride and refuse of the universe!" (#434).

————◇————

What is philosophy supposed to do now? Isn't philosophy simply over and done with? In fact, at this point Pascal takes a completely surprising turn: "Know then, proud man, what a paradox you are to yourself" (#434). There follows a downright dictatorial call to humanity to recognize that the solution of the contradiction can't be expected from man at all, is referred man to something else, which transcends him: "Humble yourself, weak reason; be silent, foolish nature; learn that man infinitely transcends man, and learn from your Master your true condition, of which you are ignorant. Hear God" (#434).

This, to be sure, is a leap. But for Pascal it is not a leap of thought, but the daring of a faith by no means irrational. Unlike Descartes, Pascal, who saw through the ambivalence of human reason, could ground his certainty not on a "cogito ego sum" (I think, therefore I am), but on a "credo ergo sum" (I believe, therefore I am). And this man is shaped not by the vision of a mathematically oriented universal knowledge, of the sort Descartes had one November night in Ulm on the Danube, but a religious border experience, a "conversion," a "vision," like Moses' when he saw the burning bush. As we know, it was only by accident that a servant, after Pascal's death, found the "memorial" sewn into his coat. It, too, stemmed from a November night. It had a long prehistory. It began with the word *feu* (fire) written in large letters, and reported of an experience of certainty, of *sentiment*, of a peace that overcame all sense of abandonment. Pascal had this experience not with the abstract "God of the philosophers and savants," but with the living "God of Abraham, Isaac, and Jacob, the God of Jesus Christ." It was not a "mystical experience" in the actual sense of an experience of unity with God, but rather the intensive, intimate experience of the divine partner in the spirit of the fathers and prophets of Israel.

And so Pascal had found a final ground of certainty that could no longer be doubted, on which one could build every certitude—not the self-consciousness of the thinking man, not a concept, some sort of idea of God, but the real, *living God of the Bible*, who is indeed always present, but externally absent. This primeval certainty in the hidden God, who reveals himself only to the believer, thus derives not simply from thought, but from belief: "God felt by the heart, not by the reason" (#278). This is not to devalue or overpower reason: "There is nothing so conformable to reason as this disavowal of reason." Why? "The last proceeding of reason is to recognize that there is an infinity of things which are beyond it" (#267). In brief, both are needed: "Submission is the use of reason in which consists true Christianity" (#267).

Pascal finds it unforgivable that Descartes isn't really concerned in his philosophy with true Christianity, with the true Christian God: "I cannot forgive Descartes. In all his philosophy he would have been quite willing to dispense with God" (#77). For Pascal, however, a triply dialectical truth is clear and distinct: "The knowledge of God without that of man's misery causes pride. The knowledge of man's misery without that of God causes despair. The knowledge of Jesus Christ constitutes the middle course, because in Him we find both God and our misery" (#526).

It is toward this middle course—in the dialectic of fall and redemption—that the rest of Pascal's fragments are oriented. All of them were supposed to form parts of his apologia—on the Old

Testament (Law, prophecies, the hidden God), on Jesus Christ (fulfillment of the prophecies, miracles, redemption and grace, morality and the ways of salvation), on the church (foundation, continuity, infallibility), and on the secret of divine love. The *Pensées* have rightly been called the "first dialogue of modern man with religion," where we can see the "highwire act that Christianity would have to do in the following centuries" (I. E. Kummer, *Pascal*, 25).

Pacal's extremely ecstatic *and* extremely deliberate experience of a new certitude of the heart came on 23 November 1654, "from around ten thirty in the evening till around a half an hour after midnight." In the same year, the year of Louis XIV's coronation, he presented to the Parisian Academy his treatises on the arithmetic triangle and the theory of probability. The ecstatic moment was for him the high point and the solution of a *crisis*. Full of inner unrest and intellectual restlessness, sick and disgusted by worldly doings in Paris, he was helped by the many conversations he had with his congenial favorite sister, Jacqueline. She had entered against his will the strict Jansenist cloister of Port-Royal, a spiritual center that would later increasingly become the spiritual antipodes of nearby Versailles.

This Augustinian *Jansenism* now became Pascal's destiny. Jansenism was a strict, theological and moral reform movement in the spirit of Augustine, which originated with the Belgian bishop Cornelius Jansen and his French friend the abbé de Saint-Cyran, the spiritual inspirer of Port-Royal. "Total submission to Jesus Christ and my spiritual director," said the end of Pascal's "memorial," quite Jansenistically. This meant that the tension between reason and faith was increased by the tension between freedom and grace. In his last years, Pascal became the most important contender in the "great dispute over grace" between the *Jansenists*, who—following Augustine—stressed God's irresistible grace against the irresistible concupiscence of man and defended the strict moral and disciplinary ideals of the early church, and the *Jesuits*, who—in a modern vein—argued for the freedom and activity of man under God's grace and for a more liberal morality (probabilism) and sacramental discipline (confession).

There followed a time when in the controversy over grace,

which extended into the salons and the theaters (Racine for the Jansenists, Corneille against), both sides increasingly showed no mercy. The little group of nuns and hermits—who did not, however, wish to become priests or monks—had to ride out the controversy—although they had many high-ranking sympathizers on their side. The "gentlemen," "friends of St. Augustine," as they called themselves, instead opened a number of little schools. For the frivolous society of the capital, they were increasingly a burdensome reproach; for the absolutist system, they were a dangerous deviation and challenge.

Only after the Jansenists were condemned by Rome (1653), and the Sorbonne, too—a good year after Pascal's vision—issued it anathema (1656), did Pascal get involved in the argument, but from the outset his commitment was complete. Overnight—here, too, he was an initiator of modernity—he became France's first great journalist. His anonymous pamphlets, *The Provincial Letters*, full or irony and caustic wit, sharp-eyed in their logic, composed in a taut, polished, superior style, were a sensation, a scandal. To this day, they have cast discredit on casuistry and Jesuit morality. They paved the way, intellectually, for the suppression of the Society of Jesus in the eighteenth century. In the very next year, Rome put the *Lettres Provinciales* on the Index of Forbidden Books. Later the book was condemned in Paris by the Council of State and publicly shredded and burned by the hangman.

Strictly opposed to any compromise with Rome, Pascal rejected Port-Royal's diplomatic tactics as dishonest. In a vehement discussion about this with his friends, he lost consciousness. Now he had only a few months to live. His conscience was caught in a dilemma—the pope and the church on the one hand, personal religious conviction on the other—and not even his incredibly keen mind could find a way out. The dispute was no longer between faith and reason, but between faith and faith.

In protest against the placing of his book on the Index, Pascal appealed to a higher court, as indicated in this note: "If my letters are condemned in Rome, still what I condemn in them is condemned in heaven! Ad tuum, Domine Jesu, tribunal appello. To your court, Lord Jesus, I appeal." Fatally weakened by a disease whose nature even learned medical treatises have not yet been able to diagnose unequivocally, as well as by reckless penitential exercises, Pascal was finally allowed, as he lay in his death agony, to receive viaticum. The priest who administered the Sacrament would later have to answer for it to the harshly anti-Jansenistic archbishop of Paris. Without recanting, Pascal died in the conviction that he was a true Catholic, only thirty-nine years of age, on 9 August 1662, nine months after Port-Royal signed its own condemnation. His last words were "May God never forsake me."

No one who has ever dealt with Pascal's person, work, and life can deny a certain perplexity. What could one add to his writings? When philosophical and theological problems become questions of fate in this way, aren't we forbidden to pass judgment on the person? Indeed we are, and the issue here is not his personality. But we must be allowed to raise questions about his position in the context of our inquiry into religion and modernity. These questions can be summed up in a single one: *Why couldn't Pascal's religion*—which managed to hold its own so sharply and shrewdly against the challenges of the new age—*become the religion of modernity*? Even in his own day, Pascal was controversial, and in retrospect many doubts about the presuppositions and consequences of his faith come up again. I shall group them around three key phrases—anthropological pessimism, moral rigorism, and apolitical privatism.

1. An understanding of religion based on *anthropological pessimism* in the sense of the older Augustine could not in the long run be sound or productive, and it certainly could not replace the high esteem for the human that, in the wake of Thomas Aquinas, humanism, and the Renaissance had become pervasive even in Scholasticism and was especially affirmed by Jesuit theologians. How could reason ever be squared with the idea that everyone, without regard to his actions, had been predestined to salvation or perdition by an inscrutable decision of God? Could human reason accept that man had been corrupted in his nature by original sin, and that his will was irresistibly ruled by evil concupiscence, which could be overcome only by God's equally irresistible grace?

2. Any practice of religion based on *moral rigorism* would have to be useless for the future of modernity. Such rigorism demands

strict renunciation and humiliation, ascetic self-torture, and an antisensual spiritualism; it rejects music and comedy (but not tragedy) and casts a suspicious, pessimistic eye on all pleasure. In religious discipline, the requirements (for confession and receiving communion) are intensified. Yet can't we view self-abasement before God not as service to one's fellow man but as self-destruction? Must we hate our own ego, in order to love God from the heart? Doesn't the Christian way to God involve turning to the Thou instead of destroying the I: love of neighbor (measured against love of oneself) as fulfillment of the love of God? As a matter of fact, in modern times this sort of external "asceticism", "exercise of abnegation, mortification, self-denial" at the price of humanity and one's fellow humans (having no foundation in the New Testament) has made belief in God and Christianity deeply offensive to persons with a humanistic frame of mind.

3. Given the shape that modernity, as it prevailed, has taken, any religion that is limited to the private realm and has too little to do with society and politics would be bound to fail. Can religion be based on *apolitical privatism*? Here we have to take one last look at the seventeenth century in France, which was not only the golden age of French philosophy, science, and literature, but also the age of absolute monarchy, of misery for the peasants, of continual revolts and their bloody repression.

There can be no question that his spiritualistic, internalized piety helps to explain why Pascal, highly sensitive as he was in many ways, still never anticipated that fourth great power of the modern world, which even in the seventeenth century was giving notice (in the secularization of politics and political theory) of its arrival—*democracy*.

Is this question anachronistic? By no means. The breakthrough of democratic-liberal ideas in the century of the Enlightenment that followed was prepared by the English and French proponents of "natural rights" in the "early Enlightenment." During Pascal's lifetime, these thinkers, under the influence of Stoicism and Spanish baroque Scholasticism, argued that political constitutions, economic order, morality, and religion were grounded in human "nature" or "reason," and they raised those principles, in the face of historical circumstances and abuses, to the status of the critical norm. *Natural rights* were now attributed to the individual. These rights were also binding on the ruler. To be sure, they were no longer viewed, following medieval and Spanish Scholasticism, as anchored in the Creator's desire for order, but in the insight of human reason.

Thus for many years there lived in Paris a Dutch Protestant emigrant, who like Pascal wrote an apologia for Christianity, with exactly the same title, though in Latin ("De veritate religionis christianae"), Hugo Grotius (1583–1645). But unlike Pascal, he stood with Erasmus of Rotterdam in defending an undogmatic, grammatical-historical exegesis. At the same time he gave independent status to natural rights, and borrowing from the Spanish baroque Scholastic Suárez, he launched the development of modern international law ("De iure belli ac pacis," 1625, put on the Index by Rome).

And Blaise Pascal himself? Under the dictatorship of Richelieu, then of Cardinal Mazarin, and finally of Louis XIV, all of whom practiced Machiavellian politics (beyond morality, religion, and confessional differences), it was practically impossible to criticize princely absolutism, exploitation of the people (Versailles later had a retinue of four thousand persons), and unceasing wars (wars of religion, tax wars, peasant wars, cabinet wars). All criticism of the *grandeur* of the one and the *misère* of the many was at once eliminated—with the help of censorship, a spy system, and sudden arrests. A number of his *Pensées* clearly reveal that Pascal, who like many Jansenists came from a family of the *noblesse de robe* (nobility of officials), is thinking more than he says. The power of kings, he writes, is based upon reason, but still more upon the stupidity of the people. Otherwise, he speaks only in general terms about rights and laws, but he finds it dangerous to tell the people that the laws are unjust.

Pascal was familiar with the enormous distress of the people, who would later greet the death of the Sun-King with curses and throw stones at his coffin. Up to the limits of what was financially bearable, he tried to help the poor every day in Paris, especially in his last years. He willed the income from the omnibus society to hospitals; he took a destitute family (including a child stricken with smallpox) into his house; he sold his horses, coach, Gobelins, silver, and furniture. He wanted to die in the Hospital of the Incurables.

Unlike Rousseau, for example, Pascal lived by what he said. But for all our respect for his person, in the long run can Christian love of neighbor, pious words, alms, and individual charity replace political commitment? Although monarchy, the greatest and most important thing in the world, had for its foundation weakness—namely, the stupidity of the people—Pascal thought it could nevertheless be amazingly secure, because nothing was as certain as the fact that the people would remain weak.

But there he was mistaken. When the "light of reason" began its work of enlightenment among the people, when the epochal misuse of religion for the benefit of the rulers was made increasingly apparent and the divine right of kings (which had prevailed in the West since Carolingian days) had been traced back to natural factors (a "social contract" subject to termination), then the hour of absolutism was over. The king was guillotined, the nobility decimated, many clerics hanged, exiled, or disciplined, and the Christian God was replaced by the atheistic goddess of "Reason."

Modernity had reached its climax, and set about conquering the nineteenth century. The political-scientific revolution had found its counterpart in the *political revolution*, and could finally put all of its gigantic power on display in the Industrial Revolution. The Christian religion, which had dominated Europe since the time of Constantine, was for the first time in European history violently persecuted and where it survived, it was at best tolerated by the enlightened, but increasingly ignored, repressed, and often even crushed.

Blaise Pascal, *homo mathematicus*, *homo faber*, the physicist, engineer, and organizer, was a thoroughly modern signpost for science, for technology, and even—in its beginnings—for industrialization. But Pascal, as *homo religiosus* and *homo christianus*, could hardly point the way to modernity in the same manner. For all his brilliant insights into the contradictory nature of man, in matters of faith, Pascal the Christian, who did not want to call himself a Jansenist, looks back to Augustine, whom he keeps praising and quoting afresh, to Augustine who laid the foundations for the medieval paradigm of theology and piety. Amid the transition from the medieval Counter-Refomation to the modern paradigm, Pascal's position remains, for us, *divided*. It is at once modern and medieval—progressive, dynamic, and forward-looking in the area of science and technology, but static, conservative, and unhistorical in matters of church doctrine, morality, and discipline. One might expect a great deal from modern men and women as far as devotion and commitment go, but surely not that they should secretly wear a belt of spikes against their bare bodies, as Pascal did, so as to press it into his skin at the mere thought of pride or worldly joy, while praising beautiful women or fondling children.

Once again, for all our respect, there is something inherently elitist, puritanical, and prudish about this religiosity. It is a spiritualized spirituality of the "chosen few" as opposed to the mass of unbelievers. "J'ose prendrele parti de l'humanité contre le misanthrope sublime." "I dare to side with humanity against the sublime hater of men." That is what Voltaire said in his "Remarks on the Pensées" (1734), in his *Philosophical Letters*. For all his mockery a moralist in the good French fashion, was he altogether wrong?

Whatever stand one may take toward Pascal on individual questions, whether with Voltaire and the Encyclopedists, with Aldous Huxley and some Marxists, who are highly critical of him, or with countless philosophers, theologians, and writers from Chateaubriand to Charles Péguy, who were full of admiration for him, one has to admit the truth about his enduring appeal. While Descartes, the most important philosopher of the seventeenth century, is today read almost exclusively by philosophers, and the court bishop Bossuet, the most influential theologian and preacher of the same century, is now at best of historical interest only, what François Mauriac said of Pascal holds true: "After three hundred years there he stands, taking part in our disputes, alive. Even his least thoughts perplex, enthrall, and irritate us, but he is instantaneously, from the first word, understood, and much better than he was in his own lifetime. . . ."

WALTER JENS

◆

Certitude! Certitude!

"Let us imagine a number of men in chains, and all condemned to death, where some are killed each day in the sight of the others, and those who remain see their own fate in that of their fellows, and wait their turn, looking at each other sorrowfully and without hope. It is an image of the condition of men" (#199).

A prophecy of horror. *L'homme sans dieu*, the godless man, positing his autonomy: For Pascal this is not only a depraved, aberrant, and desperate creature. It is the candidate for death who at the moment of truth, when it comes time to die, experiences his end as an execution, mute and hopeless in the face of the firing squad that awaits him.

In a few sentences, Pascal anticipates the mass executions of the twentieth century, with the people huddled together naked and robbed of their dignity, waiting for a bullet in the back of the neck. The loneliest death there is, the most wretched and meaningless, seems prefigured here in a way that points to the divinatory power of great poetry shaped by visionary images. How else can we read today, after Auschwitz, Oradour, or My-Lai, Pascal's description of the "last act": "The last act is tragic, however happy all the rest of the play is; at the last a little earth is thrown upon our head, and that is the end forever" (#210).

Yet this is unlike the time of fascism, unlike the period under Stalin or Pinochet. Here it is not the innocent—Jews, dissidents, and advocates of humanity—but those declared guilty in the name of religion, the godforsaken, no longer mindful of their first nature, to whom Pascal calls out his "damnati eritis in saecula saeculorum," *lost for time and eternity*. The analysis of the execution scene takes on a quite different look when we consider that the vision of bloody, violent death has the nature of a warning. What Pascal is getting at is that the man who dies his miserable, horrible death, neither looking back to the time before the fall nor thinking ahead to the possibility of redemption at the end of his days, doesn't wait till the end to die; he dies every day.

When the author of the *Pensées* describes the human condition, he chooses the position of a penitential judge, who in the last second would like to order "Stop," provoke awareness, and make possible a conversion—and this not in the form of a philosophical meditation, but in ecstatic and yet logical discourse. Such discourse suggests images for concepts, translates concepts into images, and applies to the people living thoughtlessly just as it does to one's own ego.

The *Pensées* are not precise and carefully pointed maxims of the sort written by French moralists like La Rochefoucauld or Vauvenargues, but queries, objections, memoranda, in which atheists as well as believers say their peace. They are notes that record monologues, preliminary sketches that—like Emil Nolde's "unpainted pictures" from the time of persecution—were later to be painted out and completed as a comprehensive apologia of the Christian religion. There is not just one voice speaking, but countless voices. The words of the penitent and prophetic warner mingle with the speech of the man of the world. The enlightened heir of Montaigne, the mathematician and *honnête homme*, gets equal time with the spiritual man, who while living in the world radically renounces courtly etiquette and the vain behavior of the ruling classes.

And then, all of a sudden, we no longer hear the *littérateur*, with his knack of putting on one mask after another, of playing ever more daring roles. Now the perspective takes a radical shift: Blaise Pascal is not praying to Jesus, but Jesus himself speaks up and directs an immediate appeal to the person calling upon him. "Compare not thyself with others, but with Me. . . . Now I am God in all. I speak to thee, and often counsel thee" (#554).

In other words, the *Pensées* do not speak on *one* level, with a single voice, but between heaven and hell, with whole choruses of voices, leading to contradictions and stunning breaks that resist any harmonizing or smoothing over, even of a friendly kind.

It is the essence of Pascal that he always says yes and no at once; he can never be tied down to a "thus and not otherwise," a "definitely" and "irrevocably." After writing the *mémorial* on 23 November 1654, he seems to have decided once and for all in favor of a radical practice of Christianity ("Certitude! Certitude!") But, still possessed by the theory of probability, he continued to meditate on the chances of winning at roulette . . . and not just the metaphysical kind, where the point was to risk the finite to win infinity, without losing sight of the fact that if the risk was certain, the gain was not.

With Pascal there are contradictions everywhere you look. In the *mémorial* we hear a man speaking with rapid-fire short sentences about the vision of fire that came over him—and in the process measuring the time precisely ("from around ten-thirty to half an hour after midnight"). He makes a clean copy of his jottings, and sews it into his coat, which was, by the way, not so much an eccentric as a ritualized act blessed by court etiquette—even Richelieu had notes sewn into his overcoat.

Once again he was human in his contradictions. Pascal, Kierkegaard's predecessor, invented a calculator. Pascal, who lived like an ascetic outside monastery walls, called brooms a superfluous item of furniture (which earned him a housewifely reproach from his sister). The same Pascal, as if he were a predecessor of Marcel Proust, moves about in circles of the nobility, chats with the Chevalier de Meré and the Duke of Roannez, and behaves with arrogance and condescension toward the rabble, whose ignorance he despised. Yet despite this he was the "man of sorrows," and for this reason was later viewed with pity by Leopardi and Nietzsche, because his life from his eighteenth year onward became one long physical torment.

The sick genius—a leading nineteenth-century motif—was prefigured in Pascal. "Some altogether extraordinary minds," wrote Giacomo Leopardi on 17 June 1821, "whom nature sometimes produces as if by a miracle . . . have quickly used up their bodies, their intellectual capacities, indeed even their genius itself. The extremely great delicacy of their organs causes them to be more readily consumed and more readily spoiled, since their organs are subject to those who are less delicate and more complete. The proof of this is Pascal who died at thirty-nine years of age, already the victim of a kind of madness." (Leopardi, who wrote this, himself died at thirty-nine and on the edge of mental derangement.)

Pascal, a sovereign player of games like Lessing, was a helpless, pain-racked creature, always restlessly bursting with projects. He was a man who conceived things instead of carrying them out, someone who longed to extinguish his ego for the love of God, and who nevertheless maintained an unmistakable individuality. He spoke of himself with unflagging élan as one of the most precise thinkers in the field of religious literature ("Pascal," wrote Nietzsche, "whom I almost love, because he has been infinitely instructive to me, the only *logical* Christian"), but, like Nietzsche, he was a thinker without a system.

Pascal embodied contradictions in religion, and contradictions in politics. He was the apologist of autocratic power and advocate of the status quo who had studied his Machiavelli very well: "It is dangerous to tell people that the laws are unjust; for they obey them only because they think them just. Therefore it is necessary to tell them at the same time that they must obey them because they are laws, just as they must obey superiors, not because they are just, but because they are superiors" (#326).

This power thinker from an enlightened legal family (Descartes had the same sort of roots) lays bare the ideological character of power and sets up a contrast between the meditations that are appropriate to his class and that secure the social status quo, and his "secret thoughts," which take the form of wishes, dream thoughts, thoughts of liberation from Pascal, the role-player. "When force attacks humbug, when a private soldier takes the square cap off a first president, and throws it out of the window" (#310).

But whatever Blaise Pascal did, whether he said yes or no (he preferred both at once), he always played *va banque*, in the sense of the famous dialogue on the wager: *Vous êtes embarqué*. You are on board, sir, now the bets have been placed. Choose "Scripture," take a risk, and bet that God exists. "If you gain, you gain all; if you lose, you lose nothing" (#233).

The yea-and-nay sayer, who knew all that was humanly possible about uncertainty and insecurity, was no trimmer, no "both-and" preacher, but—to quote Nietzsche once again—"in his combination of fervor, spirit, and integrity, the first of all Christians." He was a man who thought through problems, which he himself had raised, with the utmost consistency, all the way to the point that could be elucidated only by paradoxes. He took this path, accepting the danger of ending up trapped in antinomies that for someone obsessed with truth and unwilling to make any sort of compromise, as Pascal was, had to deprive him of his understanding, and literally "cost him his head." When in October 1661 the pope called for the *unconditional* signing of the formula condemning the teaching of Jansenius as heretical, and the compromisers at Port-Royal submitted, Pascal risked a war on two fronts against Rome *and* the old allies, for whose cause he had once skewered the Jesuits in the *Provincial Letters*.

Together with the jurist Domat, he sketched out—as if criticizing his old comrades-in-arms for jesuitical entanglement in the world—a "grand écrit," a last great letter (now lost), in which finally placed between God and the pope, he reproached the bishop of Rome for "having the diabolical intention of condemning the doctrine of Jansenism."

On one side was the church and its supreme head, without whom the Catholic from Clermont found a life under the sign of salvation unthinkable, and on the other side God and the truth. At the end of his life, Pascal found himself facing an antinomy that, two hundred years later, Dostoyevsky pushed to the limit in the parable of the Grand Inquisitor. Dostoyevsky, too, was animated by the same will to construct inescapable antinomies and was bound to a Manichaeism as grandiose as it was inhuman. Inhuman because it was shaped by the friend/foe thinking, the Christ/Antichrist opposition that also informs Pascal's model of argument. Pascal, says Romano Guardini, "felt both a powerful sense of personal election and a sensitivity that was in itself already a sign of a final insecurity. This inclination is connected to . . . the demonic nature of the struggle, the will to struggle pure and simple. This destructive struggle becomes instantly possible— indeed, it receives a positively religious dedication—because the opponent is turned into the absolute opponent, thus becoming the person who stands against, betrays, and misuses truth. This is the satanic opponent, Dostoyevsky's Grand Inquisitor, the Antichrist.

Pascal was undoubtedly least of all a conciliator. Instead, he was one of those people who, owing to their all-encompassing, absolutist thinking, lose sight of the here and now, of concrete history and the world in which God's creatures strive for a life in the spirit of Christ. We can sense in Pascal little of the Franciscan spirit—meaning, to be sure, in theory, not in the practice of piety, in living alongside the poor and worrying over children's chances for survival—or of compassion and love for all creatures. "Reverence and the common obligation to humanity," of the sort Montaigne had in mind, a humanity (to quote from the second volume of the *Essays*, "which binds us not only to the living, feeling animals, but even to trees and plants." Such *humanité*, which reverences the Creator in the creatures, was fundamentally suspect to Pascal, an expression of heterodoxy in the sense of a reversal of the divinely ordained hierarchy.

No wonder, with all this, that the French Enlightenment in particular, with Voltaire leading the way, raised objections to the rigid limits Pascal set for man. Voltaire protested against the exclusion of horizontal relationships—I and the world, I and Thou—in favor of the vertical relationship, the only dominant one, the only one that validates first nature, between God and man.

"Objection, sir. Your comparisons are not fair." Actually, this is how Voltaire's *Philosophical Letters* go about a point-for-point confrontation with Pascal's fragments—in truth humanity's natural destiny is *not* to be chained and strangled, but, like the animals and plants, to grow, to live for a while, and to die.

Objection, sir. I object to your thesis that one has to love God— if he exists—and only God, not the transitory creatures that led us astray from him and seduced us into thinking of anything else but him ("All that is bad"). In truth, Voltaire postulates, we are to love tenderly all created things, our homeland, spouse, children, and parents, and to do our part to perfect human society.

Was Pascal the anti-Enlightenment man and God-crazed individualist, an obsessed denouncer of human fallibility and human blindness (caused by denying God)? Was he really? I think that anyone who argues this way—from the standpoint of Montaigne and Voltaire—focuses exclusively on Pascal the penitential preacher in flight from the world, misses the yea-*and*-nay thinker (one could also say, the genuine dialectician) and forgets the *other* Pascal. This Pascal was a friend of rational thought, witty paradox, and trenchant argumentation. Despite all his skepticism toward "second nature," he spoke up for the progress of the human species in a way that classifies him more in the circle of the Encyclopedists than among the hermits of Port-Royal. Thus in an early fragment about the vacuum, Pascal writes that just as man

> stores up knowledge, he can likewise easily increase it, so that the people alive today are in exactly the same position, so to speak, as the ancient philosophers would find themselves in if they had been able to live all the way into the present and had managed to add to the knowledge they already had the information that they could have acquired by study in the course of so many centuries. This is the reason why, through a peculiar privilege, not only does the individual make progress in the sciences from day to day, but all people together, to the extent that the world grows older, continually progress. For in the succession of humanity the same thing is repeated that happened in the various stages in the life of an individual. Thus one can view the whole sequence of men in the course of so many centuries as one man who is always alive and learns continually.

This is an early testimony, to be sure, filled with Bacon's or Descartes' optimistic faith in progress. But for that very reason it is also a document that teaches us how consideration of Pascal the theologian has to be continually balanced with an eye to Pascal the scientist. He was the first postmedieval writer who dared to think and describe what infinity is and what it means for human consciousness to live at a random time and in a random place where everything finds itself in frantic movement. Pascal was the man who mathematized theology by giving a new meaning to concepts like "finite, infinite, nothing, and all," based on knowledge and not on speculation. In describing human beings, the double creatures oscillating between misery and grandeur, Pascal objectified the ambiguity shaping his own life and thought, by giving to private existence the character of the universally obligatory. This man was always, despite all the shifts between his twentieth and fortieth year, a "great Christian" when he did science (for example, writing about the equilibrium of fluids or the calculation of conic sections). And he was always a mathematician when he meditated about God and, trying to shed light on God's sunshine, worked with the concept of the "indivisible."

This much may be said: No one—not excepting Augustine and

Luther—ever presented the infinite and the finite, the possibility of God and the uncertainty of man, as precisely as Pascal did. As a psychologist and, as Nietzsche said, a friend of the "great hunt," of the reconnaissance of the human soul and its boundaries, Pascal would not find combatants who could measure with him until two hundred years later. Then a term like boredom (*ennui*), between Baudelaire and Kierkegaard, became a central category, under which one could analyze the combination of depression and distance from God, melancholy and loneliness, which Pascal had as it were discovered before everyone else. (On this point, too, by the way, he was diagnosing his own sickness as a sickness of the time. "The mathematician," says an old topos, "is a sad fellow"; the Melancholy of Bürer's famous picture has the scientist's equipment scattered around her.)

"I who spy on myself more closely, who have my eyes unceasingly intent upon myself. My footing is so unsteady and so insecure, I find it so vacillating and ready to slip, and my sight is so unreliable that on an empty stomach I feel myself another man than after a meal. . . . A thousand unconsidered and accidental impulses arise in me. Either the melancholic humor grips me, or the choleric; and at this moment sadness predominates in me by its own private authority, at that moment good cheer" (Donald Frame, trans.). Thus, in the quest for himself and beyond that for the *conditio humana* as the possible result of such a quest, spoke Michel de Montaigne in the famous twelfth chapter of the second book of the *Essays*, "The Apology of Raymond Sebond." And thus, in Montaigne's footsteps, Pascal spoke, too. Bent over himself, reflecting on the most hidden impulses of his soul, he practiced a kind of psychological art that, in his words, no one was interested in. Yet nothing was more important than to outline the human being who is neither beast nor God, neither in the dark nor in the light, helpless, but, unlike the beast, knowing his helplessness. In reality man is nothing (or as good as nothing) and yet can potentially be everything—a being who has received the legacy and the obligation of transcending himself.

Just as Plato in the *Phaedrus* has the beast in his fable grow feathers in the state of erotic ecstasy and has the dream image, seized by tenacious memory, expose the divine soul within it, so Pascal "Christianizes" Platonic anamnesis. He does this by repeatedly representing the person who, roused by the preacher of penance and his shattering paradoxes, experiences the distant sensing of his first nature as certitude. This certitude, at the same time, tells him he was made for the infinite (*ad deum creatus*) and that he has an organ that unites him, finite man, with his infinite Creator. That organ is his *heart*, which can think visions and translate thoughts into images.

Coeur is a center of sudden and total cognition—and, still more, *re*cognition, Platonic recognition. The "heart" is something that, at the frontier of highest consciousness and intuition (or, to borrow a phrase from Musil, in the state of "mysticism bright as day"), unites reason and love. The "heart" begins to think "Godwards" and therefore brings to life that which is only "scars and empty traces, pale mark, and drift-covered path": the possibility of recalling the first creature. Thus man, catapulted out of deception and delusion and distraction and boredom, again understands himself as the king he once was. The king who has dethroned himself in the garden of Eden may trust that, redeemed and freed from his chains, he will win back the throne (or rather a little footstool at God's feet).

From this standpoint, the actual (and highest) goal of Pascal's writings is to mobilize longing for the lost homeland. Pascal wants to show people—as in the Platonic allegory of the cave—that they live in a world of appearances, into which nevertheless a tiny reflection of the sun—symbolic of the divine idea—presses its way. Pascal wants to strengthen the insight that our existing misery, once it is acknowledged, makes the former grandeur all the more visible: "It is the wretchedness of a great lord, the wretchedness of a dethroned king."

Wretchedness and royalty are the terms that acquire their polyvalence, their Pascalian power of reference, through the fact that they point not only to the poles of human understanding of the world and salvation, but at the same time to the ambivalence of Christianity. Between wretchedness and royalty is where we find Jesus of Nazareth. Jesus reveals to man the sign of the hidden God, and at the same time shows him his baseness, which is his own fault and is proved by the fact that *deus absconditus est* (God is no longer visible).

Jesus, the quintessence of a person who transcends humanity, is a paradox of obscure fame. Nowhere does Pascal's ability to dramatize the truth dialectically show itself in a more brilliant

light than the scene where he describes the man without whom
the world was for him a kingdom of hell—Jesus Christ. It is to
Christ that Pascal, in the "Mystery of Jesus," sings the most
gripping, because most human, death song. This death song to a
lonely, anxiety-ridden man begins with a meditation and culminates in a dialogue, at the cutting edge of misery and royalty:

> Jesus is in a garden, not of delight as the first Adam, where
> he lost himself and the whole human race, but in one of ag-
> ony, where He saved himself and the whole human race. He
> suffers this affliction and this desertion in the horror of the
> night. I believe that Jesus never complained but on this sin-
> gle occasion; but then He complained as if He could no
> longer bear His extreme suffering. "My soul is sorrowful,
> even unto death." Jesus seeks companionship and comfort
> from men. . . . But He receives it not, for His disciples are
> asleep. Jesus will be in agony even to the end of the world.
> We must not sleep during that time. (#552)

The agony of the Redeemer is one of those paradoxes, perhaps
the most pitiless one, with which Pascal makes graphic the contradictoriness and ambivalence of man and the world, here and
now. Pascal interprets the antagonism and ambiguity that he sees
by choosing a style that plunges the reader sentence for sentence
into confusion and uncertainty. If the argument here concerns
man, there it takes God's perspective; here the method is mathematical, there it skips transitions. It is highly poetic and full of
pathos, all with the goal of provoking the reader, of never letting
him rest, but of introducing bluff, theatrical play, paradox, and
ceaseless change in tone, so as to unsettle his interlocutor (whom
he always has in mind and whom he has provided with stupendous
knowledge of human nature). And all this is carefully calculated
to settle the dispute between reason and instinctive irrationality
in favor of reason. Such reason, of course, is not the same as
pure rationality. It is a kind of thinking set in motion through
sparkling paradoxes. Robert Musil, who like Pascal was concerned with sensory-precise descriptions of ratiocinative phenomena, once said of thinking like this that, "with its claims to
profundity, boldness, and novelty," it was limited, "for the time
being to the exclusively rational and scientific realm. But this
understanding consumes what lies around it, and as soon as it has

grasped the feeling, it becomes mind. Taking this step is the business of the poet."

It is the business of the poet—or the philosopher of the sort that Blaise Pascal was. When he was criticized for basically having said nothing that wasn't already known, Pascal responded with a genuine writer's axiom—at least in his case the order was different—"In ball games everyone plays with the same ball, but some place it better."

And that, I think, is what Pascal did. He found adequate language for a situation marked by the possibility, but not the certainty, of an existing God and the possibility *and* certainty of a human being, prefigured in Jesus, who transcends humans. What Pascal found was paradox.

No doubt, Montaigne, whose essays, along with the Bible and the books of mathematics, belonged to Pascal's "last assets," would have called his descendant to order an account of this audacious paradox. He would have spoken of eccentricity and excess. Take the great, extremely human, extremely pagan, extremely enlightened finale of the *Essays*, a soft decrescendo that connects with the ancient maxim, "The more you acknowledge yourself a man, the more you are a god." This sounds like a prophetic critique of Pascal:

> It is an absolute perfection and virtually divine to know how to enjoy our being rightfully. We seek other conditions because we do not understand the use of our own, and go outside of ourselves because we do not know what it is like inside. Yet there is no use mounting on stilts, for on stilts we must still walk on our own legs. And on the loftiest throne in the world we are still sitting only on our own rump. The most beautiful lives, to my mind, are those that conform to the common human pattern, with order, but without miracle and eccenticity. (Donald R. Frame, trans.)

I believe it's useful to read Montaigne's *Essays* after reading the *Pensées*. But it's also useful, after reading Montaigne's reflections, focused on the day and the hour, to return to Pascal. No one, and this bears repeating, has gone further in space than he did—in cosmic as well as psychological space. No one has given a more precise description of what, measured by the Ptolemaic sense of the world that we all live with, it is like to lead a

thoughtful existence against the horizon of infinity. No one has
worked out a more vivid picture of how eternity could be made
experiential and, in the same breath, how the relativity of human
existence could be conceptualized in the face of the infinity of
time and space. Although we all know about that infinity, nowadays, we have by no means taken it to heart: "How many kingdoms know us not" (#207).

ANDREAS GRYPHIUS

POEMS

HANS KÜNG

◆

Religion
in the
Thrall of the Reformation

In my first blossoming. In the spring of tender days
Grim death orphaned me / and the night
Of sorrow wrapped me round / the harsh power
Of sickness consumed me. I languished in constant grief.
I divided my time / in sighs / distress and complaints /
The means / I often took for solid pillars /
They have all (alas) shivered and cracked
I bear all alone the affliction / that I bear.

Thus begins the sonnet "Dominus de me cogitat" ("The Lord
Thinks of Me") by Andreas Gryphius (1616–1664). The speaker
here (*Gedichte*, Reklam, p. 16) knows the meaning of death and
sickness, distress and complaint. Phrases like the one about "solid
pillars" that have "shivered and cracked" were for him anything
but pretty poetic pictures. They were existential experiences
transformed into poetry.

Gryphius' youth in Glogau (Silesia), Görlitz, Frauenstadt, then
in Danzig and Schönborn, was thoroughly overcast by the horrors
of the Thirty Years War. At age five he lost his father, at eleven
his mother. His closest friends, who took the place of the family
for him, died of plague as a result of war-related events. Of his
own seven children, four died very young, and two more were

hard hit by the blows of fate. Indeed, this man knew what he was talking about.

And yet Gryphius would not be Gryphius if his texts did not keep returning to this characteristic shift, this quite unpretentious, unobtrusive turn to what is pious, Christian, and God-given. The poem is gently counterpointed:

> Yet no! the faithful God still offers me eye and hand
> His heart has flamed out toward me, like a true Father /
> It is he / who at all times / must care for me, his child.
> When we find no means / we see his wondrous deeds /
> When our forces fade he proves his strength /
> Look to him / when you think / he has concealed
> 　　himself. (17)

In this section I shall have to speak at length about the origin, importance, and structure of this characteristic shift in the texts of Gryphius. I shall try to diagnose, from both a theological and a literary standpoint, what is the specific nature of this man and his works. But the theologian should at this point first exercise restraint. The Gryphius texts—particularly the popular ones under the vanity motif—can all too easily lead us to reducing the poet to existential dismay and religious emotion. Walter Jens will make the essential comments on the great texts of Gryphius, but to envision the whole person as well as the whole temporal context of his work, we also have to begin here by soberly defining our historical standpoint. I am not concerned in this book with lining up disparate religious works—though that would be interesting— nor just with presenting an individual interpretation of the texts chosen, but with shedding some light from intellectual and cultural history on the major connections between the individual epochs under the one guiding question: How did people deal with religion in the modern period, and what did religion itself make of modernity?

As early as the nineteenth century, which had little understanding of baroque literature, the literary historian G. G. Gervinus called Gryphius the "most independent and many-sided of all seventeenth-century poets" (*Geschichte der Deutschen Dichtung*, III, 349–50). But not until the research on baroque done in our time (above all by M. Szyrocki, W. Flemming, H. H. Krummacher, and W. Maurer) were the significance and importance of this Silesian poet clearly worked out. Andreas Gryphius was, to be sure, a man from provincial Germany, but his province was at the time the battleground of Europe. In an altogether different way from Pascal the Parisian, suffering from the war provoked him to great literary creation. Thus, he is for us another grand representative of this epoch in European history, which in the European context has still been given much too little attention. He may confidently be included in our group of major figures.

In Germany, too, there is a *life within a historical shift* that embraced at once ecclesiastical and political structures, theological-literary and socioeconomic developments, both religious and social movements. Of course, historians argue about the interdependence of the religious and political spheres, of theology and society. The findings of the history of religion and theology have hitherto been too little shown as internally connected with those of cultural and intellectual history, with legal and constitutional, economic, and social history.

The really controversial point is periodization, which can be done differently in accordance with different standpoints and different disciplines. In most general histories and church histories, however, after the Reformation, after the Lutheran and Reformed orthodoxy, after the Catholic Counter-Reformation and the age of confessionalism, we find a second great watershed located *in the middle of the seventeenth century*. This "continental divide" is the crisis of the Reformation (Counter-Reformation) paradigm, which led to the transition to a new total constellation, to a new *paradigm of modernity*, characterized by the new science, technology, industrialization, and democracy.

As the research of numerous English-speaking scholars (E. J. Hobsbawm, H. R. Trevor-Roper, T. K. Rabb), French scholars (R. Mousnier), and German scholars (H. Lehmann) has shown in detail, not only Germany, but all of Europe then found itself in a profound, ongoing crisis: slumping birth rates; economic decline in agriculture, business, trades; increase of illiteracy. All this was bound up with a deep uncertainty about moral values and norms. Thus, we have a crisis not only in politics and economics, but also in theology, the church, and piety. In other words, by contrast with the time of Luther and Calvin, religious and ecclesiastical demands were not so much influencing the political, economic, social, and cultural processes, as the other way around. The church's structure, religious movements, and theology were increasingly shaped by political, economic, social, and cultural factors. A further indication of the rise of modernity was that culture and religion were drifting apart. This marked the beginning of a *process of secularization* that increasingly became a controlling force everywhere.

————————◆————————

Where in this revolutionary upheaval do we find Andreas Gryphius—a German contemporary of Pascal and Descartes? Was this leading mid–seventeenth-century representative of German literature already a modern man—unlike Pascal—in the *theological* sense? Was he shaped, in his piety and theology, by the basic forces of the new science, technology, industry, and even democracy? Did he succeed in reacting more appropriately than Pascal, from a theological standpoint, to the paradigm of modernity?

New science? One of the most significant epigrams of the Protestant Gryphius is dedicated to a Catholic canon in Royal-Polish Prussia, *Nicolaus Copernicus* (1473–1543). We know that out of fear of the Index and the stake Copernicus put off publishing his life's work almost until he died. In his work *De revolutionibus orbium coelestium libri VI* (of which he is said to have received the first copy on the day of his death) he laid the foundation, as we know, of a new, truly revolutionary world system based on his own observations, calculations, and geometric-kinetic reflections—the system of heliocentrism.

This "paradigm change" par excellence first affected physics, but later had consequences for the whole worldview and even the metaphysics of the human race. This "change in the total constellation" was at first validated only in theory; and it was quickly rejected by the Reformers Luther and Melanchthon. Around this change, after definitive proofs had been provided by Galileo and Kepler, a wild struggle raged in Rome; Pascal in Paris, Descartes in Holland, and even Gryphius in Silesia followed the outcome of the conflict with the closest attention. In 1616, the year Gryphius was born, Copernicus was put on the Index of Forbidden Books.

The young Gryphius wrote an enthusiastic epigram on Copernicus—probably under the influence of his gymnasium professor

in Danzig, Peter Crüger, an important mathematician and as-
tronomer. In his first collection of epigrams (1643), this piece
occupies the symbolically important seventh place (p. 107). In
between times, Gryphius had studied (and ultimately taught) law,
philosophy, history, and even science for five years, from 1638
to 1643, thus acquiring a high level of education. For Gryphius,
Copernicus was the "thrice wise spirit," the "more than great
man," "whom neither the night of time, which can blast everything / nor bitter envy has bound / the senses / that have found
the course of the earth."

Copernicus deserved praise because he had refuted "the dream
and darkness of the ancients" and had presented "aright" (in a
mathematically convincing way) "what lives and what stirs."
Therefore he deserved fame:

> Look now, your fame is blooming, fame that, as if on a
>   wagon /
> The circle on which we stand must carry around the sun.

A thrice wise "spirit"? "Spirit" here is surely not to be understood in the rationalistic sense of Descartes. Gryphius is not, as
Herbert Schöffler tried to prove, the first Lutheran familiar with
Descartes, and certainly not the first Lutheran Cartesian. Nor in
his highly poetic sonnet "To the Stars," which he characterizes
as "God's watchmen" ("You lights / that I can never get enough
of looking at on earth / You torches that divide night and black
clouds" [7]) can we sense anything of Pascal's anxiety over the
infinite "empty spaces."

"Spirit," of course, must not be viewed in the first instance
from a biblical-theological perspective in connection with the "art
of dying," as Hansjürgen Schings does. "Spirit" here should be
understood in the context of this life, against the horizon of exploring the planet. As a "thrice" wise, a completely wise spirit,
he is willed by God, indeed, granted grace by the Holy Spirit,
and is therefore immortal:

> When that which is earthly / passes away with time
> Your praise shall stand unmoved with its sun. (p. 107)

Science meets theology. Was Gryphius, then, a modern man;
was his world picture, like Descartes' or Pascal's, primarily mathematical and scientific in its contours? Hardly. Research has

rightly shown that Gryphius, for all his scientific education, was no "scientist" in the more modern sense of the word. And Gryphius was therefore not modern, because he "at no time looked to knowledge of nature for an autonomous human activity, independent of the order of salvation. . . . Hence the determination that Gryphius' knowledge of science as a lofty, valid human achievement is not enough to justify the claim that he stood for a scientific (in today's sense) world picture or for a 'modern' (which at the time was more or less equivalent to Cartesian) world picture. Gryphius' view of science does not even show that he was a supporter of the Enlightenment. We hear talk of scientific findings even in the Protestant literature of edification" (so writes one of the leading interpreters of Gryphius, Wolfram Mauser, in his study, *Poetry, Religion, and Society in the Sonnets of Andreas Gryphius*, pp. 53, 55–56).

No doubt, the poet Andreas Gryphius knew his age. He made a long trip during the Leyden period to Paris, Florence, Rome, Venice, and Strassburg (1644–1647). He had managed to make his own many of its findings, even in the area of natural science. But they would never become for him, as for Pascal, the occasion of a fundamental conflict in theology and politics. Immediately after the end of the terrible war, he got married. He turned down professorships in Frankfurt on the Oder, Uppsala, and Heidelberg. In 1650, back in his own town, he finally became the Syndikus (legal advisor) of the provincial diet of the principality of Glogau. Throughout this time he remained a *Reformation Christian* in his thinking and feeling. He made use of the new scientific activities and discoveries, not, like other spiritual writers, merely apologetically, in a point-by-point manner, to confirm the truths of faith. Rather, as a *poeta doctus*, as a scholar and philosopher, at once a man of faith and reason, he fit them into his notions of the order of salvation history, as shaped by the Bible and the Confession of Augsburg.

Gryphius was not a modern, but a distinctly Reformation person and poet. This holds true of his attitude not just toward the sciences, but also toward the *state* and *politics*. His ethics, based on his Protestant faith, his highly developed sense of justice, his upright private and political conduct (praised on all sides) reveal him as the man he was in his day: a blameless Lutheran Christian. But at the same time it becomes unambiguously evident—indirectly in his sonnets, odes, and epigrams, quite directly in his dramas—that precisely as a Lutheran Christian, and as a jurist and politician as well, Gryphius affirmed without reservation the princely absolutism that was approaching its zenith, first in France and then in Germany as well. This was the system of the *divine right* of kings, which now increasingly bore the mark of the court and the established church, instead of a confessional tenet.

To be sure, for Gryphius even the prince stands *beneath* the positive or natural law of *God* ("jus divinum, naturale, et gentium," H. Hildebrandt, *Die Staatsaufassung der schlesischen Barockdramatiker im Rahmen ihrer Zeit*). But at the same time, he stands *above* all *human* laws and statutes, simultaneously incorporating in one person the legislature, the executive, and the judiciary without any sharing of authority.

Especially in his great moral-didactic tragedies, *Leo Armenius or Regicide*, *Murdered Majesty or Charles Stuart, King of Great Britain*, and *The Magnanimous Jurist or Aemilius Paulus Dying*, tragedies that Johann Elias Schlegel compared to Shakespeare's royal plays, one thing becomes clear: Gryphius had no time for *popular sovereignty* (and the right of resistance), as taught by Hugo Grotius in Leyden. (Leyden was where Gryphius himself had studied, although of course Grotius was driven out in 1621.) Nor did Gryphius respond to the movement toward popular sovereignty initiated by the English parliament's opposition to the absolutist Stuart kings, and championed by Gryphius' contemporary Oliver Cromwell in the English civil wars.

Naturally, real national consciousness, the prerequisite for popular sovereignty, could scarcely arise in a Germany broken up into so many little states. All during Gryphius' life, fidelity and obedience remained the most important virtues of the subordinate. Rebellion against the ruler was rebellion against God. So the judgment of Willi Flemming seems well-founded: In Gryphius' dramas we see manifested "patriarchal absolutism based on Luther, as conceived and practiced in central Germany, and as advocated by Gryphius from the beginning" (p.101).

In sum, just as Gryphius had a clear religious and denominational position, his views on society and politics were equally straightforward. He was a monarchically minded Christian, who firmly supported princely absolutism, that is, the state of being freed from (*ab-solutus*) all human laws and statutes, while struggling against princely despotism, Machiavellianism, and autonomous raison d'état. Gryphius had a profound awareness of law, as consciously based on God's eternal law.

All this has to be kept in mind when we try to draw a more precise *theological* picture of Gryphius in the crisis of his day. How did this pastor's son cope with the oppressive anxieties of life in the seventeenth century? (The reader will find excellent information about the various religious and philosophical positions of the age in Hartmut Lehmann's *Das Zeitalter des Absolutismus, Gottesgnadentum und Kriegsnot.* For the different interpretations of Gryphius, see Hans-Henrik Krummacher, *Der junge Gryphius und die Tradition.*) Where does he stand? A comprehensive portrait of Gryphius will incorporate six aspects.

1. It's quite understandable that the dreadful Thirty Years War played a particular role in evoking an apocalyptic consciousness in Christian circles. The enormous external pressure of fear was compensated for only by the expectation that the end of the world would soon arrive. Didn't the Book of Daniel in the Old Testament and the Book of Revelation in the New contain enough hints, which could be substantiated by complicated calculation? Weren't there said to be conclusive "signs of the times" everywhere that the return of Christ was not far off? The reascent to power of the papal Antichrist, the success of the Counter-Reformation, the advances of the Turks, as well as uprisings, diseases, natural catastrophes, and especially the appearance of "disaster-bearing" comets all suggested it. In the year Gryphius died, 1664, and the year that followed, 130 pamphlets were published about comets, most of them completely unconcerned with science.

But Gryphius, even though he was highly sensitive and astonishingly receptive, was no *apocalyptical enthusiast.* Much as he believed in the Day of Judgment—one of the earliest sonnets by the twenty-year-old poet was devoted to this theme—he showed little of the excited high intensity of an apocalyptically minded sectarian. As the sonnets show, he was less concerned with the

General Judgment than with his personal destiny of death, which was on his mind every day. Not surprisingly, death appeared to him as liberation, as the entrance way into eternal life.

2. Although a man of conscience, of constancy, and courageous dedication, Gryphius was also no *repressive fanatic*. He was not one of those people who—often faced, as he was, by an apocalyptic horizon—project their anxieties onto others, onto "scapegoats," and thus respond with persecution. Nowhere does he acquiesce in the persecution of Jews and witches, which reached a horrible high point in this century of external and internal uncertainty.

After the anti-Jewish bull of Paul IV in 1555, the year of the Augsburg Confession (we should not forget the anti-Jewish writings of Luther's old age), there were persecutions of the Jews in the papal states and Italy. At the beginning of the seventeenth century, there were also expulsions of the Jews from Spain and Portugal, pogroms in Frankfurt, Worms, and Vienna, and then immediately after the middle of the century the worst persecution of the Jews in Poland. Left in the lurch by their Polish master, more than 250,000 Jews were murdered and more than seven hundred communities destroyed by the rebellious cossacks.

As for *witches*, with ideological support from declarations by the popes, but from Luther and Calvin, too—from the end of the sixteenth to the end of the seventeenth century an estimated one million pitiful women (along with a few men and children) were executed for entering into pacts with the devil and harming people, animals, and property. All this was carried out in accordance with unimaginably cruel inquisitorial procedures. Because of the confessions wrung from the victims by torture, there was no way out for the accused, but healthy profits for judges, executioners, and other authorities. The first person to protest against the witch trials—five years before Gryphius' first sonnets (1631)—was the Jesuit Friedrich von Spee, the poet of the "Defiance-Nightingale." Not only did Gryphius not engage in oppression, but after the Thirty Years War in Silesia, which was once more Hapsburg territory, he himself as a Lutheran was one of the victims of the Counter-Reformation.

3. As he was neither an apocalyptic enthusiast, nor a repressive fanatic, so neither was Gryphius one of the backward-looking

orthodox doctrinaires, who poured the living message of the Reformation into a rigid, highly theoretical philosophical-theological system and thus contributed to the tension between theology and piety. In the face of the confusion of the time and the schism in Christianity, he never displayed this anxious concern over pure doctrine, the infallibility of the letter, the inviolability of denominational tradition, or the interpretation of individual points of doctrine. Gryphius—a convinced Lutheran, although in a threatened position, a true member of the community, and not an ecumenical spirit—was disinclined to orthodox bickering and denominational polemics (as were many contemporaries with his level of culture). He spoke out against discord and contention in the church, showed no particular interest in differentiating himself from either Catholicism or any other Protestant denomination. And in his poems, citing and adapting even Catholic authors, he broached many subjects that may be called common to all Christians.

4. But Gryphius was also not a *pre-Enlightenment* type. In the light of an often simplistic opposition between "Renaissance optimism" (confidence in the world and oneself) and "baroque pessimism" (hopelessness and despair), critics have tried to turn Gryphius into a precursor of the Enlightenment, only superficially Lutheran (Gerhard Fricke), even a rebel (C. von Faber du Faur). Indeed, Wolfgang Philipp characterizes him as something like a mystic of negativity, a representative of "cosmic and anthropological nihilism" (*Das Zeitalter der Aufklärung*, 15). But this approach completely removes Gryphius' "vanitas" poems from the context of Lutheran devotion. This is to absolutize one pole of his spirituality (the nothingness of the world) while ignoring the other (trust in God). It exposes him, with no good reason, to the suspicion of an abysmal inner conflict, of intellectual dishonesty, in fact.

The poem cited at the beginning of this chapter and numerous other texts are more than sufficient to refute this charge. The theme "All is vain (transitory)" has to be seen against the background of "what is eternal":

You see / wherever you see only vanity on earth . . .
Ah, what is all this / that we revere as exquisite /
But evil nothingness / but shadows / dust and wind;

But meadow flowers / that are gone when sought for.
Nor will anyone reflect on what is eternal. (5)

5. On the other hand, Gryphius is also *no mystic*. In the light
of the preferred treatment accorded mystic religiosity by scholars
of German literature and their harsh opposition to orthodox theology, Gryphius becomes the representative of mysticism in the
positive, actual sense (as Karl Vietor has said). But this poet is
not concerned about an (ultimately futile) immediate-intuitive
experience of unity (the source of revelation is less his own interiority than the Word of the Bible). He is not concerned about
the consciousness of a previously existing unity of man with the
primeval foundation and abyss, of the fusion of the "little spark
of the soul" with the "flowing light" of the deity. He does not
care about cosmological speculations à la Giordano Bruno, theo-
sophical trains of thought à la Jakob Böhme, or pansophist Ros-
icrucian visions à la Johann Valentin Andreae. But in good
Lutheran fashion—given an irreducible difference between a
kindly God and sinful man—he writes of the light granted by the
Holy Spirit, a grace that never leads to identification with God,
but to seeing God face to face:

My often storm-tossed ship the plaything of the wrathful
    winds
The ball of the bold waves / which cuts through the flood /
Which runs over cliff and cliff / and foam / and sand
    Comes before its time to the port that my soul desires.
    Often / when black night overcame us at noon
The rapid lightning burnt the sails.
How often have I misread the wind / and north and south.
How damaged is the mast / the helm / rudder / centerboard
    and keel.
Disembark, you weary spirit / disembark! we have landed!
Why do you shudder at the port / now you will be free of all
    bonds
    And fear / and bitter pain / and heavy sorrows.
Farewell / cursed world: you sea full of rough storms! /
Happiness to my fatherland / may constant rest keep it in
    shelter
    And protection and peace / you eternally bright castle.
    (9–10)

6. Thus Gryphius' works should be understood in connection with the *literature of edification* then coming into vogue. This was a literature that enjoyed an increasing vogue because of the desolate, comfort-seeking time of crisis and distress. The demand for such writing increased particularly after Johann Arndt—who, like his predecessor Philipp Nicolai (*The Joyful Mirror of Eternal Life*, 1599), was strongly influenced by medieval literature—published his multivolume *On True Christianity* (1606–1610). These works seem to belong in the category of devotional literature, which aims not at theological scholarship and objective correctness of doctrinal statements, but at depth, interiority, and practice. On the Catholic side, this approach had parallels in Francis de Sales, Cardinal Bérulle, and Miguel de Molinos, while in the Protestant world there was a matchless flowering of hymnody (Paul Gerhardt), accompanied by a flood of consolatory pieces, funeral sermons, elegies, and the collections of prayers.

It is true that recent research (P. Böckmann, E. Geisenhof, K. O. Conrady, A Schöne, H. H. Krummacher, D. W. Jöns, H. J. Schlings) has established Gryphius' connections with the literature of edification (especially with Arndt, Heermann, Herberger, Meylart, Stegmann) and to the closely related Lutheran "Reformed orthodoxy." And yet Gryphius is not really an edifying writer, someone aiming to provide spiritual consolation. At the end of an epoch of dispute over religion and faith, and on the threshold of a new age of knowledge and science, he was a poet with a *strongly rational orientation*. It was characteristic of him that out of deep personal faith he linked together Lutheran biblical piety with humanistic-rhetorical education, so that he could, above all, address an elite group of educated people.

Thus, although he was actively committed, and at the same time highly conscious of reality, in his poetry he did not wish simply to communicate pious feelings, to present personal experiences, or to produce lyrics about his own life (he was very restrained even in his portrayal of Jesus). Instead, as a philosophical poet, he tried to pass on *sophia* (poeticized knowledge, wisdom) through his art. In language that was terse and compact, both artistically polished to the last degree and yet full of powerful images (Walter Jens will analyze this in detail) he understood how to make clear, in continually different contexts, *the standpoint of man on this planet*. Gryphius illuminated the human condition within the whole enormous structure of order, shaped by time and eternity, darkness and light, life and death, salvation and perdition.

What, then, are the distinguishing features of this man, who was no apocalyptic thinker (despite all the apocalyptic travail of the age), no fanatic (despite all the period's horrible religious struggles), no orthodox believer (despite all his unconditional ties to the Protestant-Lutheran faith), no pietist (despite the great personal warmth of his texts), no mystic (despite the world-denying reflection on the bedrock of human existence)?

Indeed, what distinguished him, this man who was more melancholic than mystical, more spiritual than intellectual, who was called *theoreticus* and *practicus*? It was, we have to say, his superior wisdom, and thus his amiability, his magnanimity, his *lack of fanaticism in a fanatical age.* His texts show how he always maintained a tight control over himself despite all his passion, a strictness toward himself despite all his feelings, a reserve despite all his bewilderment. He was not a man to indulge in boundless, hopeless outcries. In his texts as in his faith, he remained rational and measured (he bore the mark of Stoicism). In many ways he could be compared to Johann Sebastian Bach. Thus, just as his emotions do not burst the bounds of classical measure (alexandrines, sonnets), so the upheavals of his day do not shatter his faith. Despite all those upheavals, there is a final unshakableness; despite all the setbacks, there is an unconditional trust in God, the rock of steadiness.

> Up, my heart! Awake and bethink you
> That the gifts of this time
> Are yours only for a moment.
> What did you enjoy before?
> It has run off like a stream /
> What is to come: Whose will it be?
>
> Laugh at the world and honor /
> At fear / hope / favor and learning /
> And beseech the Lord.
> He remains king forever,
> Whom no time banishes
> Who can forever bring oneness.

Blessed is he who trusts in him!
He has built right soundly /
And if he falls here at once,
He will stand there yet /
And never pass away
Because strength itself upholds him.

To put it in more modern terms, amid a grand *crisis of orientation*, in which all standards and the meaning of life are threatening to fall by the wayside, this many-sided man with his practical politics, a committed, learned poet, wished to offer *Christian guidance* (W. Mauser) in high poetic form without lamentations or false pathos. What he had was not new theological theories, but a new meaning, new standards, a practice anchored in Christian faith. Practically speaking, this meant the imitation of Jesus Christ in a time of distress.

Perhaps it is this remarkable mixture of an *awareness of crisis and an unshakable confidence in God* that makes Gryphius at once close to and remote from us, who find ourselves in a similar crisis while making the transition to a new paradigm. This Gryphius evokes in us both agreement and distance. In reading the texts, we agree with the description of all the uncertainty of our life, all the anxiety, fear, and concern. We agree with the description of the crises of our time, with the acknowledgment of the fact that our life before God is, in the final analysis, vain and transitory. It will fade away like smoke blown by strong winds. We agree, then, that Gryphius' faith is tied in with the perception of crises; it cannot be thought through or lived out while disregarding all the thousandfold threats he faced. This man is close to us because we, too, live in an "age of anxiety" and have come to know the apocalyptic destruction of the world as a technical possibility.

Agreement, yes, but distance as well. We are put off by the fact that the diagnosis of crisis, the awareness of anxiety, and the analysis of danger in Gryphius cannot take place without a radical depreciation of the world, that his hope in God must be purchased by gloominess toward the world. Gryphius, to be sure, could bear the catastrophes of the age because he was sure of his God as the place of asylum, as the harbor of peace, rest, and harmony. But Dostoyevsky and Kakfa are in many respects closer to us. In the crises of their time, God, too, was in a crisis. As early as the eighteenth century, *theodicy* became a key word, but Gryphius himself was not yet familiar with the concept in the seventeenth century. And the full awakening of human reason to modern autonomy—as we shall see it in Lessing—would, on the one hand, enormously revalue the world and humanity, and, on the other, call into question not only the medieval Catholic faith in God, but the Reformers' faith as well. And it would do this in a way that Gryphius and the last generation of the denominational age could not anticipate.

But the fact that the paradigm would now change in Germany, too, takes nothing away from the meaningfulness of his Reformation faith. Some of the deeply pious prayers from Gryphius' time have held up till this day; some of the powerful old chorales still belong to contemporary hymnody, although we have to retranslate almost everything into the language of our time:

> Now give thanks, all of you, and give honor, you people in
>   the world,
> To him, whose praise the angel hosts in heaven constantly
>   proclaim.

Although this reflects a bygone paradigm, it is still the same Christian faith. This holds true of the chorales of Paul Gerhardt as well as of the poems by his contemporary, Gryphius. As I conclude, let me make that point clear once more, by means of an often-ignored sonnet, to which Walter Jens called my attention. It is an opus posthumous, written on the occasion of the birthday of his daughter Maria Elisabeth and the Feast of Concordia. It was composed in the later Glogau period, in any case after the end of the war (*Complete Edition*, M. Szyrocki and H. Powell, eds., I, 112).

Once again the reader has to realize the situation. In his childhood, Gryphius was forced to witness the expulsion of his father by Catholic troops. In his revered patron Schönborner, he came to know a highly cultured, but religiously torn, man. This taught him what it meant when the Counter-Reformation was imposed by continual threats, trickery, and violence. All his life, Gryphius was a victim—now more actively, now more passively—of Catholic repression. On another occasion he complained about the compulsion, which no one approved, of unconstrained souls, and about the perversely violent conversions. Still, he never let fall a word of hatred or hostility. "No wrathful word will ever be found in my mouth"—what he says to his daughter is true of him, too.

Although he had to watch the Christian churches themselves rending each other "in raging full quarrel," he unswervingly faced the fury and the wrath, the quarrels and the divisions, the whole chaos of unrestrained behavior, in Christian faith. He countered all this with the image of harmony and peace, "dear union"— "Concordia!" Gryphius' faith lived in the confident belief that God is peace, that the spirit of the one God is the spirit of harmony, and that in this spirit one can become the daughter of God, in other words, the child of God.

This text is moving not only as a Christian, profoundly human programmatic contrast to the separateness of nations and confessions; it is also moving as a humble withdrawal of oneself in the face of God: "But if I ask so much / Then do stay bound to your God in harmony." What could this mean except that, even with the breakdown of peace in the world and the church, peace with God is still possible? But concord with God, Gryphius is saying, must be matched by concord with men; the inner and the outer world must be reconciled. This is in fact a deeply Christian, a truly ecumenical, text—a promise that to this day has yet to be fulfilled:

Come, pledge of harmony come / the wrathful nations
     storm /
  In raging full quarrel / the Church is split /
  And by that very band / that takes the name of Christ /
You find nothing here / but unrestrained morals. /
Ah if men can beg the heart of the Highest Lord
  That he / who knows only the means of harmony /
  Through the fire of his spirit / which burns only in peace /
Will calm the mind of all men / while you yet live.
  If it be possible, then let it come: But if I ask too much /
Then do stay bound to your God in harmony /
  Dear unity be the goal of your thoughts /
Let no angry word be found in your mouth.
  Should you gain this wish / you will be not only mine:
  No, but thrice more / the daughter of the Most High.

WALTER JENS

◆

The Sword into a Plow

Tübingen, 350 years ago. An autumn day, the great war was drawing to a close. Many villages had been laid in rubble and ashes, marauding troops swung through the country, the fields were devastated, the herds of cattle driven off, pestilence and disease reigned all about. This was the time when a professor of mathematics and Orientalism, Wilhelm Schickard (who later won fame and honor as the designer of a calculating machine), made this entry in the minutes of the faculty: "Abandoned by every-one—even the councillors and the noblemen had fled—we gathered trembling in the senate in the middle of the night and submitted to the mercy of the conqueror in order to spare the blood of innocent children."

Abandoned by everyone. In the Thiry Years War, that meant to be helplessly exposed to the bands of military ruffians (Schickard's elderly mother was cut down), to have to pay disgraceful contributions, to live in disease-ridden houses that no doctor would enter. "O good Jesus," Schickard wrote in the university register, "to what end have we been spared?"

Germany in the seventeenth century, around the middle of the Thirty Years, shortly before the Peace of Westphalia. In Swabia at that time, blooming fields had turned into moorland and swamps. A messenger riding from the Electorate of Saxony to Berlin would spend an entire day, from early morning to night, passing through unplowed land and dense thickets of conifers. There wasn't a single village where he could rest.

"Because of the wretched and troubled circumstances in these

two years and more, not one child has been born into the world."
This note from a parish register in the Coburg district stands as
an example of the catastrophe brought on by a war in which two-
thirds of the population in Thuringia, the Palatinate, Mecklen-
burg, Pommerania, and Würtemberg had been sacrificed. There
were no seeds to be sown, no cattle, no work; for years to come
there would be no prospect of rebuilding.

"Was there ever heard, since the foundations of this great
world were laid, such grim tyranny and horror? Is there anything
that has not been destroyed by war, the sword, flames, and the
spear?" Andreas Gryphius, the man who wrote these lines in a
festive sonnet for the twenty-fifth Sunday after Holy Trinity, knew
whereof he spoke. He had experienced the meaning of war, burn-
ings, plague, murder, the loss of his nearest and dearest, religious
distress and the pillaging of body and soul. His life has the character of a solemn reminder, as shown by his funeral discourses,
memorial sonnets, and elegiac odes; as does his description of
the plague of Glogau—a song of tears and thanksgiving after
danger has been overcome, in which the destroying angels dialogue with the stricken humans. Before the angels of the covenant
finally appear, we find in the middle of the poem not the Father
of Peace, but the terrible God of Wrath, so close to the war, the
God of Job—"Why do you hide your face and take me for an
enemy?"—whom Gryphius quotes in a lament that verges on an
accusation: "Ah, he hides his countenance! In deepest affliction
lays me low / He forces me into battle / He has conspired in
enmity against me, / Chosen me as the target of revenge! Yet I
am nothing but dust and vapor."

If there ever was a writer who described war, with all its retinue,
as the quintessence of man's oblivion of salvation, as the calling
down of wrath from heaven—it was Andreas Gryphius. He was
orphaned early and thrust about hither and yon. Later forced to
study abroad since Silesia's Protestants had no university, he was,
according to his first biographer, Baltzer Siegmund von Stosch,
a child without a homeland: "Since all over Germany everything
was devastated, turned upside down, he . . . found no room in
the inn." Glogau was laid waste. Freystadt was destroyed, like
those German cities in the Second World War, one of which
(Hamburg) Erich Nossack describes in his account of the destruction of Hamburg in such a way that the model, Gryphius' poem

about the destruction of the city of Freystadt, can still be recognized. That poem closes with the verses: "What the plague has not taken, the rifle and saber have! What they do not get, the fiery blaze consumes! What have the greedy flames left of Freystadt? What you see, the handful of dust and ashes."

No doubt, looked at in this way, in a German peace library—like the one imagined by the pacifist and physician Georg Friedrich Nicolai at the time of the First World War—Andreas Gryphius would receive a place of honor. He would be featured there a little more prominently than other writers who, with a similarly clear voice and without ideologically glorifying terror, have described what the absence of peace means for human beings. One such writer would be Friedrich von Logau, who composed an acrostic with the first letters spelling war (KRJEGS in the original German):

> Trouble that consumes the marrow /
> Robbery that lays waste possessions /
> Woe that perverts the mind /
> Misery that weighs down the body /
> Cruelty that brings injustice /
> Are the fruits that war provides.

In fact, any interpretation of Gryphius' poetry *sub specie religionis* that forgets that, at the time of the Thirty Years War, hell was an ever-present reality (Logau: "Because war like fire burns, because men are devils") would a priori lose sight of its object and stand in danger of losing itself in airy, empty speculation.

War meant the dominance of evil all over the world, not only on the field of battle. For writers, war was equivalent to a threat to their existence, both physical and intellectual. War meant, for example, preaching in the outdoors or in makeshift churches (in Silesia alone, 650 Protestant churches were closed by the Catholics). War meant sickness and early death. None of the great German poets in the seventeenth century, Opitz, Logau, Gryphius, Grimmelshausen, lived past fifty-five. But, last of all, war meant dreaming the great dream of peace in the form of a transcendent vision, the dream of universal reconciliation. At the time, this vision conjured up a country that to the writers around 1650 was at once infinitely far away, located more in heaven than on earth. And yet thanks to a lightninglike, extremely realistic countervision, this country was close and reachable: Switzerland.

It is staggering to read how Grimmelshausen's Simplicius and his companion Heart-brother, "fitted out with long black coats, pilgrims' staffs, and rosaries," go as pilgrims from Swabia to Switzerland. There they enter a different world, seemingly located in distant constellations and yet as close and palpable as Lake Constance: "The country seemed so strange to me, compared with other German countries," Simplicius the pilgrim informs us,

> as if I had been in Brazil or in China. There I saw people trading and walking about in peace. The stables were full of cattle, the barnyards were full of chickens, geese, and ducks running about, the streets were safely used by the travelers. The taverns were full of people who sat there enjoying themselves. There was no fear whatsoever of the enemy, no concern about plunder, and no anxiousness about losing one's property or life. Everyone lived securely beneath his vine and fig tree, and indeed, measured against other German countries, they lived in pure voluptuousness and joy. I took this country for an earthly paradise.

Here it becomes evident *ex negatione—ex negatione belli*—how amiable peace is and how close to paradise, as attested to by the biblical terms vine and fig tree, the earthly here and now could look. This is a small, very tender, very concrete vision à la Bertolt Brecht ("an earthly Paradise, although it seemed to be rather rough of its kind"), a poetic anticipation of sensations that three hundred years later, in fascist Germany after 1939, were to become a kind of collective dream: Simplicius and Herzbruder's hermitage—a Garden of Eden on a star, whose nearness, since it was unreachable, constituted its distance: "There was no fear at all of the enemy . . . and no anxiousness."

The heavenly Jerusalem is mirrored in the likeness of a Swiss peasant's peaceful field, where Helvetian ducks and geese waddle around vines and fig trees, which seem at once real and unreal, and point to the everyday biblical realm, to Palestine and such things, with a poetic salto mortale, quickly through the air.

How differently, and yet in keeping with this vision of Grimmelshausen's does Andreas Gryphius' war lament sound. Originally composed in 1637, "The Lament of Devastated Germany," seven years later called "The Tears of the Fatherland / Anno

1636," was published within the framework of the Leyden sonnet
cycle:

We are now wholly—nay more than wholly—devastated!
The band of presumptuous nations, the blaring trumpet,
The sword greasy with blood, the thundering cannon
Have consumed everyone's sweat and industry and
    provisions.
The towers are on fire, the church is cast down,
The town hall lies in ruins, the strong are maimed,
The virgins raped, and wherever we look,
There is [nothing but] fire, plague, and death that pierces
    heart and mind.
Here through the bulwarks and the town ever-fresh blood is
    running.
Three times six years ago the water of our rivers
Slowly found its way past the corpses that almost blocked it;
But I will say nothing of what is worse than death itself,
More dreadful than the plague and fire and famine—
That so many have been despoiled of the treasure of the
    soul.

                    (Leonard Forster, trans.,
                    The Penguin Book of German Verse)

"The Tears of the Fatherland" is a poem that presents experiences, but is no poem of "experience." It is a sonnet that teems
with elements of reality, but nevertheless is anything but "realistic." It is a poem in which the writer incorporates himself into
the text—"we are devastated"—and yet is no piece of confession
pointing to an individual with unmistakable features or even to
a lyrical "I" tuned to radical subjectivity. Anyone looking in
Gryphius for a twin of his contemporary Pascal, a domineering
ego (though capable of humility) operating against others in clear
confrontation, is on the wrong track.

"The Tears of the Fatherland" exudes no feelings, but carries
out a highly pathetic spiritual exercise: exact, rational, and comprehensible. The sonnet form prescribed twice four, then twice
three verses, with the obligatory rhyme of the first, fourth, fifth,
and eighth line, and then of the second, third, sixth, and seventh
verse. It usually called for but did not require rhyming correspondence of the ninth and tenth, eleventh and fourteenth lines,

and in addition the twelfth and thirteenth. This schema was described by Martin Opitz in Chapter 7 of his book on German poetry, which spurred on Germany's authors to try to match strides with illustrious artists in the Romance languages, from Petrarch to Ronsard. It left no room for extravagances, original thoughts, and highly private feelings incapable of objectification. The sonnet could not do this, with its fourteen lines, nor could the (again habitual but in no way required) alexandrine with its twelve or thirteen syllables of iambic meter and the dramatic caesura after the accentuated sixth syllable: "Wir sind doch nunmehr *ganz* / ja mehr denn ganz verheeret. Der freschen Völker *Schar* / die rasende Posaun, das vom Blut fette *Schwert* / die donnerende Cartaun hat aller Schweiss und *Fliess* / und Vorrat aufgezehret."

Everything is calculated down to the last detail. Feminine and masculine rhymes, paired or crossed; caesuras that demand a structuring of the text by antitheses and parallelisms. This leaves as little opportunity for cheating as the obligation each poet has of organizing his poem according to the scheme of *proposition*, *argumentation*, and pointed *conclusion*, best of all with the help of a surprising final twist.

Read "The Tears of the Fatherland." What presents itself at first glance as an individual description is in truth a school piece of rhetorical craftsmanship. The thematic assertion ("We are now wholly—nay more than wholly—devastated") is followed by cogent analysis in the form of a description designed to bring the assertion presented at the outset closer to the hearer and reader by listing striking details so that both see the event as it were immediately before their eyes: "The towers are on fire / the church is cast down. The town hall lies in ruins / the strong are maimed."

Amplification through organization, differentiation, and clear illustration of the theme is the key to poetic craft. Gryphius uses amplification through description of things, persons, and places, amplification with the intention of making the reader an eyewitness of the event, as described, differentiated, interpreted, narratively explicated: "Here through the bulwarks and the town / the ever-fresh blood is flowing."

In this way there gradually arises, in the main section of the sonnet, a plastic image that at the end, in a twist reserved for the tercets, is given a surprising interpretation that brings the picturesque description into sharp focus—an interpretation through correction. Gryphius shows that however horrible the devastation of the earth may be—a devastation that even brings water, the essence of movement, to a halt ("the water of our rivers slowly found its way past the corpses that almost blocked it")—worse than the destruction of the body is the endangering of souls, which the sonnet writer mentions almost in passing in the form of a dramatic *praeteritio*. He does so precisely to give it a relevance achieved through silence rather than through conjuring up by means of "hundredweight words": "But I will say nothing of what is worse than death itself, More dreadful than the plague and fire and famine—That so many have been despoiled of the treasure of the soul."

Here the *political* poem suddenly becomes a *religious* poem. Here the devastation, or more precisely the condition characterized by the rhetorical figure of hyperbole ("more than devastation") is related to the loss of faith, to forced or voluntary conversion, to the abandonment of conscience and the betrayal of the Reformed confession. Not fire, plague, and death, but failure under the cross, the renunciation of fellowship with Jesus Christ, lies at the secret core of the sonnet. From the standpoint of the periphery—the final verse—it becomes clear that the actual, and final, horror of the war consists in eternal death, brought about by the loss of faith and the damaged soul itself, in the death that stands not for entrance into God's glory, but for damnation *in saecula saeculorum*.

"The Tears of the Fatherland" is a war poem that, when seen from the standpoint of its conclusion, proves to be a sonnet whose significance derives from something not mentioned—the cross of Christ, which guarantees the inviolability of the soul's treasure. It is the war poem of a Christian, then, who understands the great quarrel among men as a triumph of fallen nature, paid for by the abandonment of eternal life.

It is a pious song—and this bears repetition—the work of a master singer, academically correct and carefully thought through, pregnant with images, and exactly calculated. Gryphius was, like Pascal, a precise thinker and a comprehensively educated man, a jurist and scientist, an adminstrator, a lay preacher, anatomist, and poet into the bargain. He was a learned gentleman and not a profound thinker (as he would later be seen), rather a humanistically trained Protestant than a Faustian precursor of expressionism (as he has also, of late, been interpreted to be).

While he might despise the world, he knew it well. And he knew how, once he came to public office and official business, to establish himself in that world. Gryphius was no romantic enthusiast. When he describes death—as he does over and over again—calling it "pale," "black," "bleak," "cold," "dreadful," "insolent," he speaks—above all in the "Graveyard" thoughts—as one who knows how experts dissect cadavers, and which function to assign each bone in the skeleton. For Gryphius first came the seeing, then the metaphorical interpretation; first the reality, then its allegorization in the image that transcends reality: *primum vivere deinde philosophari*, first live, then think.

"I remember," Gryphius says in his discourses on death, "that in the world-famous anatomical theater at the University of Leiden there is among many other skeletons one bearing a banner with the familiar words, *Nosce te ipsum*, Know thyself."

Gryphius' style of pathos is a pathos of sobriety, not of visionary ecstasy. The terrifying phantasmagoria in the "Cemetery" does not disguise the fact that the writer at work here knows firstly all about the morgue and, secondly, aims to come as close as possible to the rhetorical ideal of *evidentia* (brilliant plasticity) through the most true-to-life description. In this way, he can satisfy the prescription "Ut pictura poesis" ("The poet's art is identical to the painter's technique").

The result is an exhibition of monstrosities and the spectacle of death as a demonstration of artistic talent by a Protestant poet competing with the Jesuits in their archetypal field: the mise-en-scène of the great theater of the world under the aegis of Director Death. Like a young Schiller, Gryphius appears, the rhetorician trained in the *theatrum anatomicum* at Leiden, linking together literary kitsch and metaphysics in a pious doctrine-cum-horror-show poem:

> The eyes' extinguished light
> Begins to move hideously /
> Through the stirring of the worms within /
> The nose turns up and breaks apart.
> The tender cheeks cave in /

Jaw, tongue, and teeth are bared /
The coral glow of the chops /
Is quite done in with black spots.
The forehead bursts open. The snow of the neck
Has won over the harsh frost
And gleams more hotly from its height.

What whispers through the windpipe?
What do I sense hissing in the breasts?
Methinks / I hear snakes
Mingle their dreadful whistling with adders.
What an unbearably foul thick smoke
Rises through the disquieting air.

No, Gryphius was by no means a man careful with words, an advocate of "interiority," and of mystical elevation. He was no less familiar with the pomp of the Jesuit theater, whose practices he thoroughly mastered (as shown not least of all by the stage directions of his dramas), than with the Protestant hymn. He learned from both forms; he was an artisan who had masters on both sides. He went to school with both, whether the master be Johannes Heermann, by trade a Protestant writer of edifying songs, or Jakob Balde, a Jesuit, whose cemetery poems Gryphius deftly translated into German. Gryphius always sought to legitimize the causes he thought just by a maximum of artistic craft, and to apply the most advanced techniques where the point was to give faith its proper rights in the forum of the educated world. Hence the playing with antitheses, chiasmus, metaphors, oxymorons in the alexandrine; hence the preference for difficult forms, the sonnet, the epigram, the Pindaric ode, whose mastery showed that the faith of the Christian man was most convincingly represented not in murmuring and stammering on the verge of silence, but in richly informed discourse and formally perfect verse.

Goethe's principle "Reason and right thinking express themselves with little art" would have struck the baroque poets of Gryphius' stripe as madness and blasphemy. The code of seventeenth-century art dictated that the more witty, the more artistically polished, indeed, the more full of courtly charm was the presentation of any theme, the higher its rank and the greater its power to convince. "I have no sympathy for the opinion," we read in the Introduction to the book of odes called "Tears over the Suffering of Jesus Christ," "that bans all the flowers of eloquence and the embellishment of poetic art from God's church." Gryphius was especially convinced of this in view of the fact that "the Psalms themselves are nothing but poems, some of which express the most heavenly mysteries in an exceedingly lofty way and with the fairest modes of speech. . . . The most exquisite blessings of the Most High are not so much described as sung by the Ancients. The holy sister of the great Lawgiver needed at once tongue and drum when the great tyrant drowned in the Red Sea. Moses himself had no better way than poetry for praising this miraculous rescue to the skies, and his last prophecy is to be found in his last song."

For centuries, a dispute had been going on about the poetically appropriate presentation of biblical situations. In this environment, unlike the worldly domain, the smallest and most inconspicuous item—which, as something consecrated, could not actually be small or inconspicuous—might need a dramatic, indeed a pathetic-ecstatic rendition. On the other hand, the sublime, the crucifixion and resurrection, could be most readily presented through movingly simple description. This controversy over the proper way to clothe the most sacrosanct things in appropriate language was decided by Gryphius in the Prologue to the "Tears over the Sufferings of Jesus Christ," in a comprehensive historical retrospective. Gryphius argued that poetry's sphere is unlimited and the pen dipped into the "blood of the spotless Lamb" can record both biblically plain and rhetorically convincing material. In each case, the poetry had one goal—"to make the Muses sing around the cross of the Lord."

In whatever ways Gryphius wrote, in sermons, tragedies, comedies, odes, epigrams, church hymns, and satirical verses, he never engaged in composing as he went along, in self-expression or self-realization in the act of writing, which in the seventeenth century was taken for granted.

Nosce te ipsum was also Gryphius' personal motto, the slogan of a writer who wanted to take the means uniquely available to him: discourse. He enthusiastically celebrates speech in the first "Reyen" (a kind of choral song) of the drama *Leo Armenius* as man's most excellent gift, the one that distinguishes him from all living creatures. With this gift, he aimed to bring his readers to self-knowledge, to an understanding of the world and to insight into the role that fell to the individual within the framework of the Christian theater of the world. Gryphius shows us life down on the "race course," in the "show fortress," with a view of the "school" (cemetery), in the "game of time" *sub specie aeternitatis*, on the boards of this world, where death plays the lead and God at most enters the picture as an infinitely remote spectator, enthroned somewhere high above: "Play then this serious game, while time still permits."

Andreas Gryphius was a poet, but at the same time he was also, in Luther's footsteps, a spiritual orator, a preacher of penance, an imploring warner in the final hour—a writer who tried with truly obsessive energy to interpret the world from the standpoint of its end, and earthly existence from the standpoint of death.

Gryphius conjures up terror-stricken visions of a Christian in the Thirty Years War: "The world is the royal city of the tyrant Dracula, studded and ringed round with spears, gallows, and wheels of torture, from which the blood, the putrefaction, and the pus of the innocents who have been strangled stream away. . . . It is a vast and spacious charnel house, with nothing inside but the withered bones of departed souls. It is the torture chamber, wherein one hears nothing but the threatening of the judges, the crying out of the hangmen, the pitiful whimpering of the tormented, the clank of the chains, and the stink of lit sulfur candles."

Gryphius' world is made up of a kingdom of the dead, among whose paradoxes is the fact that people, despite all the tortures and atrocities, are unclear about the nature of the place they inhabit. They mistake the most fleeting things for permanence and time for eternity; they confuse a few seconds' happiness with constant well-being. Although they have been branded by death, marked as ephemeral, and poised for departure, at no time are they aware how much they live in a state of insecurity and precariousness. They have forgotten that with every passing moment the chances for gaining eternal salvation diminish. Whence Gryphius' *Great Teaching*, his insistence on the topoi *vanitas vanitatum* and "all is vain"; whence his quoting of medieval Dance of Death motifs (which sometimes degenerate into a list of stereotypes); whence his determination to look upon the here and now from the perspective of the end of time and the Last Judgment, and to interpret contempt for the world ("I must praise affliction") as the Christian's fitting preparation for the day of all days; whence the closeness of his accurate, eloquent phantasmagoria on death to the descriptions of the "hellish Sodom" and the "last trumpet" from the pen of the preacher and poet Johann Matthäus Meyfart; whence, finally, his spirit of *metanoeite* (repent and do penance) in his references to the moment as the second enabling man to understand this counterimage of eternity as a likeness that illuminates it, even while distorting it.

Meditation on Time

The years which time has taken from me are not mine;
The years which may still come are not mine either;
The moment is mine, and if I pay attention to that,
Then he is mine who made time and eternity.

(Leonard Foster, trans.)

Gryphius' theological and political goal was to think time and eternity into unity. Through oxymoron, which shows that contradictions are reconcilable on a higher level, he illuminates light and darkness to let the sign of eternity shine in the "blockhouse" and the "torture chamber" of this world as the rebuttal to our temporal life. This, and just this, was Gryphius' theological *and* political goal. Night and day he would name the reality of Golgotha and the possibility of Bethlehem; he would relate them as connecting and limiting each other. It is no accident that the sonnet "To the Crucified Jesus" is preceded by a poem, also in the sonnet form, that shows how consistently Gryphius used literary paradox to bring the new age's cancellation of natural contradictions, as guaranteed by the night in Bethlehem, into the light of poetry and hence, as he saw it, into the brightness of truth.

Night, brighter-than-bright night! night brighter than the day;
Night brighter than the sun, in which that light is born
Which God, who is light, dwelling in light, has chosen for
     himself:
O night, which can defy all nights and days!
O joyous night, in which wailing and lamenting
And darkness and everything that conspires with the world,

And dread and fear of hell and horror all were lost.
The sky breaks open, but no thunderbolt falls now.
He who made time and nights has come this night
And taken upon himself the law of time and flesh,
And has given our flesh and time to eternity.
The dismal night of sorrow, the black night of sin,
The darkness of the grave must vanish through this night.
Night, brighter than the day! Night, brighter-than-bright
    night!

                    (Leonard Foster, trans.)

Once again, typical of Gryphius, we have a pious *and* artificial poem. We have proclamation, Christian paraenesis in the form of a rhetorically executed intellectual operation that reaches its goal in the last line, reversing the opening line. The original assertion, that night can be brighter than day, has acquired the character of proof through a theological analysis of God's holy place. The thesis, that there is a sun of the night and a light of darkness (*of* and not just *in* the darkness), is established through the recourse to Christ, who abolishes the night, black and heavy with sin, the night of the grave, by making it his own and thereby annulling it. In an audacious, almost tightrope-walking confrontation with the lines from John ("And the light shines in the darkness, and the darkness has not overcome it," "And this is the judgment, that the light has come into the world, and men loved darkness rather than light") Gryphius names the night, not the light, the sun-night of God, as the messenger of redemption. The eternal night defies earthly days and nights, because it represents the arrival of him who is before all times and nights. Jesus is a maker of confusion in the light; through his birth, God and man are reconciled because eternity is realized in time and flesh. On the other hand, flesh and time after Bethlehem are capable of self-cancellation and transcendence.

Through fourteen verses, in ever newer, bolder variations on the basic theme of "night brighter than day," a battle is staged between night and the nights, the sun-night and the darkness, the day-night and the darkness of the grave, misery, and sin. This conflict is staged as a versified showpiece, a demonstration played out on the level of thought. In contrast to a sonnet like "The Tears of the Fatherland," the real elements—the emperor's decree, the stable, the manger, the child, and the Magi—remain out of consideration. It is not the *imago*—to be explained at the end—the graphic picture, but only the *significatio*, the interpretation of the meaning-content, that shapes the structure of the poem. Where others indulge in description—sometimes idyllic, sometimes sober—of the event, Gryphius has confidence in the reader's knowledge of the situation and places all the stress on the salvation-history analysis of a *kairos*. Once and therefore forever, in this sacred moment the child of night, founding the *ordo Christianus*, let humans take part in the light of God.

I wonder if "Christian poetry" (or rather poetry by a writer who understood himself to be a Christian) ever went any further in the sensualization of theology than in this Christmas sonnet. If anywhere, Gryphius, in his poem, published in 1643, on the birth of Jesus, reached a limit in which image (son, thunderbolt, bursting sky, darkness of the grave) and thought become akin. Here he displays a power of abstraction that shrinks back from no bold excess (using "night" fifteen times in fourteen verses), and brings off something that to this day scarcely any other writer has succeeded in doing: to write poetry in the manner and on the level of meaning of John the Evangelist. He was dimensions ahead of all retellings of the episode of Jesus' birth as offered by the Synoptics.

Andreas Gryphius disdained reason and continually defended the thesis that the truly wise man had to laugh wisdom to scorn if he wished to be a human being, that is, the child of God. This same Gryphius was a poet, a "rationalist" of the highest rank, a sober master craftsman (consider the ingenious technique of his sonnets, the reworkings from one version to the next), an artist of strong thoughts and strong language, adept at appropriating and transforming his material, a master of clever construction, a rhetorician who put reason to work. He especially liked to use "hundredweight words," insistent naming, metaphorical expression and exclamations ("Oh," "Alas," "Up"), so as to create high pathos and heart-stirring effects. He was a disputant, trained in suffering, an artist and Cartesian, so far as the discovery of "brilliant" figures, tropes, and rhyme schemes went. And yet at the same time he was still a man of childlike piety, who, like Pascal, carried on a lifelong conversation with the Man of Sorrows. Jesus the martyr provoked him to ever-fresh representation, while the Risen One in glory was represented by Gryphius rather academically in the traditional manner. But Jesus the *companion*, Job's brother on the cross, who, although God's son, fell into temptation, was something else again. Jesus, the adversary of the "cruel God" (Gryphius says in the *Dissertationes funebres*, ". . . what would one have to suffer from God, should he transform himself into a cruel one"), Jesus, to whom only seven sonnets in Gryphius' posthumous works are dedicated—the lowly one, pathetically conjured up in threnodies, strophic meditations under the cross and passion songs—was for Gryphius the key figure. In the shadow of this Jesus, Gryphius—as the sonnets for Sundays and feast days show—translated the texts underlying the pericopes into contemporary terms. He did so by going along in the steps already laid down by the Gospels and at the same time revealing his interest in the stories through paraphrase, didactic reworking, and confessional variations on the model turned round and round. That interest guided his understanding; it looked to concrete time and persons. And he made these stories his own, as shown by the example of the sonnet on the Good Samaritan, a variation on the parable in Luke 10:30ff.:

Wounded unto death / lacerated / battered / crushed
I languish and disappear / now my face dwindles /
My weak body expires / my spent heart breaks;
My weary mind fades in a thousandfold griefs.
My veins have already gone stiff / my mouth can no more
     weep.
Death hovers over me / I myself simply do not know
How heavy the pain is! O light of true life!
Lord Jesus, wilt thou ask for me ever so little.
As priest and levite, ah, Samaritan, come
And pour oil and wine on me / the stream of blood and
     water
From your side! The rough deserts
Of the murderous world only increase my distress /
I will go to the church / where at your command
I can be freed from death through word and sacrament.

Here we find joined once again pious pathos and allegorical art, simple prayer and the descriptive approach with its enumerations. Here as elsewhere, those enumerations consist in prefabricated set pieces, particles to be ticked off from a catalogue of sufferings. And then, suddenly, the turnabout: interpretation of the parable according to its spiritual sense. Jesus is seen as the Samaritan, oil and wine as food from the body of the butchered Lord, the inn as a church. The inn becomes the "host's house" (*Wirts*haus), God's house, in which the pastor, an eloquent Protestant Christian, protects the soul in need of salvation, in good Lutheran fashion, through word and sacrament, fending off eternal death, which is the loss of the treasure of the soul.

This is Protestant poetry, represented by a man who always thought of himself as an obedient administrator of his regional church. It is poetry written at a time of religious schism and a great war. It is an expression of longing for peace in Christ's church spoken from the perspective of the oppressed creature who at the moment of its extreme distress recognizes its helper only in the Man of Sorrows and its home in a church that is not a temple but an inn and a hospice. The church is a hospice for those victims in whose name Andreas Gryphius articulates, in a dark time (see "On the Destruction of the City of Freystadt"), the vision of a future home, shaped by the spirit of Jesus Christ: "The spear, the half-rusted sword will be turned into an axe and a plow."

This vision was written as a daring utopia, in 1637, in a situation where Christendom was further removed than ever from reforming the "murderous world" in the spirit of the Good Samaritan. On the contrary, an epigram by Friedrich Logau points out, as opposed to Gryphius' irenic vision of swords turned into plowshares and reconciliation under the sign of the martyred Rescuer, what was the reality at the end of the Thirty Years War:

> Lutheran, Papist, and Calvinist
> All these three faiths
> Are on hand, yet we may doubt
> Where Christianity is.

GOTTHOLD EPHRAIM LESSING

◆

NATHAN THE WISE

HANS KÜNG

◆

Religion
on Trial
in the Enlightenment

*T*he young lad was twelve years old when he sat for his school's entrance examination. He was asked to do a Latin translation on the influence of Christianity in overcoming ancient prejudices toward barbaric peoples. After the assignment was finished, there was still some time left over, so he added on his own a few well-phrased sentences—still in Latin—which showed even then astonishing intrepidity, penetration, and eloquence.

It is barbaric, he argued, to distinguish between nations, since all have been created by God and furnished with reason; it is particularly fitting for Christians to love their neighbor. According to Christ, our neighbor is the one who needs our help, and thus, he concluded, since we all need one another's help, we are all neighbors one to the other.

"Hence let us not condemn the Jews, although they condemned Christ" ("Itaque nolumus damnare Judaeos, quamquam Christum damnaverunt"), the twelve-year-old demanded. "Let us not condemn the Mohammedans; even among Mohammedans there are decent people" ("nolumus damnare Mahometanos, etiam inter Mohametanos probi homines sunt"). "Finally, no one is a barbarian, except for those who are inhuman and cruel" ("Denique nemo est barbarus, qui non inhumanus et crudelis est" (shared with me by E. A. Diller, quoted in K. Aner, p. 14).

It is remarkable what internal continuity emerges from these sentences in the life of this externally discontinuous person. One might have expected them as the motto of his very last drama, whose production he never lived to see. The playful boy, so quick to learn, who was born into a tolerant but highly orthodox pastor's home in Saxony in January 1729 and died in 1781 (the year of Kant's *Critique of Pure Reason*), became the most feared literary critic of his day and at the same time its most inventive and thoughtful dramatist. He was Gotthold Ephraim Lessing.

But let's pause for a moment and flash back. Pascal and Gryphius died at practically the same time (1662, 1664). While they were still alive, Baruch de Spinoza (1632–1677) was working in total seclusion. His book, when it was published at the end of the decade (1670), was met with vehement rejection. Four years after publication, it was forbidden even in liberal Holland. As early as 1656 (the year Pascal was condemned by Rome), its author was excluded from his own religious community. In his *Tractatus Theologico-Politicus*, this disciple of the rabbis and the most accursed religious philosopher of early modernity, made extremely radical demands that went far beyond anything the Reformation had brought:

1. unlimited freedom of religion for the individual, whether Christian, Jew, or whatever vis-à-vis church and state;

2. criticism of the Bible itself as a human (and often contradictory) document of Judeo-Christian religion; and

3. a new understanding of God, purified from anthropomorphisms, a God no longer outside but in this world, embracing everything, ruling everything, being everything.

Of course, what in 1670 was still considered fully unacceptable, indeed, worthy of condemnation, was now, one hundred years later, largely accepted by Lessing. People (that is, broad circles of educated people) had become—to borrow an expression from eighteenth-century France—*modern*. Meanwhile, times had in fact changed in a fundamental way, and the paradigm change that set in around the middle of the seventeenth century, from Protestant and Counter-Reformation orthodoxy to modernity, had imposed itself on Europe's intellectual elites. This change was fostered rather than arrested by the interiorized, individualistic movement called Pietism and by pious English natural theology ("physico-theology"). And along with the political stabilization there came an improvement of economic conditions, of nutrition, and life expectancy.

We may criticize Paul Hazard's precise dating of the *Crise de la Conscience Européenne* (1935) from 1680 to 1715 as too narrow, but there is no denying that we are dealing with a change from the ancient to the modern in the intellectual culture of Europe, a change from orthodoxy to new forms of faith. The cultural centers of gravity were shifting from the south to the north. This was a transformation in whose wake belief in the devil, witches, comets, and miracles was driven back, and ideas of the natural law and the social contract, valid for all men and women, increasingly prevailed.

This turnabout was likewise unmistakable in the fundamental religious mood and the period's whole response to life—as incorporated in the philosophy of, say, Leibnitz, the first modern German philosopher of European caliber. For his famous *Theodicy* (1710), the Jesuits coined the word *optimisme*. This was a change, then, "from the century of anxiety to the century of hope" (H. Lehmann), in Germany as well as in the rest of Europe.

In Gryphius' day, there was still an atmosphere of anxiety, of transitoriness, and futility, of the consciousness of guilt and the need for grace. But in Lessing's day—this is quite palpable in his writings—we find an atmosphere of hope in life and trust in the goodness of human nature. Self-denial and self-contempt give way to self-affirmation and self-realization. Hostility to the body and sex gives way to naturalness and joy in the senses. Instead of denial and renunciation of the world, conquest of the world comes to the fore. We have the opening up of North America and the English colonization of India (European history becomes world history), as well as Isaac Newton's sketches of the world as seen by classical physics.

◆

Enlightenment became the magic word of the epoch—enlightenment, which began in Holland and England, quickly veered in France (after Voltaire's visit to England) to opposition to the church and Christianity, indeed, to atheism and materialism. In the Germany of Leibnitz, of Christian Wolff, and then of

Lessing, the movement took, of course, a much more moderate
(antimaterialistic-theistic-deistic) path. The challenges posed by
the Enlightenment to the traditional image of the world, God,
and man were also unmistakable. The world, "God's creation,"
became the world machine, God became the highest reason, and
in contrast to all anthropological-theological pessimism (original
sin!) the dignity of man moved onto center stage. This was a
dignity based on man's inborn awareness of God and the natural
law, the freedom of the will, and the immortality of the soul. In
short, Enlightenment religion was a naturally ordained natural
religion for the sake of "virtue" ("usefulness" for the good), of
good morals, and for promoting noble human qualities.

Does this mean enlightenment *through* religion? Recent literature by Enlightenment scholars has called attention to the fact,
specifically in connection with Lessing, that the many-layered
process of the "siècle des lumières," "Aufklärung," "En-lighten-
ment" had important religious roots and components. All the talk
about light can in fact be traced back from the pietistic religion
of illumination and the light-saturated transcendental experience
of English natural theology through Bonaventure and Augustine
all the way to the philosophy of Plato (see the extensive docu-
mentation in A. Schilson, 1974).

And yet this changes nothing about the fact that the crucial
element and the characteristically modern feature of the Enlightenment, which in Germany concentrated primarily on philosophy
and theology, is its power as a critique of religion—the religious
and political emancipation from tradition and dogma, from the
church and Christianity, in other words, the enlightenment of
religion. The daring choice of intellectual adulthood is thus quite
in keeping with the classic answer that Immanuel Kant—consistently following the line of Descartes' Cogito—gave three years
after Lessing's death to the question "What is Enlightenment?":
"Enlightenment is man's release from his self-incurred tutelage."
"Tutelage" here is understood as man's inability to make use of
his understanding without direction from another" (Lewis White
Beck, trans. The Library of Liberal Arts).

If anyone realized the motto of the Enlightenment, "Sapere
aude!" ("Have courage to use your *own* reason"), in an exemplary
manner—as opposed to what Kant points to as "humanity's lack
of resolution and courage"—it was Gotthold Ephraim Lessing.

Karl Barth rightly called Lessing "an eighteenth-century person complete in himself and helping to complete others" (208).

What was Lessing, the child of the Enlightenment, concerned with in his religious sensibility? Lessing's first theological sketches (some striking thoughts on the community of the Herrnhuter), written when he was twenty-one and a prototype of the freelancer and journalist, make clear the direction he was headed in. Man, he said, was "not made for hairsplitting" but "for action" (*Werke in drei Bänden*, Hanser-Ausgabe, III, 272). As opposed to orthodoxy, both Pietists *and* supporters of the Enlightenment (often falsely seen only as enemies) are intent on the idea that true Christian faith proves itself not in reasoning but in right *praxis*. Faith is working for the good of humanity, its happiness. That is why Lessing always stresses action more than theology, morality more than dogma.

Lessing freed himself from tradition and dogma early on. As a theology student who preferred philosophy, philology, archaeology, and, finally, medicine, the traditionalism of his home was already behind him when he attended the University of Leipzig. But he also kept his distance from each of the distinct theological forces of his time—Lutheran orthodoxy, Enlightenment philosophy à la Wolff, and neology.

One can't blame him for this. Lessing thought that Lutheran orthodoxy was extremely "penetrating," but it demanded blind obedience. Despite Luther's attacks on reason and despite a fundamental harsh opposition between reason and revelation, Lutheranism had once again called upon, of all thinkers, that great "prestidigitator" Aristotle, though only for the sake of expanding its theological system. But, of course, modern physics and philosophy were now about to consign Aristotle permanently to the dust heap. As for the popular Enlightenment philosopher Christian Wolff and his theological followers, they had, in an almost Thomistic fashion, harmonized the order of reason and the order of revelation. But they put the accent on reason, and hence were suspected, with good cause, of Catholic sympathies. Then, finally, there were those contemptuously labeled "neologians" (new theologians"), who did subject the dogmas to criticism. In the first instance, they attacked the dogma of original sin, which offended the optimistic anthropology of the Enlightenment, but later they also scrutinized the Trinity and the Incarnation. The neologians rationalized away the contradictions between revelation and reason in a "newfangled fashion." As Lessing saw it, they had produced nothing but a "patchwork of bunglers and half-philosophers."

For consistent thinkers had long asked themselves this question: If the *machina mundi* is supposed to be a shapeless infinite thing without a center or limits, as Nicholas of Cusa, Marsilio Ficino, and Giordano Bruno had already foreseen, and as was thought to be true since the time of Galileo and Pascal, then the heavenly hierarchy of both the ancient church's Hellenistic paradigm and the medieval Roman Catholic paradigm were no longer tenable. According to the new image of the world, it was impossible for God the Father to be throned "up above," topographically speaking, in heaven. Nor could the Logos, the Word, the Son descend to the center of the universe (the earth), going down all the way under the earth (into hell), only to mount up again on the day of his ascension. But if that was untenable, then much else is shaken, too—not least of all the divinity of Christ, which Patristic and Scholastic writers overstressed in almost Monophysite fashion.

In the Catholic restoration, to be sure, an ersatz heaven was created in baroque vaults, baroque cupolas, and baroque dogmas, as if Ptolemy and Aristotle were still capable of supporting the Bible, supposedly infallible on all matters. For Lessing, meanwhile, all theological questions ever posed could be settled by *exegesis*. The important point here is that he no longer took the Bible—as Pascal still did, in the spirit of ancient and medieval theology—as a divinely inspired, encoded book, full of symbols and puzzles that could be decoded by the allegorical method, already practiced by Origen and Augustine. Instead, Lessing understood the Bible as a very earthly document of human authors in the spirit of Spinoza and Richard Simon. In 1678, shortly after Pascal's death and long before all Protestant scriptural scholars, Simon (1638–1712), a pious Oratorian priest, founded modern Bible criticism with his *Critical History of the Old Testament*. After his book was suppressed (thanks to Bossuet's influence), Simon was promptly ejected from the order, which needless to say did not prevent him from continuing his scholarly labors.

And Lessing? Exactly a hundred years later, he didn't do much better. In 1778—after eight years of service as the office librarian in the ducal library of Wolfenbüttel—he published the scandalous *Anonymous Fragments* by the Hamburg Orientalist Hermann Samuel Reimarus. Reimarus had composed them in secret under the direct influence of the religion of nature and reason preached by the English deists (Locke, Toland, and Tindal, among others). Lessing got them from Reimarus' daughter after her father's death. In a relentless rationalistic critique, Reimarus had uncovered the contradictions in the biblical texts, attacked the credibility of the disciples and the authors of the Gospels, and by raising questions about the original Jesus of Nazareth had radically challenged existing ecclesiastical Christianity. With the publication of the Reimarus fragments began the historical investigation in Germany of the life of Jesus. This proved to be an epic journey that Albert Schweitzer has masterfully described, though in a grotesque omission he did not discuss Lessing's arguments.

The controversy over the *Fragments* was carried on, to the dismay of the orthodox and contrary to all the academic rules of the game, in German, in a manner that could be understood, and hence in full view of the public. This dispute, which occupied Lessing's last years, has been called the strongest jolt to the church in Germany since Luther. Indirectly, it was also a threat to the absolutist state. As in the case of Galileo with the Catholic church, here the controversy, as far as Protestantism was concerned, amounted to a decisive battle for the *modern paradigm* of theology. While it continues to be rooted in its biblical origins, modern theology still must accept the results of modern natural science (Galileo) and take into cognizance modern historical research (Reimarus-Lessing). Despite all the storms of outrage, of contempt, protest, and calls for censorship, Lessing defended his anonymous author, but by no means totally identified with him on the basic question of the relation between reason and revelation.

Reimarus had argued against dogmatic orthodoxy; Christian truths of faith or dogmas (the resurrection of Christ, for example) were incredible, he said, because the corresponding accounts by the evangelists contradicted one another. The orthodox, on the other hand, were historically helpless. They maintained that the Christian truths of faith were believable, because the reports by the evangelists were *not* contradictory. Lessing took issue with both sides, and nowadays critical theology agrees in principle with him. *Although* the accounts do contradict one another, the resurrection of Christ can be credible. Lessing put the problem this way: Weren't there "proofs of the spirit and power" at the time of Jesus Christ? Yet how should Christian truth be plain to a person today, when such proofs no longer exist, except in reports? How am I supposed to leap over the "nasty wide ditch" so as to get from Then to Now, and from the accidental truth of history to the necessary truth of reason?

From a contemporary standpoint, we would say that Lessing (siding with Reimarus against orthodoxy) rightly rejects the doctrine of literal inspiration as a theologoumenon, because Scripture contains undeniable natural and historical contradictions and errors. At the same time, Lessing (here turning against both the orthodox and Reimarus) rightly rejects *historical proofs* in favor of the Christian truths of faith. One should not suspend all of eternity on the thread of a spiderweb. But our question to Lessing today has to be: Is it really given to human reason to understand the truths of revelation from within, in their eternal rational truth, independently of the testimony of the Bible? And if that should not be possible, what then? We shall come back to this question in connection with Kierkegaard.

In any case, it is strange to think what would have happened if the churches had taken a man like Lessing seriously. Would the unity of religion and thought in modern times not have come apart so quickly? Wouldn't the life of the mind and religiosity have developed less independently of the established churches? What would have happened if the problems that have now accumulated like an avalanche had been worked out and fresh knowledge been accepted, instead of mulish, humorless, dogmatic clinging to the traditional understanding of God, the Bible, and the world, in the manner of Lessing's adversary, Pastor Goeze? As his letter to the Jewish Enlightenment philosopher Moses Mendelssohn, in Berlin, attests, Lessing himself had already made a breakthrough to a new orientation around 1750. He writes that he had to fetch back many things that he had earlier thrown out because of certain prejudices.

Lessing was neither the brisk rationalist that earlier research (Karl Aner, say, in his *Theologie der Lessingzeit*, 1929) made him out to be, nor the Lutheran Christian that theologians, in reaction to this, tried to incorporate into their number. He was—as seen in the growing consensus of recent studies—a genuinely *dialectical thinker*, strictly logical, and yet not a system builder. Lessing has often been understood to be speaking *dogmatikôs* (in principle), when, engaged in sharp polemics, he merely wished to speak *gymnastikôs* (i.e., tactically, for the sake of exercise). To that extent, he was not altogether dissimilar to a man like Martin Luther.

Would not Luther, that "great, misunderstood man," were he placed in a new time, likewise adopt Lessing's position? At the high point of the controversy, Lessing cried out to Melchior Goeze—the head pastor of Hamburg and one of the most prominent representatives of orthodoxy in those days—"I simply will not be slandered by you as the man who does not mean as well for the Lutheran Church as you do. . . . Who will finally bring us a Christianity as you (Luther) would teach *now*; as Christ himself would teach! Who—" (III, 441–42). Finally, Lessing directed at Goeze his "knightly *renunciation* in brief": "Write, my dear pastor, and let write, for all you are worth: I write too. If I give you your rights in the slightest matter concerning myself or my anonymous author, where you are not right, then I cannot let my pen rest" (III, p. 443).

Four months later, "the pen" was destined to rest. After eleven anti-Goeze pamphlets, the freedom from censorship of the Wolfenbüttel librarian was cancelled by a cabinet order, which was equivalent to a ban on any publications dealing with theology. Like Pascal's *Provincial Letters*, his pamphlets were polemical literature on the highest level.

On the same day, however, on 8 August 1778, when Lessing answered the duke about the deprivation of his freedom from censorship, he announced a new project; the intrepid, resourceful hand-to-hand combatant and "amateur of theology" (as he always modestly styled himself) was now more than ever ready for battle. The work in hand was a verse drama, *Nathan the Wise*. "I have to try and see," he wrote Elise Reimarus, the daughter of his Anonymous Author, "whether they will at least let me preach undisturbed in my old pulpit, the theater" (*Gesamte Werke*, P. Rilla, ed., IX, 798–99). The only thing he had changed, then, was the battleground, and this with the express intention of "playing an even meaner trick on the theologians than with the ten fragments." The work went rapidly forward; half a year later *Nathan the Wise* appeared—Lessing had circumvented the censor.

All through the five acts, as usual, the definitions are subtle, the arguments are entertaining, and the thinking is enlightened. But now it all takes place in supple blank verse. As a dramatist, Lessing remains a sharp-tongued dialectician, a man of profound conversation, of passionately witty give-and-take. Yet this conversation is carried on not in any old poetic time and space, but in a place that must have seized the imagination of the spectators, as it still does today: Jerusalem. *Nathan the Wise* is set in the holiest place of Jews, Christians, and Muslims during the High Middle Ages; the scene of the Crusades and persecutions of the Jews; the scene of the unholiest conflicts. This is the holy city that has been wooed, quarreled over, and fought for to this day.

With his eye for large perspectives, Lessing shifted the confrontation with religion to a higher plane. He was no longer interested in the often petty conflict between an orthodox head pastor and an enlightened writer, but in the dramatic conversation between the three world religions of Semitic origin and prophetic character, presented in vivid stage figures full of wit and understanding. The protagonists were an enlightened Jew (Nathan, the first noble Jew in a German play), an enlightened Muslim (the eminent Sultan Saladin), and an immature, but ultimately enlightened, Christian, a young Crusader. At the same time, Lessing offered (in the simple monk) a counterimage to the authoritarian church (represented by the infamously clerical "Patriarch"), which guarantees its claim to absolute truth by means of power politics. This church burns people at the stake when necessary and keeps men and women in obedient tutelage. What is the issue in this didactic drama, which against all the rules of art is a comedy and tragedy in one? Let us try to approach this question in three cautious steps, working from the outside in.

————◆————

What first may appear to be an individual *family drama* proves in fact to be a *drama of humanity* as a whole. This has to be stressed in the face of theological interpretations that take the sting out of Lessing's position by displacing his basic approach to the questions, whether of human existence or of divine providence. Two limitations are necessary:

First, the Protestant interpretation of Lessing by Helmut Thielicke certainly deserves recognition. As early as 1936, Thielicke, with his studies on Lessing's philosophy of religion under the significant title *Revelation, Reason, and Existence* (5th ed., 1967), had introduced a theological "rescue" of Lessing. The relationship between reason and revelation, between the truth of reason and the truth of history, was rethought. It became clear that with Lessing we cannot speak of atheism. Lessing clung tightly to God, freedom, immortality, and virtue—as did the whole German Enlightenment. And yet Thielicke falls prey to a typical existentialist narrowing of his day, when both here and again in the chapter on Lessing in his recent book on *Religion and Thought in Modern Times* (1983) he argues that human existence and the perils it runs are Lessing's "fundamental problem." ("How can I, a rational creature, accept myself as a historical creature without thereby falsifying my existence" [124]). Thielicke goes astray, too, when he treats Lessing's Nathan in the context of subjectivity (121). Here, in discussing the claim to truth of the various revelatory religions, he contents himself with the bare remark that this is "the most profound problem of the parable of the rings" (143), once again dismissing what Lessing sees as the central problem of religion.

A second limitation: The Catholic interpretation of Lessing by Arno Schilson, which also saw the light in Tübingen, doubtlessly has its importance. Under the shadow of antimodernism, one hundred years passed without the publication of a single book on Lessing by a Catholic theologian. This one is probably, among the recent Catholic interpretations (e.g., B. Bothe), the most comprehensive. It appeared under the title *History Against the Background of Providence* (1974). And yet it seems to me an attempt to minimize Lessing's posing of the problem, when "Providence"—which was doubtless an important truth of reason for

Lessing and the German Enlightenment—suddenly becomes not the "background" (as in Schilson's title) but the center of Lessing's philosophy of history. In this way, *Nathan* becomes simply— as Schilson puts it in a recent book on *Lessing's Christianity* (1980)—a "play about Providence" (65), which completely wipes out the problem of religion.

Thus, what to one scholar—in the good old Protestant style— is an existential dialectic is to another—in the good old Catholic style—the problem of theocentrism and anthropocentrism, of belief in providence and freedom. But the *basic problems* raised in the play about Nathan the Jew are lost sight of: the trenchant criticism of the church as a patriarchal institution of power, the problems of Christianity and Judaism, important desiderata for theological study of the Enlightenment, and, above all, the especially uncomfortable question for theologians concerning the world religions, namely, which is the *true* religion?

Hence it is no wonder that Lessing, a nonacademic Enlightenment critic of revelation, is simply passed over. This happened both in Catholic theology and in most modern Protestant histories of theology. According to I. A. Dorner (1967), it was not until 1947 that Karl Barth devoted a chapter to Lessing, which was sympathetic but in the end rejected him. Here we see coming to light "narrowings," "whose aftereffects continue to be felt to the present day. We find these primarily in late Barthianism, among those who invoke the 'Reformation legacy' in a very narrow sense, and then among the fundamentalists" (W. Trillhaas, 62).

In the very first act of his analytical drama, Lessing shows concretely what the theological task of Enlightenment means. In witty, ironic fashion he does away with some prejudices—prejudices against Nathan, who is "only a Jew," and yet contrary to all clichés is "honesty, generosity itself" (I, 1), indeed a Jewish anticapitalist. Instead of taking interest, Nathan gives money away. Every kind of delusory belief is concretely dismissed: "Sweet delusion gives way then to the sweeter truth . . . a man is ever more dear to man than an angel" (I, 1). The faith in miracles of the "people hungry for wonders" is rejected: "The greatest wonder is / That to us all the true and genuine wonders / Can come to be so commonplace, and should" (I, 2, Bayard Quincy Morgan, trans.). Instead, Lessing refers to praxis: "It's easier to swoon in pious dreams / Than do good actions" (I, 2, BQM).

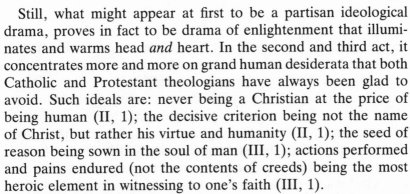

Still, what might appear at first to be a partisan ideological drama, proves in fact to be drama of enlightenment that illuminates and warms head *and* heart. In the second and third act, it concentrates more and more on grand human desiderata that both Catholic and Protestant theologians have always been glad to avoid. Such ideals are: never being a Christian at the price of being human (II, 1); the decisive criterion being not the name of Christ, but rather his virtue and humanity (II, 1); the seed of reason being sown in the soul of man (III, 1); actions performed and pains endured (not the contents of creeds) being the most heroic element in witnessing to one's faith (III, 1).

Humanity as the human race's ideal of itself flashes out in the figure of Nathan: "Jew and Christian, Muslim and Parsee, it is all one to him" (II, 2); "How free his mind of prejudice; / His heart how open unto every virtue, / With every beauty perfectly attuned" (II, 3, BQM). "Are Jew and Christian sooner Jew and Christian / Than man? How good, if I have found in you / One more who is content to bear the name / Of man!" (II, 5, BQM).

According to this play, then, who is "the Wise"? It is not simply the "clever man" (III, 5), the man of reason with his egotistical calculation and ironic moralizing, his "cold book learning" (V, 6). It is the man with a head and a heart, tested by suffering, a battler, who has managed in reason to bring his will into agreement with the will of God and precisely in this way can deal with his fellows, working out of superior knowledge in selflessness. This is Nathan the Jew, who in the drama of life appears more Christian than the Christian: "O Nathan, Nathan! You're a Christian soul! / By God, a better Christian never lived!" (IV, 7, BQM), says the Friar (V, 7). But Nathan immediately turns the argument around: "And well for us! For what makes me for you / A Christian, makes yourself for me a Jew!" (BQM). It is not being a Christian or a Jew, if these things cast shadows on humanity, but being human, with the values of qualitative humanity potentially common to both, that is crucial here. And beyond this, another crucial point is that Lessing grounds humane behavior in religion—unlike Voltaire, he was not a skeptical mocker of religion without moral seriousness (in his *Dictionnaire Philosophique* Voltaire characterizes the Jews as "the most abominable people on earth").

———————◆———————

Nevertheless, what might at first appear to be an indifferent drama of tolerance proves in the end to be a utopian drama of reconciliation. Even in the optimistic eighteenth century, there was an unmistakable background of suffering and misfortune, executions and the night of pogroms. And against this there streams forth profound humanity and love, "uncorrupted love, free from prejudice" that makes survival possible, affords strength and greatness. In truth, *Nathan* is concerned not just with a general God-man or existential dialectic. Nor, as some superficial interpretations would have it, does the play deal just with the political-religious utopia of a better future for humanity, symbolically mirrored in the feast of embraces among men of different faiths at the end. The point, altogether in the spirit of Lessing's future-oriented thinking about history, is the vision—inspiring even today—of peace among the religions as a prerequisite for peace in the human race as a whole. This great religious vision of peace raises *Nathan* far above all the works of writers like Klopstock, Herder, or Wieland, Lessing's contemporaries, and continues to stir audiences today.

To be sure, this noble vision of the future presupposes one thing: The question of the true religion has to be resolved. "Of these three / Religions only one can be the true one" (III, 5): Lessing solves the problem, as everyone knows, with the help of the old parable of the three rings. This was borrowed from Boccaccio's *Decameron*, but completely reshaped. Its central importance is underlined by its position in the center of the drama (III, 7). If theoretical explanation is of no use ("the genuine ring was not / Demonstrable"), which ring, therefore, is the right one, which the true religion? The answer is that only the test of practice counts, and "Let each aspire / To emulate his father's unbeguiled, / Unprejudiced affection" (BQM). Then the power of the ring is proved "with all humility, / With benefaction, hearty peacefulness, / And with profound submission to God's will!" (BQM). Faith can be proved true then, only through devout humanity in life itself. In a word, every religion is genuine, is true, to the extent that in act and in fact it proves it has the "miraculous power" of making its followers "agreeable to God and man." But is this a clear standpoint?

One may wonder whether this drama might not be anything more than an illustration of the remark by Frederick the Great advising everyone to get to heaven in his own way. Is that what Lessing meant? No, that would be to trivialize his religious vision of peace and to underestimate the refinement of his thinking. As far back as a letter written a good ten years before *Nathan* to Friedrich Nicolai, a supporter of the Enlightenment in Berlin, Lessing had opposed Berlin's reducing freedom of thought and expression to the "freedom to bring as much foolishness to market against religion as one wishes" (*Gesamte Werke*, P. Rilla, ed., IX, 327).

Lessing does not see the great religions, as Reimarus does, from a vulgar Enlightenment perspective, as provisory envelopes of reason or nature, later to be cast aside. He doesn't think unhistorically; he doesn't simply want to get rid of religions as they have historically developed in favor of a purely rational universal religion. On the contrary, he is concerned with thinking about reason and history together, reason and tradition together, reason and revelation together, so as to overcome the unhappy split in consciousness that his age experienced between reason and religion. Despite all the historical difficulties, Lessing did not want to strip away Christianity like an old skin. He wanted to reinterpret it and boldly transpose it forward from within.

For Lessing sees Christianity, along with Judaism, as the "part of the human race that God had wished to comprise in *one* plan of education" (#54). Lessing was always more interested in questions of principle than of detail, and this idea is what he presented in his momentous final programmatic piece, *The Education of the Human Race* (1780). That book grew out of his confrontation with Reimarus, and was published (in the camouflage of anonymity) a year before he died. The concept of "education" in the broadest sense was in the air during the Enlightenment—an "age of education." Of course, the theological topoi in Lessing's essay go all the way back to the patristic era. Both the idea of a "historical plan" (an "economy of the one and the same God," #88), as well as the idea of God or Christ as a "pedagogue" of humanity,

can be found in the Greek church fathers (whom Lessing knew
well). On the other hand, the notion of the three ages (Old Covenant, New Covenant, Eternal Gospel) is found in Joachim de
Fiore and subsequent medieval "enthusiasts" (#87).

But still Lessing was convinced that a person who didn't know
history remained an inexperienced and endangered child. He was
the first to risk a philosophical, scholarly sketch of all history
(oriented to Judeo-Christian history), thereby paving the way,
especially for Hegel, toward the philosophy of history. As no one
had before him, he understood revelation as a process of education by divine providence, as a "new directional impulse for
human reason" (#63). Hence he consistently saw all of human
history as focused on the future: as a *revelation to reason*, which
progresses in millennial steps from childhood (Old Testament)
through boyhood (New Testament) all the way to manhood (fulfillment). In the process, the "revealed truths" gradually become
internally intuitive "truths of reason" (#76).

As in drama, so too in theology Lessing was less a revolutionary
than a reformer who always made deft use of the old to legitimize
the new. More than anyone else he was conscious of being on
the *way*: first of all on the way with all of humanity to a "full
enlightenment" (#80), that "time of completion," in which man
will do the good not because it is rewarded, but "because it is
the good" (#85). Lessing self-mockingly characterized himself as
a pagan in his head and a Lutheran Christian in his heart, but
did he finally rely on his head or his heart? We don't know. He
revealed his ultimate thoughts and feelings to scarcely anyone.
But this much is certain: The poet of *Nathan* remained faithful
to the dreams of his youth. He died, only fifty-two years old, in
the arms of a Jew, who had been robbed and imprisoned owing
to arbitrary injustice, and whom Lessing had freed through his
personal intervention.

———◆———

But can theology today be satisfied with the solution of *Nathan*,
with Lessing's serious appreciation, but, at the same time, radical
relativization, of the positive religions? This question cannot be
answered in a few words. Still it is certain—even though theologians like to dodge such a realization—that since Lessing the
theological absolutism that poses one's own truth ab-solutely, re-

moved from all other truths, has become *untenable*. That standpoint of exclusivity that lumps all the non-Christian religions together and condemns them as untrue appears simply as an unproved theological postulate. It is no different from any other claim to superiority that rates one's own religion a priori morally or intellectually loftier than the rest.

Catholic theology and, particularly on this point, Protestant theology, too, is faced with the task of making distinctions that Lessing in his day could scarcely find a satisfactory answer to. While avoiding absolutism, how can we also avoid *the sort of relativism that makes all values and standards a matter of indifference*? For it is equally true that the modern "anything goes" pluralism, which slowly came to the fore and is today intellectually popular and which approves without distinguishing one's own religion and all others too, can no more invoke Lessing than the indifferentism to which all religious positions and decisions are equally valid. It merely spares itself the trouble of "discerning the spirits." The borderline between true and false, we must say in the spirit of Lessing, does not run simply between Christianity and the other religions, but within each of the religions. This calls for a multilevel religious criteriology, which has been an unfulfilled desideratum since Lessing's day. Yet such a system can be developed only if one does not mix "the religions" together in judging them, but submits to the endless toil of coming to grips with the coarse and fine structures of each individual religion.

Modernity culminates in the Enlightenment of the age of Lessing. One may criticize this Enlightenment, the way some theologians and church spokesmen customarily do, as superficial, trite, and insipid. But such verdicts glance off the epochal figure of the man who launched the age of German classicism and stands for liberating rationality, incorruptible morality, and comprehensive humanity.

We may, to be sure, join Hans-Georg Gadamer in characterizing the great prejudice of the Enlightenment as its prejudice against prejudices. But all hermeneutic reflections, preliminary or posterior, howsoever justified, cannot do away with the historical fact that in Christianity, without the struggle of the Enlightenment against prejudices, the rack and the Inquisition would still be functioning, the church's faith would be imposed from above even more harshly, and every conceivable kind of prejudice and obscurantism would be tolerated. All those nowadays who think they have long since put the Enlightenment behind them might consider three points:

1. So long as the Roman Catholic church has not yet put into practice within its own house the human rights, freedom of thought, and removal of censorship that Lessing demanded, although it continually demands them from others outside it,

2. and so long as the World Council of Churches does not dare to give any positive answer to the question of the eternal salvation of the Jews, the Muslims, the Hindus, the Buddhists, and all the other hundreds of millions of living persons, although it has, paradoxically, issued guidelines for dialogue with them,

3. and so long as a theology that poses as modern uncritically works with ostensibly suprarational Christian "mysteries" (on the Catholic side) and "paradoxes" (on the Protestant side), that are alien to the Jesus of the New Testament: *then to that extent these churches and theologians do not have Lessing behind them, but before them!*

Of course, Lessing, who was an upright man with a keen intellectual flair, would presumably be one of the first today to demand an *Enlightenment on the Enlightenment.* He would be one of the first to warn about uncritical trust in human reason and science, as a guide to the knowledge of the truth and the humane shaping of life, just as Pascal did vis-à-vis Descartes. Today, doubts about the realization of rationality in the modern world have swelled to immense proportions. And after the slaughter of Jews in Auschwitz, after Hiroshima, and after the Gulag Archipelago, it has become simply impossible to understand the course of human history as an ongoing evolution toward a higher state, as an autonomously progressive revelation to reason. If Lessing had lived longer, we may assume that he would likely have become attentive to the "dialectic of the Enlightenment."

I would like to close with one of the moving paragraphs at the end of his *Education of the Human Race*: "Go your imperceptible pace, divine Providence! Only let me not despair of you because of this imperceptibleness. Let me not despair of you, if even your steps should seem to me to be going backward!" (#91).

WALTER JENS

◇

Nathan's Attitude Has Been Mine All Along

Writing to his brother Karl from Wolfenbüttel on 11 August 1778, Lessing noted:

> I still don't know what the upshot of my business (with Johann Melchior Goeze) will be. But I would very much like to be prepared for every possible one. You well know that one can't be better off than when one has money, as much as needed. And so this past night I had a foolish notion. One time many years ago I sketched out a play, whose content has a sort of analogy with my current controversies, one that I never dreamed of at the time. If you and Moses (Mendelssohn) think it's good, I'll have the thing printed by subscription.

The "thing" was *Nathan the Wise*. Lessing preferred casual talk, offhandedness, a practically deprecating approach, when he spoke about his own work. "More the product of polemics than of genius," he would later say; a writer really can't talk about nascent material more offhandedly. Lessing chose to make the leap from the pulpit to the theater not out of enthusiasm, seized by *rabies poetica*, but for more down-to-earth reasons. First of all, he wanted to get around the censorship that, had he continued the battle against Goeze in theological pamphlets, would have finished him off (and not only in Brunswick). Second, he wanted at the same time not to drop his polemic, but to give it the character of a public affair, one that also (and especially) affected ordinary people. Third, he wanted to improve his finances.

Thus, *Nathan the Wise* was written because a quarrel promised to make some profits, and Boccaccio's parable of the wise Jew Melchisedek was versified as a play about Enlightenment theology. An impoverished writer, the miserably paid librarian at Wolfenbüttel made six hundred thaler a year, while the director of the Brunswick ducal opera received thirty thousand, and a solo dancer made over six thousand a year, more than ten times Lessing's salary. This destitute poet and Christian put himself in the place of a wealthy Jew and businessman like his friend Mendelssohn. And in this transformation, he didn't dodge Goeze's question, "Where do you stand, Lessing, on Christian faith?" Instead, with the help of tactical twists, but radically and honorably (while protected by a mask and ambiguous allusions), he gave his answer.

For Goeze *had* asked, with the precision of an Inquisitor, *had* insisted on a distinct demarcation of religion from true Christian faith. He had pointed out that it was up to his opponent to give a clear and definite explanation *in puncto puncti*, to "explain himself as an honorable man," to stop "blowing all sorts of blue haze into the [reader's] eyes."

Driven into a corner as he was, what could Lessing do but with all requisite precision assure the public that by the Christian religion he understood the teachings "that are contained in the creeds of the first four hundred years of the Christian church"? This was a sly answer, to be sure, an answer that portrayed the accused as clinging to his strict separation between the spirit and the letter, religion and the Bible. But at the same time, for Lessing, it was also an awfully Catholic thesis. *Scriptura et traditio*, revelation fixed in Scripture and living religious tradition shaping the community, were peacefully united. Gotthold Ephraim Lessing, the minister's son from Kamenz, was following in the footsteps of the second-century fathers of the church! Irenaeus and Tertullian were summoned as star witnesses in the struggle against a Protestant pope! Was Lessing, as a victim of the Protestant-style tyranny of the letter, ultimately on the way to conversion? Or was the adherence to the *regula fidei* an expression of the spiritual cynicism displayed by the most famous convert of the eighteenth century, Johann Joachim Winckelmann? When

Winckelmann left the Protestant house of God for the Catholic church, he announced to the world:

> At first, when some heretics . . . saw me kneeling at mass, I was ashamed, but every day I become bolder. . . . My father, as I now began to notice, had not wished to make a Catholic out of me. He gave me a sensitive knee-leather that was altogether too thin for what one must have to kneel in Catholic fashion with good grace. . . . In the summer I shall . . . therefore have to bring a pair . . . of gloves with me, in order to kneel with devotion. I can see how much is still lacking to my blessedness. When I am supposed to make the sign of the cross with my right hand, my left makes itself felt to the annoyance of those standing nearby. . . . On Ash Wednesday I received the ashes: Out of fear of doing it wrong, I jerked my head, and the sanctified dirt almost got smeared in my mouth.

Was Lessing, then, following in Winckelmann's footsteps? Although a true son of the Catholic church, Winckelmann would not leave off his habit "of singing one of our good Lutheran hymns" in the morning while he prepared his breakfast. "Why should I fret?" he asked, a Protestant treble sung to the ringing of all the churches in the Holy City. Of course, Lessing was no convert after the manner of Winckelmann; on the contrary. But to camouflage himself, to feint, and placed as he was at the boundary separating the religions, to trim his cape to the wind with the necessary artfulness, he was not spared the indignity of the comparison.

Lessing subscribed to the *regula fidei*, the "confession of faith of the oldest Fathers" as the rock, on which the "Church of Christ is built." This statement was written with the intention of rattling the Imperial Privy Council, the highest censorship authority in Germany. A Protestant attack on Lessing for denying the principle of "sola Scriptura" would hit not just Lessing, but also the greater part of the religious authorities who still adhered to the old church. That majority—so the man from Wolfenbüttel calculated—could not be provoked with impunity: To hell with all the Goezes.

On 23 July 1778, Lessing wrote to his brother Karl: "I have a

sure means of dividing the Imperial Privy Council and leaving it
at odds with itself, just as Paul did with the Sanhedrin. Since most
of the members are Catholics, I can only present my case so that
the condemnation the Lutheran ministers pronounce over me
actually contains a condemnation of all papists, who do not want,
any more than I do, a religion based on Scripture and Scripture
alone. With this intention I have already written a sheet."

"With the Catholics against Goeze" (to make him "capot")
was Lessing's motto. Anyone who had to fight against censorship
around 1788–1789, least of all the theological writer, evidently
was not allowed to be too squeamish in his choice of allies. He
had to look for fellow fighters wherever he could. The main thing
was that the cause of reason was advanced by such allegiances.
And the broad position Lessing had adopted, regardless of all the
necessary tactical twists, must not be abandoned by so much as
a hand's breadth.

Not by a hand's breadth, indeed. This is the thesis argued in
Lessing's "Necessary Answer to a Highly Unnecessary Question
by Head Pastor Goeze in Hamburg": "This regula fidei and *not
Scripture* is thus the rock on which the church of Christ was built,"
". . . This thesis aimed at Lutheran orthodoxy was immediately
followed by the parallel principle. Now the Catholic dogmatic
theologians were the target." "This regula fidei and *not Peter and
his successors* is the rock on which the Church of Christ was built."

First a slap on the cheek to the right, to make the leftists laugh,
then a slap on the left, to make the rightists laugh (and vice versa):
In this way, Lessing, fighting the battle against powerful literary,
political, and religious institutions, divided up his strokes. He was
at once plucky and careful, ever intent on avoiding total confrontation. And so he spoke in parables, fairy tales, and ambiguous images that could be variously interpreted, rather than in
"affirmative" discourse, letting the truth rumble around the
house, with a loud fracas, the boom of orthodoxy.

> H'm! h'm!—how strange! I'm all confused.
> —What would
> The Sultan have of me?—I thought of money;
> And he wants—truth. Yes, truth! And wants it so—
> So bare and blank—as if the truth were coin!—
> And were it coin, which anciently was weighed!—

That might be done! But coin from modern mints,
Which but the stamp creates, which you but count
Upon the counter—truth is not like that!
As one puts money in his purse, just so
One puts truth in his head? Which here is a Jew?
Which, I or he?—But stay!—Suppose in truth
He did not ask for truth!—I must admit,
Suspicion that he used the truth as trap
Would be too small by far.—Too small?—What is
Too small for one so great?—That's right, that's right:
He rushed into the house incontinent!
One knocks, one listens, surely, when one comes
As friend.—I must tread warily!—But how?—
To be a Jew won't do at all.—
But not to be a Jew will do still less.
For if no Jew, he might well ask, then why
Not Mussulman?—That's it! And that can save me!
Not only children can be quieted
With fables.—See he comes. Well, let him come!

(BQM, trans.)

If there is any passage where the identity of the author and the protagonist is clear, then it comes in Nathan's famous monologue that serves as a prelude to the parable of the rings. These twenty-six lines (parlando, rhythmic prose approaching the purely colloquial) and twenty-one dashes indicate a shift of thought between "H'm! h'm!" and "Well, let him come!" When the moment of decision comes, Lessing doesn't press forward; he slows down, considers, pauses and begins again, poses questions, raises objections, brings his partner into the game, develops alternatives, and presents a dialectical exercise in his peculiar act of thinking out loud. The essence of the reflections is that truth is not a coin that can be quickly counted, at face value, on the counter. Truth wants, at the least, to be carefully weighed ("And were it coin, which anciently was weighed!— / That might be done!"). Truth cannot be quickly minted and then made available. Its value is not measured through any calculations that comply with the dictate of any reckoning, of addition and subtraction. Truth is not a result in the sense of a balance, but best acquires its profile, if it does at all, in dialectical activity and mutual response, in listening to one another, in other words, in Socratic conversation among friends. Truth must not be reduced to formulas and axioms; it should only be moved into purview, parables, and images, as a good to be striven for but never possessed.

In a word, Lessing thinks truth is never something you "have," but at most something you at some time or other gain. But that means we can speak of truth only with extreme caution, especially amidst those people intent on the *one* beatific, politically valid truth. And so someone who has to deal with the ambivalence of truth has to play roles (the way Nathan plays the Jew that he has long since ceased to be, or Lessing—*regula fidei!*—played the orthodox person he never was). Fairy tales have to be told, and silence for the sake of threatened truth is more reasonable than unguarded statements. "You are already familiar with truths that are better kept quiet," says the Freemason Falk to his partner in Lessing's *Ernst and Falk, Dialogues for Freemasons*. To which Ernst answers, "But one *could* say it." Falk: "The wise man cannot say what he does better to be silent about."

He can't *say* it, to be sure, but he can suggest it, paraphrase it, and hint at it in riddles—quite well, at least in play. Drama makes possible what writings about theological controversy (at that certain point where the center is touched and it begins to "burn") can no longer do. Drama can speak about basic questions *e contrario*, as it were, in a cheerful to and fro, with surprising allusive links between trenchant seriousness and a gaiety that guarantees a sense of worldliness and urbanity. In this way, Lessing shifts his allusions between the highest pathos (Nathan, reporting about the pogrom) and amusing ethos (the chess game, the friendly skirmish between Saladin and his sister Sittah, meditations on the advantages of spying, wealth, and amusing schemes for one character's benefit and the harm of his opponent).

In the long run—and not just with a view to censorship—Lessing was tired of opposing "theological scholastic language." "I am an admirer of theology and not a theologian," he writes in the Introduction to his *Axiomata*. "I have not had to swear by any specific system. Nothing binds me to speak a different language from my own. I pity all honorable men who are not so fortunate as to be able to say this."

Lessing was fortunate; Johann Melchior Goeze was pitiable. The pope of Hamburg never stopped fulminating against the thea-

[margin handwritten note: or Jens the "tolerant" (?)]

ter as the devil's pulpit, occupied by the Jesuits (Goeze was thinking of Protestants who preferred the opera to church). Goeze
vainly polemicized against the passion felt by those young ladies
"who found in theater incitements, instructions, and opportunity
for an extremely detrimental understanding of love." Meanwhile,
Lessing could finally do what he had long been dreaming of. He
could sing the hymn of natural religion in a language entirely his
own, and at the same time he could demonstrate the narrowness
of the religious truth that had been revealed and thereafter declared to be absolute.

One imagines Lessing, the pastor's son from Kamenz, giving
free rein to the anger inside him ("Well now, my dear irascibility!
Where are you? Where are you hiding? You've got free play. Just
break loose! Have a good romp! . . . gnash my teeth, strike me
in the forehead, bite my lower lip!"). One imagines him stopping
and remembering his hotblooded father ("How often you told
me: Gotthold! I beg you, take an example from me: be careful.
For I fear, I fear. . . . Indeed, old man, indeed").

In fact, scarcely had the play begun when we seem to see him,
the pious heretic Gotthold Ephraim Lessing, all over the country.
He launched a powerful subscription campaign. He heightened
tension through carefully measured communiqués and advance
publicity. He staged "fine collections" between Austria and Denmark. He made his opponent tremble by means of contradictory
announcements, and then appeased the censors. When things got
ticklish, in Vienna for example, he withdrew the subscription. In
the middle of the campaign (with the outcome of the play still
uncertain), he kept both the clergy and the gentlemen from the
ministry in suspense. Lessing once remarked, "My play has nothing to do with today's parsons," and another time, in reply to the
question "What will be done with Goeze?": "Well, I'll have a
patriarch come on stage!"

Lessing was rehearsing a masterpiece of refined self-dramatiz-
ing, without resources and support from the powers that be and
with only a handful of friends and an honest printer. How lonely
he was, in his great theological battle in the theater, how absolutely on his own, can be illustrated by a comparison between
Nathan and the play destined to replace it in the esteem of Germans, Goethe's *Faust:* On 24 March, 1800 Schiller wrote to Cotta,
"I am afraid that Goethe will completely neglect his Faust, so

much has been done already, unless he is induced . . . to finish
. . . this great work. . . . . Naturally, he is counting on a large
profit, because he knows that people in Germany are keenly
looking forward to this work. I am convinced that by brilliant
offers you can get him to . . . finish this work."

How different with Lessing. He did not have a powerful pub-
lisher, money, or outside offers. He was harried by disciplinary
measures. *Nathan* was forbidden in Würzburg, Augsburg, and the
core provinces of the empire. He was brought into contempt,
after his death, by curious compromises in the script (the patriarch
transformed into a commander). And, nevertheless, he *wanted* it
that way, *wanted* to provoke the enemy by making him ridiculous.
Lessing had edited the account of the great patriarch Heraclitus,
knew it in detail, and translated part of it. He now transmogrified
that historical figure into a fat, red-faced, friendly prelate. Lessing's prelate is a man who proves to be a dull dogmatist, engages
in church politics like a small-time Cesare Borgia. Beyond that,
he quotes lines from Goeze verbatim, now refers the Templar to
the theater and speaks of "theatrical drolleries" (Goeze himself
spoke of "Herr L.'s theater logic"). Fixated on power as he is,
the Patriarch's thoughts turn to Sultan Saladin: "And easily I'll
make him see what danger / Lies for the state itself in lack of
faith. / All civic bonds dissolved and rent asunder, / When men
need not believe." (What Johann Melchior Goeze originally said
was: "The only person who can look upon undertakings 'of Herr
Lessing's sort' as something indifferent is the one . . . who refuses
to see that the happiness of the civic constitution is immediately
based on itself.")

The target was hit, the man was disposed of—and with him the
"church," in the sense of an official, empowered institution. Lessing wanted his play to expose that church to merry laughter. He
wanted to expose it not least of all from the perspective of the
pious Lay Brother, who, sworn into the religion of Christ, unmasks the thing calling itself Christian religion by a description
of its administrator: "I've often wondered how / A saint who lives
in heaven otherwise / Can condescend to be so well informed /
On worldly things. That must seem bitter to him."

Thus, the Patriarch is a caricature, a preposterous advocate of
positive religion, whom Nathan disposes of. And we may ask
whether Lessing doesn't join Nathan here ("Nathan's attitude,

opposing *all* positive religion," Lessing wrote in a sketch for a prologue to the play, "has always been mine").

Was the Patriarch designed to mock a Pharisee who—like the bigoted Daya—thinks he knows the only true way to God? Was he Goeze in theatrical costume: a sinister representative of an established church mourning its old privileges? "O happy times," says Lessing in the fifth anti-Goeze pamphlet, "when the clergy was all in all,—thought for us and ate for us! How gladly would the Head Pastor bring you back again in triumph! How gladly would he wish Germany's rulers to join with him in furthering this sacred intention!"

Was the Patriarch a substitute for the Christian spirit of the world, whose hour had passed once and for all? *This* Patriarch— the point must be stressed—was the mortal enemy of the great religious community of Jews, Christians, pagans, and Turks, which Lessing had already legitimated in his early piece "The Saving of Hieronymus Cardanus." There he transforms the good arguments of the mathematician, philosopher, and physician Cardanus into even better ones. (Cardanus' essay was titled *De subtilitate*—and subtleties certifiably issue from Nathan in the play: Lessing the *poeta doctus* leaves his calling card.) But, beyond that, our Patriarch primarily represents the dogmatic types in his own ranks. He stands for the rigid pedants glossed by Lessing in the "parable" in which the example of a palace ("from the outside a bit incomprehensible; from within light and coherence everywhere") serves to comment on the absurd behavior of men (read, with a Christian mentality). Misled by the ugly exterior and the many blueprints handed down by tradition, people forget the beauty of the palace, which is illuminated from above. Instead of heeding the interior, they turn their attention to external events. They are bad administrators of the building, because they are so busy with all sorts of exegesis that they lose sight of the object of their efforts. They do not listen to those few individuals who are familiar with the interior of the palace, its structure, and its ways, and who remonstrate with the dogmatizers: "What do we care about your ground plans? This one or another, they're all alike to us. It's enough for us to experience every moment that the kindliest wisdom fills the whole palace, and that it spreads nothing but beauty and order and well-being across the whole country."

The Patriarch, then, is a narrow-minded orthodox type who was never in the palace, never in the sphere of light where reason and revelation meet one another. I think this characterization best fits the man who, in contrast to all the other figures in the play, remains outside every context of communication that creates humane qualities.

For Lessing, the Patriarch is the only one who does not know how to speak with others. He is incapable of dialogue because he confuses people with chess pieces. The Patriarch is a man who exemplifies the end result of spiritual leadership by a church that can only recognize dialogue with God alone or Scripture or the penitent in confession. Besides, these forms of dialogue are based on command and obedience. They are, in other words, nonconversations, in which every humane-urbane sentiment, all exchange arising in the give and take between people with equal rights, is fundamentally suspect.

Spontaneity, individual expression, special situation-oriented discourse, discovery of the I in the Other, affective conversation that relativizes one's own project will not be found where patriarchs exercise the power that is so hostile to conversation, to pleasure, and to laughter.

From this standpoint, the Christian Patriarch stands for sociability denied, whereas Nathan the Jew stands for its triumph. While the Patriarch—imprisoned in rigid power structures—closes himself off, Nathan, who is conscious of everyone and brings everyone close to the truth with the appropriate means, appears as a personalized example of an "open" instruction. How else, to take the lowest level, could he bring the starry-eyed Rachel to reason? How else, on the middle level, could he do the same for the Templar, with all his advantages? How else, finally, on the highest level, could he win over his (potential) alter ego, Saladin? And how could Nathan do all this from a pedagogical position that Lessing considered the only rational, enlightened, and humane one? At the boundary line between the "not yet" and the "no longer" (at a point, in other words, where, in the language of the dialogue *Ernst and Falk*, the individual labeled as *such and such* a man becomes the generic creature *mere* man), at this crucial border point, then, one must affirm a humane Both-And. This means denying neither the Almost-no-longer-a-Jew (Christian, Muslim) nor the Not-yet-purely-and-simply-a-person. Lessing was bent on demonstrating this sort of coexistence at a time of upheaval. He wanted no biased insistence on one's own standpoint as the presumably sole sacrosanct one, but he also wanted no vague philanthropism.

As things stood in the eighteenth century, according to the dialogue between Ernst and Falk, only dreaming enthusiasts could think of overcoming the religious divisions. Realists like Lessing, swept forward by a "communal feeling of sympathizing minds," had to think of ways to bridge the split in religious communities, states, and social classes. We may disregard the fact that Lessing, in *The Education of the Human Race*, has an anonymous person plead for the Third Gospel (the Gospel of Reason, following the Old and New Testaments); or that in *Ernst and Falk* Lessing imagines a Grand Lodge in which "every worthy man, without distinction of fatherland or civic class," might contribute to the advance of humanity; or that, finally, the author of *Nathan* in bold anticipation has the natural become real in a society of free and equal persons. Lessing has, in fact, no interest in vague, ubiquitous utopias, only in concrete ones. He supports no revolutionary activism, only gradual reforms.

"The Freemason" is basically *Ernst and Falk* all over again. The "Freemason" himself is interchangeable with "advocate of natural religion" or "defender of rational truths": "The Freemason peacefully awaits the sunrise and lets the lights burn as long as they want. It is not for the Freemason to extinguish those lights and, when they have been put out, to perceive that one must light the candle stubs all over again or set up other lights."

This is not the Freemason's business, nor is it Nathan's. He remains a Jew and *as such* is a man who is neither a dyed-in-the-wool Jew nor a complete ex-Jew. He teaches the Christian *and* the Muslim fidelity to one's origins *and* transcendence of them, confessing the accidents of one's birth. This means, in other words, acknowledging history, one's cultural heritage, socialization in the here and now *and* striving to relativize it through comparison and criticism. These things do not exclude but presuppose one another if humane behavior is to become the law of the world.

One cannot say it often enough that *Nathan the Wise* is not, any more than Lessing's youthful work *The Jews*, a philo-Semitic drama. It is rather a play that, in the sense of Moses Mendelssohn's Foreword to Manasse Ben Israel's *Saving the Jews*, aims by glorifying an oppressed minority to prove that one cannot press for human rights without at the same time calling for the rights of all minorities, even the most despised, the most chained to its prejudices.

Once again, readers who wish to see *Nathan* as a philanthropic ballad with a decidedly pro-Jewish slant are wrong. Lessing seeks not to write a pious apologia in favor of the Jews, but to destroy in exemplary fashion the Christian-derived ideology of election that, as Mendelssohn said, would prefer to make "all people who are not Christians" out to be "assassins and brigands."

Using the example of strangers to teach his own people a tolerance that proves itself in practice, Lessing set forth his intention of presenting the problem in a mode of demonstrative "alienation." He would argue not through Christians, but through an evangelist of the Age of Reason in *The Education of the Human Race*, through a Freemason in *Ernst and Falk*, and through a Jew in *Nathan the Wise*.

Nathan is a counterimage of Shakespeare's Shylock, a Jew, a master of commerce and a wise man of the world, pregnant with reality ("coin," "tax," and "minting" trip from his tongue as readily as "God," "Christ," and "reason"). Nevertheless, he is also an artistic figure: a father who sings the hymn of adoption and declares that by contrast natural generation is second-rate; a father, who thanks to the limitations of Christian society, takes over the mother's role as well. (Great actresses, like Ida Ehre, call Nathan their ideal part, and are by no means as ill-advised as they first seem.)

Lessing had his women speak precisely, emphatically, and powerfully—*too* precisely, emphatically, and powerfully, in Mendelssohn's judgment. The writer who created Sara Sampson, Emilia Galotti, Minna von Barnhelm, and Franziska, forged in Nathan the ideal father, a figure who had neither usurped authority, nor any kind of masculine superiority. "As a mother comforts her child, so will I comfort you," and "I will cry aloud like one giving birth, I will call out and cry"—thus Yahweh presents himself, in the interpretation of the prophet Isaiah, as a father who is at once man and woman in one person: "Thou hast drawn me from my mother's womb," Zion says to its king. Like Yahweh—compared to a wife who "has compassion on the child of her womb"—at once the male ruler and the woman of sorrows, so Nathan presents himself as a father. In the great speech about the genocide unleashed by the Christians, he takes on the soul-stirring majesty of the Pietà: Jew and Jewess, father and mother at once, weeping for the murdered children.

There is no glorification of the hypermasculine father. *That* is what the Patriarch is: a domineering antifather, committed to ruling (*archein*) rather than being a father (*pater*). Lessing is no more interested in hypermasculine fathers and God the Father than he is in the apotheosis of the Jews. His intention is rather to show the Christians how far they still have to go to reach humanity, since through a long religious education they have become fixated on preestablished role models. The humanity he has in mind is guaranteed only by the respect under whose aegis the religions tolerate one another (and that means *acknowledge*, not just condescendingly *put up with*).

A nothing-but-a-Christian would be for Lessing a monster with a stupid tongue, unsociable and incapable of dialectic, which was practically considered a mortal sin in Wolfenbüttel. Christian education without comparison with other forms of instruction is something even the Lay Brother would not go along with: ". . . Children / have need of love—and were it but the love / of savage beasts—much more than Christian teaching. / For Christianity there's always time."

For Christianity there's always time. Lessing was deadly serious about this, and at the same time this line, if delivered well by the actor, generally provokes hearty laughter from the public. And why not, since there is no play in German literature that, despite the pogrom scene, despite the theological subtleties, despite all the philosophical, economic, and genealogical disputes, is as witty, brilliant, ironic, cunning, and amusing as *Nathan the Wise*. Hugo von Hofmannsthal was right when he pointed out that "this play . . . has never been put on as it would have to be: as altogether the wittiest comedy that we have, altogether focused on the incomparable tension of this dialogue, this lying in wait for a word from one another, this repartee, this fencing with the understanding (and with the feelings disguised as understanding), that the whole play . . . is full of."

I wonder what writer, before or after Lessing, dared to bring on the stage the most difficult theological topics, along with the program of tolerance and education underlying them *in usum omnium Christianorum*. And Lessing does this not in a solemn linear style (yet not farcically either), but with a light touch, ambiguously, in the form of a moving tragedy, a "primer of higher cynicism" (Friedrich Schlegel), and a serious comedy.

Who besides Lessing could have dared to describe the obligation to practice piety and to warn against every kind of escapism—whether on the Ganges, in the monastery, or while playing chess? And who could have done this in lines that, since they are in blank verse, point to poetic distance—to the East and the legendary world of history. On the other hand, since the meter is broken and the nonchalantly handled rhythm approaches prose, those lines evoke the present, the here and now: Germany in the eighteenth century?

Who, beyond this, would have dared to make the basic statement of the play, contained in the ring parable? (The key lies not in the bequeathing of the ring, but in the way it is acquired; not in the possession, but in the striving to show oneself worthy of the gift; not in the object, the piece of jewelry, but in the person made in the image of God. That person in the act of love of neighbor proves himself to be a rational pedagogue aware of his limits, whatever religion he may belong to. The key lies in the fact that not the object but the subject determines the happiness of the individual.) Who, I wonder, would have dared to present such lofty philosophical theses on the unity of theory and practice, so wittily, so pertly, so boldly, as Lessing did—to Schiller's irritation. Lessing's stylistic freedom and use of colloquial speech must have grated on the ears of the poet from Weimar, who was so intent on the strict separation of genres and levels of speech.

In a word, one would have to be Lessing—and more than Diderot—to stage the pedagogical play (Nathan does what Falk teaches) in the form of a comedically interlaced drama of humanity, shaped both by "very serious jokes" (in the Goethean sense), and populated by a colorful and highly problematic (as far as character goes) society. This drama of humanity is at the same time disclosed by detective work to be a family play. All the leading characters in it, except for Nathan, are related to everyone else: uncle, aunt, nephew, and niece united in peace—and not one of them married. A widower, three spinsters, and five bachelors—that's what I call a family play, if there ever was one.

But this very point is dubious. There is in any case no happy ending, no wedding feast (as in the sketches for the play), no thundering finale with bride and bridegroom led out on stage, the lifting of the veil, and tender blushes. Instead of that, we have a silent round of embraces on all sides, no speeches, no merriment, no mere contradictions indicating the presence of *such and such* persons. Only courtly ritual and measured repetitions of the same thing over and over again. No chess-playing Parsee and no babbling Lay Brother enliven the feast. The characters celebrate a family festivity, wordlessly and without arguments, in the waxworks. A melancholy conclusion, I think.

It becomes clear that the way to the reconciliation of the religions and the emancipation of reason, which one day will no longer need revelation, after revelation has paved the way for it, is still a long one, which is what Lessing intended to show.

In between the gray mists of prehistory and the new age that perhaps in a thousand thousand years will usher in the kingdom of general emancipation from self-incurred tutelage, lies an intermediary epoch. During this time the intolerance and fanaticism of the positive, politically legitimated religions and ideological communities can be named in treatises and games, and will be deprived of unlimited dominance. But it will be long before such evils can be reduced to absurdity in favor of natural religion.

Realist that he was, Lessing had no illusions about the effect of his literary-theological undertakings. "As yet I know no place where this play could now be put on," he wrote. And he clearly realized that the Christian religion, which insisted on its historical power, would never cease to block the view of that reliable and well-vouched-for religion of Christ. By that he meant the religion that Jesus "as a person himself acknowledged and practiced, the religion that every person can have in common with him, the religion that every person must all the more wish to share with him, the more lofty and lovable he conceives Christ's character as a mere man to have been." N.B., as a mere man (not as God and not as *such and such* a person)—as an incarnation of humanity, in other words, and not as its accidentally limited personification.

On the issue of Christianity and humanity, it is moving to see how Lessing, like Pascal and Gryphius, focuses on Jesus, whom he apostrophies as a pedagogue in *The Education of the Human Race*. This is the Jesus who *never* ceased being a human being, the man from Nazareth, who was not by accident the subject of one of the last sketches on the playwright's desk. A few weeks after the appearance of *Nathan*, Lessing wrote in a letter to Elise Reimarus that he was thinking of working out a *Good Samaritan*, a tragedy in five acts. This would be a play "according to the invention of the Lord Jesus Christ." He added that "the Levite and the priest would play quite a brilliant role in it." We can see that Lessing, who championed the practice of piety that most reliably fulfills God's providential plan leading to reason, remained at the same time, up until his death, the theological polemicist. He was enrolled among the fathers who—this is the meaning of the parable of the rings—voluntarily resign their authority and leave it to their sons, of whatever religion, to lead a Samaritan existence through love of neighbor as the form of humane sociability most pleasing to God.

Lessing was enrolled among the *wise* fathers, but also the *wrathful* fathers. He inexorably challenged to battle the priests, Levites, patriarchs, and Goezes of this world, who one and all place pure doctrine and pious enthusiasm over good works. They do this, although, Lessing claims, it must be clear that good works are not to be measured by denominational standards. In *Nathan*, the Muslim pardons the Christian, the Christian saves the Jewess from the fire, the Jew accepts, on the highest level, the Christian woman whose fellow believers had just before this extirpated his family. "Or smile and let her keep this one belief, / Which Jew and Christian share with Moslem too;— / A sweet delusion, if it be no more"(BQM). This is Daya speaking about Rachel, after the appearance of the Templar. Lessing knew that, the way the times were, the *illusion* could become *truth* only by way of appearance, only in the anticipatory dreams of art. Only in the theater could be realized the autonomous society of those sympathetic minds that no longer needed any government, any worldly tyranny, or any religious discipline.

A few weeks before his death, Lessing recommended to his friend Moses Mendelssohn an immigrant, a Jew named Daveson, who had been subjected to the same mistreatment by Jews and

Christians: "He wants nothing from you, dear Mendelssohn, except that you suggest to him the shortest and safest way to the European country where there are neither Christians nor Jews . . . as soon as he successfully arrives there, I shall be the first to follow him." This, reduced to a formula, was the testament of an admirer of theology in the age of Enlightenment, on whose tombstone the words of Bertolt Brecht might stand: "He made suggestions."

To this day, these suggestions have yet to be accepted, much less translated into reality.

FRIEDRICH HÖLDERLIN

◆

HYMNS

HANS KÜNG

◆

Religion
as the Reconciliation of
Classical Antiquity and Christianity

If one could have a living experience anywhere of the meaning of the ancien régime, of the premodern "system," or of the paradigm of Protestant theology, church, and state, it would be in the Tübingen Seminary under the despotic Duke Karl Eugen in the time of Friedrich Hölderlin (1770–1843) and his friends Neuffer, Magenau, and Stäudlin. After 1790, Hegel and Schelling joined the group.

Traditionally orthodox, even though refinished in the modern style, theology in Tübingen presented itself in the form of the "older Tübingen school," headed by G. C. Storr. At the time of Gryphius, Lutheran orthodoxy and seventeenth-century Catholic baroque Scholasticism were in league with Aristotle, while the enlightened theology of the eighteenth century took its stand with Leibnitz and Wolff. Storr himself called in no less a figure than Immanuel Kant to get apologetic security for his "biblical super-naturalism": Since "pure reason" was not competent to deal with truths of faith such as the Trinity, the incarnation, and the resurrection, it was also incapable of critically probing into them. It was that simple.

Hölderlin, Hegel, and Schelling, who after all lived in the same room, would have nothing to do with this fictitious compromise between dogma and criticism. "Nowhere is the old system so faithfully propagated as over there in Tübingen," Hegel wrote to Schelling afterwards, mocking this pseudomodern orthodoxy that "tries to direct the water of new ideas into its own clanking mills." "This is how it goes: 'Yes, that's rather clear,' they say. They take a nap, and in the morning they drink their coffee and offer some to others, as if nothing had happened" (Lasson-Hoffmiester, ed., XXVII, 16 December).

Hölderlin, who had been brought up already in his narrowly pietistic environment to deny rather than affirm his ego, soon felt repelled by the intellectual compulsion of late orthodox dogmatism and moralism. Christianity increasingly and inevitably struck him as an exhausted religion. But Greek antiquity—Hölderlin's "hobbyhorse" from his youth—replaced Christianity with a new, frankly religious fascination. The ideal Greek world of "noble simplicity and silent greatness" as rediscovered by Winckelmann was German classicism's ideal of beauty—of the light-filled, blessed gods, of natural piety and harmonic humanity.

What a contrast this made with the Tübingen Seminary and its rather gloomy ecclesiasticism and Christian style. The more orthodox the theology, the more strictly disciplined was the church and the better supervised its new brood of pastors-to-be. Subordination was the watchword everywhere; an authoritarian church supported the absolutist state. In the seminary, a former Augustinian monastery, there was, according to Hölderlin, "unhealthy air," "bad food," "chicanery," or, in Schelling's words, a "moral despotism." There was a system of discipline and punishment that easily led to servility and hypocrisy, behind which stood the authority of the duke and the powerful Stuttgart consortium. The authorities felt serious concern over the critical attitude of some of the theology students toward church-state authority, order, and discipline.

For Hölderlin, Tübingen meant a crucial turn; he quickly became an opponent of the feudal institutions of church and state. He was basically antipathetic to the clerical profession. Only for his mother's sake did this waxen pale "moper" stand the pressure: "The fact that I am still in the monastery is due to the request of my mother. For her sake one can well louse up a few years" (2 vol. ed. of *Works and Letters*, Insel-Ausgabe, II, 803–4). In his student years, he was weak and moody, but extraordinarily ambitious and hungry for fame, besides being continually torn by doubt that he would rather have studied law.

The administration of the seminary was liberal only with respect to study circles, particular friendships, and reading material. The 1770s—Lessing's last decade—contained the American war of independence and the "late Enlightenment," which had been politically radicalized by Klopstock. The "Sturm und Drang" authors Goethe and Schiller had attracted attention among the German intelligentsia with their *Goetz von Berlichingen* and *The Robbers* respectively, spreading the liberation mentality and hatred of princes. In Württemberg, Schubart, Conz, and Staüdlin—all personally known to Hölderlin—were also active along these lines.

In the seminary, the Bible was read in public, Rousseau in private. While the classic biography of Hölderlin by Wilhelm Michel (1940) grossly neglected this political dimension, more recent research (W. Binder, C. Prignitz), prompted by the studies of Pierre Bertaux, has shown how much even Hölderlin's earliest poems were stamped not only by the Christian-pietistic-otherworldly spirit of the family and the boarding school, but increasingly by the freedom-loving spirit of Klopstock (first revered as "God's great singer" as well), and directed against the feudal structures of injustice.

As early as 1788, one year before the French Revolution, Hölderlin composed "Men's Rejoicing," which, completely oriented as it was toward the "Daughters of God," the ideals of "Justice" and "Freedom," as well as "Love of the Fatherland," also betrays a pronounced anticourtly feeling about the "curses of despots" and the "rage of clerics," along with a new speech about a "God of the gods":

> There glimmers in us a spark of the divine;
> And these sparks shall not be torn from
> Man's breast by the power of hell!
> Hear this, you courts of despots, hear this!" (I, 257)

A year later in Paris the great revolution began with the constituting of the French National Assembly, the storming of the Bastille, the imprisonment of the king, the proclamation of the Rights of Man, and the nationalization of church property.

The French Revolution bound together the idea of the nation and the universal ideals of humanity with bourgeois interests. The *paradigm of modernity*, which had already achieved classic shape in philosophy with Leibnitz, Hume, and Kant, in physics and chemistry with Newton and Boyle, and in political and social theory with Montesquieu, Voltaire, and Rousseau, began to make itself felt in the realm of *practical politics* as well. Neither the French proponents of enlightenment nor Lessing had considered the possibility of a violent revolution, and the French Revolution seemed at first to be a bloodless one.

That was not the least of the reasons why in crisis-ridden Germany the revolution won the approval of individuals in the middle class and in the bourgeois intelligentsia. It won over philosophers such as Kant, Jacobi, Fichte, writers such as Klopstock, Herder, Wieland, Novalis, and Friedrich Schlegel, and, needless to say, theology students such as the three young members of the opposition from Tübingen, who likewise cherished illusions about a voluntary change in the form of government on the part of the reigning princes. They were well informed about developments in France by a small group of students from Mömpelgard (Montbéliard), a French-speaking area that belonged at the time to Württemberg. Students in the seminary were gripped by the ideas of the revolution and passionately devoured French newspapers. They inscribed the pages of their albums with remarks like "In tyrannos!" "Vive Jean-Jacques!" "Vive la liberté" and similar things. Hegel, who was an enthusiastic spokesman for freedom and equality, is supposed to have joined Hölderlin, Schelling, and others in planting a freedom tree in or near Tübingen.

Hölderlin's enthusiasm for revolutionary ideas found clear expression in the *Tübingen Hymns*. The highest ideals of humanity—harmony, beauty, freedom, love—are experienced here at this early date as powers really believed in, as divine revelations and figures who address the poet and are addressed, praised, thanked, and enthusiastically celebrated by him. Here, too, for the first time there appears—in the "Hymn to Humanity" (1791)—"the God in us." The aim of these political-religious hymns is the renewal of human society. In the first hymn to Freedom, the "Daughter of Heaven" (1792), we read:

Then at the sweet, hotly won goal,
When the harvest of great days begins,
When the seats of tyrants are desolate,
And the servants of tyrants have rotted away,
When German blood and German love glow
In the heroic band of my brothers,
Then, O Daughter of Heaven, I shall sing again,
Sing to you, as I die, the last of the songs.
(Athenäum Study Edition I, 106)

Of course, everything became different when the revolution took a radical turn. There was Louis XVI's attempted flight in 1791, the September massacres of 1792, the guillotining of the king, and finally Robespierre's reign of terror in 1793. All this led to a shift of opinion in Germany. In 1793, on orders from the consistory, an inspection was carried out to repress the democratic spirit: One seminarian was dismissed; the sovereign personally gave the community a dressing-down in the refectory. Schelling, who had translated the "Marseillaise," had to apologize and did so with a double-edged quotation from the Bible: "Your Majesty, we all err in many ways." In the end, the proclamation of new, stricter regulations embittered few people as deeply as it did Hölderlin. In his hymns, he voices the cry that the fatherland must be "wrested away" from "the robbers" and tyrants.

Immediately after getting a high pass on his final examination in theology, Hölderlin—like Hegel and Schelling—definitively renounced the clerical profession and with it Christianity, too—at first, anyway. The personal God, just like the figure of Jesus Christ, receded into the background. Hölderlin began to find his own way, and we have to wonder whether he just wasn't one of those natures who would at no time and in no intellectual-religious situation "have adapted to an existing religious, intellectual, ecclesiastical order." Emanuel Hirsch thinks Hölderlin *was* such a nature, and calls attention at the same time to the historic rupture taking place in this epoch:

Hölderlin would have gone his own way as a heretic, mystic, or religious enthusiast in earlier centuries as well. Around 1700 he would have become a radical Pietist. Instead of *Hy-*

perion he would have written an autobiography, and instead
of odes in the Greek style he would have given voice to
pious Christian cries from the heart. The fact that he took a
completely different path was a sign of the time.

The crisis of transformation, as early as 1800, had pulverized a considerable part of the self-evident validity of the
Christian scheme of things. The inner power of Christian
faith, even within pious Protestant Germany, was much
weaker in matters of state, church, and theology than people
thought. (p. 455)

In this phase, Hölderlin was penetrated more than ever by the
ideal image of Greek religion, art, and mode of life, by the ancient
belief in fate (see the elegiac complaint over the downfall of
"Greece" in 1795), by the creative presence of the natural universe, and by the new idealistic philosophy. For around three
years, the three students—Hölderlin, Hegel, and Schelling—
working together confronted the leading representatives of the
new era, Leibnitz, Rousseau, Jacobi, Herder, Fichte, and above
all Kant (mediated, for Hölderlin, by Schiller).

The upshot of this was an extremely momentous event in intellectual history, a *new orientation in the understanding of God.*
Without it, one cannot comprehend Hölderlin's hymns from the
middle and late period. Once again, Lessing was the redeemer.
Speaking of Lessing, the philosopher H. J. Jacobi had written in
his public letter "On the Teaching of Spinoza" (1785, 2nd ed.
1789) to Mendelssohn, claiming that in a private conversation
shortly before his death Lessing told him he had given up the
orthodox concepts of divinity, had come to understand God as a
nonpersonal soul of the universe, and now believed in Heraclitus'
"Hen kai pan," a pantheistic formula meaning "One and all,"
which as far as Jacobi was concerned clearly amounted to atheism.
This led to a great "dispute over pantheism," but to this day it
has not become quite plain what we are to make of Jacobi's piece.
Did he really understand Lessing, the great dialectician? The only
thing certain is that since then Lessing has had a public reputation
as a "Spinozist," as the founder of a peculiarly German variety
of dynamic pantheism. That is why in the period that followed,
many, and not least of all the three Tübingen men, would adopt
the "Hen kai pan" for themselves.

Does that make Hegel, Schelling, and Hölderlin adherents of pantheism? To be sure, all three turned away from the biblical God, the ruler who keeps all human beings in subjection, as they turned away from the God of dualistic deism, who is thrust off into a distant transcendence as a mere "opposite number" set off against us (an ob-jectum). No, even Hölderlin did not engage in pantheism; for him, God and nature do not simply coincide. One would have to speak more precisely in his case of panentheism, of "all-things-in-God." The divine One is active in all things, and things are based on the one God: a differentiated unity of life understood as divine, of love, of the all-embracing spirit—these are characteristic concepts at least for the later Frankfurt period of the friends. No doubt, with this understanding of God, they thought they had cast aside the rigid doctrines of Christianity like an old skin—a metamorphosis of the divine. Instead of speaking about God as the creator and ruler of the world, the Great Watchmaker, it became possible to speak of the deity in a new and fresh manner as the All-Embracing, the Absolute, the Divine, in whom Zeus, Yahweh, and God the Father are subsumed, while leaving behind the idea of a "personal God" as a crude anthropomorphism.

Thus something decisive had taken place for religion in the modern world: The three men from Tübingen—as Goethe did, too, in a different way—drew upon the scientific presuppositions of the new paradigm to reach, for the first time, clear, though perhaps not yet sufficiently discriminating, conclusions for a new understanding of God. This new thinking would make itself felt all the way down to the days of Teilhard and Whitehead. God, the deity—or however one wishes to call the very first and last, realest reality—may no longer be thought of in naive anthropomorphic fashion as a God *outside* the world, in a physical heaven. God is thought of adequately only *in* this world and this world *in* God—the infinite in the *finite*, transcendence *in* immanence, the absoute *in* the relative. God is the all-embracing, all-governing reality in the heart of things, in man, in the whole world. The upshot of this had to be a very different feeling for life, nature, and the self.

———————◆———————

In any event, this new understanding of God was in the background when Hölderlin, after saying good-bye to Tübingen, and now not a vicar but a private tutor in Waltershauden near Jena, wrote to Hegel, who at the time was a tutor himself in Berlin: "Dear Brother, I am sure that in the meantime you sometimes think of me, since we bade farewell to each other with the watchword 'The Kingdom of God!' I believe that after each and every metamorphosis we would recognize each other by this watchword" (Insel Edition, II, 82). The *Kingdom of God* was a biblical-eschatological motto (inspired by the Swabian Pietism of people like Bengel and Oetinger, and by the chiliastic expectations that were widespread at the time and shared in secular-rational form by progressive thinkers like Lessing and Kant as well. It expresses in a comprehensive way the great goal of the society that was to be renewed. This was a goal that ought not to be abandoned even if it couldn't be immediately realized in political terms. And after the political revolution in France had run its disappointing course, the friends strove more and more for a *revolution of the mind* that was meant, of course, to embrace all domains, first of all philosophy, literature, science, and art, but religion, too, and finally politics.

Altogether in this spirit, Schelling sketched out, after a reunion with Hölderlin in Tübingen, the "oldest systematic program of German idealism" (1795–1796). A fragment of it is contained in a copy made by Hegel (II, 647–49). In the section on the "moral world," in opposition to every kind of "superstition," and "priestcraft, which lately feigns to be rational," Schelling promotes the "absolute freedom of all minds," "who bear the intellectual world within themselves, and are allowed to seek neither God nor immortality *outside themselves*." Evidently inspired by intuitions of the poet Hölderlin, the program of the philosopher Schelling culminates in the "Platonic idea of beauty," which unites truth and goodness, and hence in an "aesthetic philosophy," which is ultimately overtaken by poetry, the "teacher of humanity."

The common conviction was that mankind needed not only rational enlightenment, but—an early idea of Hegel—a "new religion" that must be a "sensory religion," able to speak to the "great multitude." Concretely, this is what Hölderlin found among the Greeks: "monotheism of reason and the heart, polytheism of the imagination and art, this is what we need!" Or, in other words, for the people and the educated, the enlightened and the unenlightened, we "must have a new mythology, but this mythology must be in the service of ideas, it must become a mythology of *reason*." That way the goal would be reached: "No power will be suppressed any longer, universal freedom and equality of minds will prevail!—A loftier spirit sent from heaven must establish this new religion among us. It will be the last, the greatest work of the human race" (II, 649). The triad of sensory religion, mythology of reason, and poetry as the educator of mankind characterizes Hölderlin's understanding of religion and poetry, which in turn shapes his hymns.

But how is this to be translated into reality? In another essay that was likewise left as a fragment, Hölderlin continues reflecting systematically "On Religion" (II, 635–41). The modern world strikes him as completely typified by the contrast between the "physical, mechanical, historical circumstances," the domain of empirical matters of fact, and the "intellectual, moral, legal circumstances," the domain of abstractions, values, and knowledge. And where does the poet stand? Should he deal in naturalistic fashion with "mere data, facts," or in the idealistic mode with "mere ideas or concepts or characters"? No, he should fuse "both into one" in his poetry. He should present what usually escapes representation, and thus make the timeless and permanent current. Then he would be translating into reality "religious circumstances" that "in their representation are neither intellectual nor historical, but intellectually historical, or mythic." All religion is thus "poetic by its nature." Hölderlin's great hope is that the poet could restore the lost "connection between men and spirits," that he could find once more the unforced Greek connection with nature and the divine, the "God of myths," whom he had experienced so vividly in his youth:

> In my boyhood days
> Often a god would save me
> From the shouts and the rod of men;
> Safe and good then I played
> With the orchard flowers

And the breezes of heaven
Played with me.

And as you make glad
The hearts of the plants
Then toward you they stretch
Their delicate arms,
So you made glad my heart,
Father Helios, and like Endymion
I was your darling,
Holy Luna.

O all you loyal,
kindly gods!
Would that you knew how
My soul loved you then.

True, at that time I did not
Evoke you by name yet, and you
Never named me, as men use names,
As though they knew one another.

Yet I knew you better
Than ever I have known men,
I understood the silence of Aether,
But human words I've never understood.

I was reared by the euphony
Of the rustling copse
And learned to love
Amid the flowers.

I grew up in the arms of the gods.

(I, 40, Michael Hamburger, trans.,
*Friedrich Hölderlin: Poems
and Fragments*)

For interpreters of the history of art and literature concerned
with more than just works and their forms and modes of procedure; for anyone aware of the fact that the history of art and
literature attests not just to matters of fact but to living human
beings, the depiction of their life will leave only cold hearts un-
moved. In the case of Hölderlin's "In My Boyhood Days," it is

impossible for the reader, given the boy's later career, to do an impassive analysis of the poem. I am speaking here not about the poet's end, wrapped in so many mysteries as it is, but with an eye to the project he undertook at the height of his powers. And I am not offering my support here for a Hölderlinian romanticism, and still less for a new national or quasi-religious Hölderlin cult, of the sort that has marked our century, even before the arrival of nazism. Up until the centenary of the poet's birth (1870), only eight thousand copies of his work were sold, while eighty thousand were sold in the year 1921 alone. This cult celebrates Hölderlin the "explicator," the "seer," the "priest," the "lawgiver," the "mediator," and at the same time the "victim" (W. Michel, 566). No, I am not arguing for the cultivation of Hölderlin as an ersatz religion, but rather for a self-critically reflective, empathetic, sympathetic interpretation.

"In my boyhood days / Often a god would save me": Hölderlin invokes memories of childhood as a time of intensive union with nature in a Swabian landscape that was still preindustrial, and in undisturbed premodern piety. The man reflecting here has been equally disappointed by theology, the church, and the state, and has rejected the whole orthodox Protestant paradigm, accepting modernity under the influence of his idealistic friends and intellectual comrades. But what was this modern "Hyperion" supposed to do, a man who was a poet and nothing else? Unlike his friends, he could not find his salvation, the meaning of his life in philosophical speculation and a secure job as a university professor. But neither could he, like increasing numbers of modern men and women, find that meaning and security in science, technology, and the industrial world. Nor could he find it as others do nowadays in politics, in the struggle for the realization of democracy. Hölderlin consciously retreated to the experiences of his youth, when he felt that he was "in the arms of the gods." The image of youth becomes a critical mirror of his contemporary world, in which the divine seems to have fled from the life of busy individuals and from nature altogether.

But what does a poet have to throw into the balance against the Godless age? What does he have at his disposal to make a bold synthesis of religion and poetry, and to strive for a better humanity? With all his abounding power of language, Hölderlin tried—and not for dreamy aesthetes, but for his whole threatened "fatherland"—to reawaken the "genius of Greece" (his last Tübingen poem in 1793 was entitled "Greece"). In a flight of nature mysticism, he tried to reawaken also the powers of life: earth and light, aether and sea, rivers and valleys, friendship and love, everything that, having taken his distance from Christianity, he called *"the gods."*

But he doesn't simply name the gods. He invokes them, appeals to them, and reveres them. He borrows from pre-Homeric, archaic Greek mythology, and he borrows from Pindar and the choruses of the tragedians. Ever since Paul Böckmann's foundational research into *Hölderlin and His Gods* (1935) and Romano Guardini's studies (1939), we know that these "gods" are not just "elements" (Obernauer) or "personifications" (Gundolf), not just mystical connections with the cult of souls and ancestors (Pigenot), and also not just poetic-aesthetic formations (Böhm). They are rather the basic forces of nature, the permanent powers of life that control extrahuman nature as well as human relations.

It is true that these gods of nature lie beyond our personal experiences. Still they can be felt, in faith, by in-spired individuals and can be recognized as real and *celebrated in the word*, in songs. Hölderlin's goal was not the pathetic propagation of great ideals as in Schiller, but hymnodic praise along the lines of Klopstock. "The primal meaning of myth is restored for Hölderlin insofar as 'mythos' in the first instance means both word and discourse and 'mytheisthai' means both speak and name. And at the same time the actual meaning of the hymns is recovered, since 'hymnein' is to be translated as extol, praise, glorify," as Paul Böckmann says in *Hölderlin's Mythical World* (1944, 20).

In doing this, Hölderlin has no intention of creating and presenting a new mythology in the sense of an autonomous, self-contained world of the gods. Instead, he wants to express *pietàs*, or religious loyalty, which humans can experience toward the higher powers of nature. For Hölderlin, myth is not, as it is for Lessing, Hegel, or the idealists as a whole, simply the untrue, unreal preliminary form of the truly real reality of the idea. It is the genuine experience of the manifestations of the one Divine, whose power is at work all through the universe.

At the high point of his creativity—especially in the time he spent with Suzette Gontard, the wife of a banker in Frankfurt and the incarnate dream figure of Diotima in *Hyperion*—Hölderlin saw himself temporarily at his goal. In Diotima, his yearning seemed to be fulfilled; the lost past and the possible future became present. In his beloved, the purest incorporation of his ideals, the divine appeared to him, the mythic Greek world in a new form, the morning gift of a regenerated world:

> Now I have found you!
> More beautiful than I, anticipating, saw,
> Hoping in the feast day hours,
> Lovely Muse, you are there;
> From the Heavenly one on high,
> Where the joy flees upward,
> Where raised beyond aging,
> Ever cheerful beauty flowers,
> You seem to me to have descended,
> Messenger of the Gods! . . .
>
> (I, 28)

But when the relationship, violently disturbed from the outside, had to be dissolved, Hölderlin's breakdown was in the wings:

> But do I not know it? Woe is me! You loving
> Tutelary spirit! Far from you they soon play to me,
>   lacerating,
>   On the strings of the heart,
>   All the spirits of death.
>
> (I, 33)

The intoxication had vanished. In the autobiographical and programmatical epistolary novel *Hyperion, or The Hermit of Greece*, memories are conjured up from the days when the Divine and the Earthly were still one. But that didn't solve the religious crisis of modernity—an increasing distance from God. "Hyperion's Song of Fate" soberly confesses the permanent distance between the "Heavenly ones on high" and himself, the unbridgeable gap between the divine powers and suffering human beings:

> You walk above in the light,
>   Weightless tread a soft floor, blessed genii! . . .

> But we are fated
>   To find no foothold, no rest,
>   And suffering mortals
>   Dwindle and fall
>   Headlong from one
>   Hour to the next,
>   Hurled like water
>   From ledge to ledge
>   Downward for years to the vague abyss
>
> (I, 44, M. H., trans.)

Unrest, suffering, blindness, "thrownness," uncertainty: With this sketch, the author describes himself—wearing the mask of Hyperion. His life from now on would stand under these signs. It would now become increasingly clear that Hölderlin had little success in bringing together program and practice, idea and reality, aesthetics and reality, poetry and society. He became increasingly accustomed to his mythic universe, but that universe increasingly began to take on an independent existence and to alienate him from the real world.

Of course, the more the illusion of a restored Greek world in a restored Germany faded away, the more Hölderlin questioned his presupposition of the structural identity of the German and the Greek spirits. The more the return of the celebrated gods was overdue, and the more he strove for a new *synthesis between Hellas and Christianity*, the more there emerged—in painful reminiscences—alongside the old gods the figure of the One who had shaped Hölderlin's youth.

> Much have I suffered
>   On your account
>   And on your son's, Madonna,
>   Since I first heart of him
>   In my sweet youth
>
> (I, 208)

Thus, the incomplete hymn to the Madonna. But even as early as this poem, we hear the note granting equal status to the Son and the gods of nature that will be characteristic of the late phase:

> For you, our Lady, and
> For the son, but for the others also
> Lest as from slaves by force
> The gods
> Should take what is theirs
>   (I, 211, M. Hamburger, trans.)

"The Archipelago" was the last great poem written out of the purely ancient spirituality. Even in the fragment of a drama, *The Death of Empedocles*, we see in the maturation of different versions (1798–1800) a progressive Christianization of the figure of the Greek philosopher who ultimately plunges into Etna, offering himself as a sacrifice for the many; Empedocles has the features of Christ. It is to him, the One, that Hölderlin's *last hymns* before his derangement are primarily dedicated. Walter Jens will deal with these in greater detail. Here, to complete the circle, I would like to select one that celebrates the return of Christ (so long believed to be far away) in a downright heart-wrenching fashion as the *reconciler*: as a Friend, the Immortal One, blessed peace, whose majesty drives the poet to his knees:

> Conciliator, you that are no longer believed in
> Are here now, assuming the shape of
> A friend, immortal, yet indeed
> I recognize   what exalted power
> It is that bends my knees . . .
>   (I, 156, M. H., trans.)

For the poet who has already sat so long in darkness, deprived of peace, briefly stirred to enthusiasm by the Peace of Lunéville between France and the German Empire (1801), the visit is an unexpected "gift." The person who appears is unequivocally more for Hölderlin than an individual, a wise man, or a friend:

> And almost like a blind man I
> Must ask you, the heavenly, for what
> And whence you have come to me, blessed Peace!
> This one thing I do know, a mortal you are not,
> For much a wise man or one of
> The loyally gazing friends may elucidate, but when
> A god appears, on heaven and earth and ocean

An all-renewing clarity shines

>   (I, 156–57, M. H., trans.)

Thus, "a god" appears, not "(the) God." Here, of course, we should immediately recall that in the New Testament, too, the Logos is called only "god" (theós), while the Father alone is called "(the) God" (ho theós). Here too Hölderlin recalls his youth, the Sunday mornings with prayer and song by the community, his doubts and fears. Still, "It was preordained. And God smiles," the "All-sustainer," "the God of gods," now called the "Father," who at the close of antiquity intervened when the "Sacred Fire" at the feast of the gods was almost extinguished:

> When swiftly kindling, the Father sent down the
> Most loving of all that are his

>   (I, 158, M. H., trans.)

And this envoy fulfills his vocation in death. However, after the men and women in the time that followed forgot about heaven in their self-sufficiency and arrogance, a new generation was now to come that would experience "the fullness of time." To this generation, the secret would be revealed: the return of Christ as the last of the gods in the evening of time, and the reconciliation of the gods and man in a new community of love.

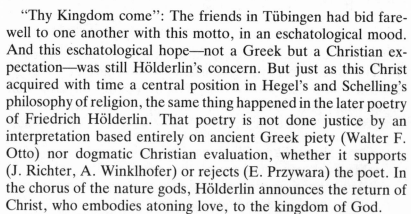

"Thy Kingdom come": The friends in Tübingen had bid farewell to one another with this motto, in an eschatological mood. And this eschatological hope—not a Greek but a Christian expectation—was still Hölderlin's concern. But just as this Christ acquired with time a central position in Hegel's and Schelling's philosophy of religion, the same thing happened in the later poetry of Friedrich Hölderlin. That poetry is not done justice by an interpretation based entirely on ancient Greek piety (Walter F. Otto) nor dogmatic Christian evaluation, whether it supports (J. Richter, A. Winklhofer) or rejects (E. Przywara) the poet. In the chorus of the nature gods, Hölderlin announces the return of Christ, who embodies atoning love, to the kingdom of God.

It is idle to discuss whether and to what extent Hölderlin's Christology agrees with Christian dogmatics. It does not and has no intention of doing so. According to Hölderlin, Jesus' death was not a sacrificial death of atonement for guilt incurred by sin, and his return would not be an act of judgment. But these traditional ideas are quite problematic nowadays, and the controversy over the orthodoxy of Hölderlin's "theology of mind," which swirled around the committed Protestant pastor Heinrich Buhr in Tübingen twenty-five years ago, would presumably arouse less furor today.

In any event, Hölderlin did not ultimately just return to his pietistic beginnings. In the end, he was quite deliberate in seeking both in one: a revitalized Christianity *and* a restored antiquity, Christ *and* the gods of nature. For Hölderlin, the gods were not, after all, as they were for Schiller, a beautiful poetic fiction, but a celebratred reality. To be sure, Christ and the gods are not completely coordinated. Christ is "the most loving mode" of the Father and "a god," who is atoning love itself. He is now more valuable than all others. But at the same time, as the higher god in the evening time of the world, Christ still belongs as much as ever to the ancient race of the gods that Hölderlin believes in.

Still, how are both elements to go together? Can we in the long run maintain Christianity alongside a mythical Hellas, the Nazarene alongside Dionysus, the Crucified next to Heracles, indeed, the one God alongside the God of the gods, and not break down over the internal contradiction? Is it an accident that not a single one of these hymns to Christ was ever finished? We can see the outline of Hölderlin's final failure here, and we shall have to say that just as he failed in his programmatic approach to poetry and politics and in his private and personal connections, so Hölderlin failed in religion, too. The new era never arrived. The great synthesis would not come off, neither politically nor religiously. In fact the

fusion of the pagan-divine element with the Christian, which arises out of dissatisfaction with the ancient gods, is one reason why Hölderlin broke down. The main reason, however, was his attempt to really grasp the divine in song and to name, here and now, the new day of the gods when the heavenly ones and the inner community of love come to stay. The hymn "Conciliator, you that no longer believed in. . . ." aims to achieve this and fails. It remains a fragment. Its faith and its proclamation did not correspond to reality.

These remarks are by Robert Thomas Stoll (150), who presents a still more compelling and philologically more precise interpretation of Hölderlin's hymns to Christ than did Romano Guardini.

But the failure here involved more than just Hölderlin with his grandiose poetry, which bit off more than it could chew. What failed, or *threatened to fail*, was also the *specifically modern piety* that, in its disappointment with, and alienation from, actually existing Christianity, attempts to take new paths. It does so with the help of an idealized Greek world (or idealized Germanness, too), a mystical nature piety, and above all a new humanism. If Hölderlin's fate had been taken more seriously, doubts would have had to be raised in advance:

1. about the chances for success of that adjustment between ancient natural piety and Christianity, where antiquity is no longer subsumed into Christianity, but where, conversely, Christianity is subordinated to antiquity;

2. about the efforts to bring about the "kingdom of God" under the conditions of modern society with a quasi-religious synthesis of philosophy and aesthetics; and

3. about the poet's ability to conjure up the divine and give it a contemporary placement in this world through his word, a superhuman task. "Woe is me!"—a "false Priest" (I, 137) were lines written on scraps of paper during his derangement.

A "needy time," Martin Heidegger wrote, in his interpretation of Hölderlin: "was the time of the vanished gods *and* the God to come" (49). The way Hölderlin fell silent so early should have warned not only those who were readying themselves to carry out the reform of the study of classical Latin and Greek—a surely much needed reform—and to develop methods of interpretation for ancient literature and culture, but also those who followed Winckelmann, Rousseau, Herder, Wilhelm von Humboldt, Goethe, Schiller, and Hölderlin himself in introducing the hyper-Enlightenment educational movement under the sign of German classicism and a renewed humanism. The *new humanism*, with its literary, aesthetic, and historical orientation, dominated our "gymnasiums" and universities for an entire century. Indeed, it largely became the ersatz religion of cultivated people in the modern era: the "Goethe-religion" of the educated German bourgeoisie. For this group and this time, art, seen in close connection with ethics, stands in the center and is supposed to have a redeeming, reconciling function.

Now that the modern paradigm has fallen into a crisis in our century with the epochal upheaval of the two world wars, it seems a starry-eyed theory to maintain that aesthetics can *replace* revelation, poets can replace priests, theater the liturgy, museums the churches, in short, *art and poetry can replace religion.* With the downfall of philosophical idealism, with progressive industrialization and democratization, this modern humanism had fallen into a crisis itself. Its apolitical individualism, its aestheticizing glorification of the self, as well as its educational egoism and the elitist essential features of its educational program were subjected to intense criticism from anthropology and sociology and, in the first instance, from both existential philosophy and dialectical theology.

Such criticism is justified from the theological-ecclesiastical standpoint only when it takes seriously the ideals of this humanism (personality, completeness, cheerfulness, beauty, humanity). It is justified when it does not battle exclusively the "damned Catholic 'And' " (Karl Barth's opposition to faith *and* works, Christ *and* Mary, Christianity *and* the church), but takes Hölderlin and his premature silence seriously. This means when it does not, with all its learning, fall back behind modernity into the earlier paradigm of the Orthodox and Pietists whom Hölderlin called "the scribes and Pharisees of our time": "They make out of the dear Holy Bible cold twaddle that kills the mind and heart." They "murder Christianity worse than the Jews because they turn his word into dead letters, and him, the living one, into an empty idol." In his "sincere, living faith" he wished to keep silence "in the presence of the *professional* theologians (meaning those who are theologians not freely and from the heart, but from the compulsion of their conscience and on account of their office)." He also felt compelled to silence "in the presence of those who do not wish to hear about all this, because from their youth on all religion has been spoiled for them through the dead letter and the terrifying commandment to believe, even though religion is the first and last need of every person . . ." (*Collected Works,* Stuttgart, ed., VI, I, 309–10).

Religion "spoiled"—and "the first and last need of every person." An inextinguishable longing for genuine, true, human religion, for God's real presence, runs through the life of this young man, who was destined, five years later, to fall into mental derangement. He was all of thirty-six years old, and would live for another thirty-seven years in his tower in Tübingen. Hölderlin's statement is reminiscent of the remark by Sigmund Freud that in religion the "oldest, strongest, most urgent wishes of humanity" find fulfillment. Is it all an illusion? All projection? To be sure, much in Hölderlin's religion was projection; much of it was, as Walther Killy put it, "private mythology." But not all. If Hölderlin failed in his attempts at synthesis, he remains unrefuted in his visions. To us postmoderns, Friedrich Hölderlin remains the witness who proclaims and who falls silent, the man who, driven to the abyss at a time of modern distance from God, refused to give up trusting dependence on the divine, on God in *this* world.

WALTER JENS

◆

. . . And Look upon Peace

"**M**inds must everywhere communicate with one another. Wherever even one living breath stirs, they must unite with every element not deserving of expulsion, so that out of this union, out of this invisible Church Militant, may come forth the great child of the time, the day of all days, which the man of my soul (an apostle whom his current mimickers understand as little as they understand themselves) calls the *future of the Lord*." Thus runs the creed, dated 9 November 1795, of Friedrich Hölderlin, a writer who was one of the most self-willed of the many pious eccentrics in which Swabia has always been uniquely rich—conventiclers, Adventists, speakers in tongues, and persons possessed by the Spirit.

Between his studies in the Tübingen Seminary and his stay in the house of master carpenter Ernst Zimmer (a few stones' throw from the seminary), Hölderlin met the church officials and gentlemen of the Consistory with horror and contempt. As a young man, he was dependent on them, much to his regret. At the same time, he was nevertheless a Christian who could match his superiors not only in spirituality but also in knowledge of the Bible and sovereign mastery of the text, especially the Pauline and Johannine writings.

The "enthusiastic seer" and "poet struck by Apollo" was in the first instance an expertly informed preacher and theologian, a *homo religiosus*. He dealt familiarly with the author of the Letters to the Corinthians (the "man of my soul") as with an equal. Hölderlin was capable of producing rich and varied adaptations of traditional metaphors, concepts, and images. He was not a dreamy enthusiast but a poet who knew a thing or two about the art of making his own individual vision clear as something uniquely different along lines paved by the past.

If we count up the names of pastors' sons who contributed to German poetry, we find that the list is long: Gryphius, Gottsched, and Gellert, Wieland, Lichtenberg, Matthias Claudius, Lenz, Jean Paul, and the Schlegels, Gotthelf, and Nietzsche: a powerful pantheon with a distinctly Protestant stamp. To this group must be added Hölderlin, the child of a Swabian family of officials and ministers. Trained in Denkendorf, Maulbronn, and Tübingen, Hölderlin remained a theologian all his life (*theos* and *logos*, God the Father and the Johannine Word, are key concepts in his work). The monastic pupil from Nürtingen could have held his own with every one of his Lutheran-educated fellow authors in debates where expertise in the Bible was at issue. The passages in his work that appear at first glance to be inspired naming often enough prove, upon closer inspection, to be modified quotations from Paul or John, embedded wherever possible, as in the case of the hymn "Patmos," in Pietist discourse (which is treated, to be sure, in a sovereign, unorthodox manner).

It is easily forgotten that Hölderlin was always on the road, a wanderer and hiker. He spoke of the "thorn staff," his beloved walking stick, as an "indispensable piece of furniture." Fifty kilometers a day was no great strain for him; so he could travel quickly from Tübingen to Switzerland. "I'm thinking of taking along three shirts, three handkerchiefs, and three pairs of socks (on account of the tearing) in a little knapsack. Since we three are traveling, it can't cost us very much as we go from one main place to another to have a man who can carry the laundry and show us the way."

He was always rambling through his homeland, "over hill and dale, as though led by instinct." He liked to talk about the "highway," farewells, and reunions in open country—this wanderer who crossed whole regions on foot ("on the much feared, snow-covered heights of the Auvergne, in storm and wilderness, on ice-cold nights, with a loaded pistol by my side in the rough bed"). According to one eyewitness, this vagabond was "pale as a corpse, emaciated, with wild sunken eyes, long hair and beard and dressed like a beggar," when he returned to Stuttgart in the summer of

1802. This friend of the "open road and the open world" was at the same time always a man of the cloister, always at home in cells, seminary rooms, modest chambers; he was on the move for scarcely more than ten years, while he spent forty, over half his life, in the condition of a hermit, tied down to Zimmer's house on the Neckar.

"So I'm back here again! I'm back in the silence—after so many diversions back in the monastery again." This sentence comes from a letter to Immanuel Nast, in Maulbronn, in the summer of 1786. It anticipates Hölderlin's way of life, and points to the interplay of longer excursions and meditative self-absorption, worldly and spiritual existence. Now Hölderlin would be on "difficult ways, rich in experience"; now he would put on the black cowl, the seminarist's cape, or his oft-described "simple doublet" throughout the four decades of his life as a hermit.

To understand him rightly, we have to imagine him *reading*, bent over the Bible and the Homeric writings. Or we can picture him in the pulpit, where he was disposed "to speak straight from the heart," or in his room, where he walked up and down and "wrote poetry with great effort." He wrote extraordinarily slowly, with enormous exertion, tinkering away, wrestling to find the words rather than pouring them out.

Hölderlin was no Büchner or Rimbaud, not the sort of writer whose first sketch went off just right. He had to pay dearly for his wisdom. His early poems, pious, conventionally rhymed studies, betray little genius. Hölderlin's religious style gets its peculiar tone not from his acquired enthusiasm for God's omnipotence or from his contrition in the face of human misery: "Lord, what art thou, what are the children of men. Thou art Jehovah; we are weak sinners." It derives from his rage at the scribes and Pharisees who administer the kingdom of God from their offices.

The older he became, the more striking his break with the bureaucratically managed church proved to be. Beyond that, his rupture with insipid Protestant monotheism likewise proved momentous. This faith was by turns sweetly pious and logic-chopping. In its concern over adoring the one God, it forgot about nature and history (shot through with God's activity though they were). For the sake of an "abstract absolute," his faith had to take into the bargain a world totally devoid of any divine presence.

Hölderlin's answer to this problem was to Hellenize the Christian sphere by expanding it, liberating it, and opening it up. Such Hellenization aimed to contradict dogmatic single-mindedness, and to understand the living multiplicity of the cosmos as the radiation and mirroring of the divine. Thus, Hölderlin's program called for no direct naming of the Christian God, no preaching by means of poetry, but for transforming of the One into pivotal images.

Christian material had to move into the reader's field of vision from the distant margin, from an alienating perspective, not unmediated, but multifariously broken up. In the years of his maturity, from *Hyperion* onward, Hölderlin erased the boundary line between poetic reference and sermonizing proclamation. In 1798 in Frankfurt, having had a religious relapse, he wrote the poem "To My Venerable Grandmother on her Seventy-Second Birthday," where he says:

> Alas, they don't know how the Lofty one walked among the
>   people,
> It has almost been forgotten what the Living One was.
> Few do know him, and often the heavenly image
> Appears to cheer them amid stormy times.
> All-reconciling and silent he went along with the poor
>   mortals,
> This single man, divinely in the spirit.
> None of the living was excluded from his soul,
> And he bore the sufferings of the world on his loving breast.
> Befriended with death, in the name of the others
> He went back from pains and toil in victory to the Father.

A pious poem—and a bad one. It offers accurate glorification and devout description of Jesus' activity with the help of prefabricated set pieces, conventionally strung together: "heavenly image," "poor mortals," "single man," "loving breast."

This is the poetry of edification that instead of transposing the given material into an image, aims at rhythmic doubling, and contents itself with reduplication where metamorphosis is called for. Jesus, deprived of all contradictions, oppositions, and breaks, becomes a seraphic spirit, a cult figure whose portrait points toward Hölderlin's orthodox effort to appease his addressee, rather than toward poetic ambition.

This then is *vers d'occasion*—and a swan song besides. Until he fell silent for good, Hölderlin would no longer speak of Jesus as Christian dogma understands him. Yet he would never stop evoking Christ, though now of course he did so in a thoroughly idiosyncratic, highly unorthodox, indeed occasionally audacious, way. Christ was now the alter ego of Empedocles, the brother of Greek heroes, the demigod, child of the heavenly Father and an earthly mother, who accompanies Dionysus and Heracles as the third and highest member of the trio. Christ is now the torchbearer and the god who appears in storms.

This, then, was the *other* Christ, the counterimage of those pious souls whom Hölderlin made Empedocles condemn in the figure of the unmerciful priest Hermocrates: "I cannot see before me the man who does holy things as if it were a trade, your face is false and cold and dead, as his gods are."

This is the *other*, the *Greek*, Christ: This is the great possibility that Hölderlin puts in place of the little reality that owes its modest existence to the literalist spirit of various modes of Protestant orthodoxy. Such orthodoxy reflects the narrowness of men of God who, as he wrote in a letter to his mother in January 1799,

kill Christ worse than the Jews do, because they turn his word into a dead letter and turn him, the living one, into an empty idol. . . . Everything had to come to pass the way we now find it in general, and especially in religion. When Christ appeared in the world, religion was in almost the same situation it is in now. But just as after the winter spring comes, so, too, after the spiritual death of men new life appeared, and the holy still remains holy, even if men do not heed it. There are probably many people who are more religious in their heart than they are willing and able to say.

If we particularize the concept of "religious" with the word "Christian," then the sentence, "there are probably many people, etc. . . ." would refer to the peculiar nature of the figurative discourse about Jesus that shapes Hölderlin's spiritual poetry around the turn of the century (1798 to 1802). "Figurative discourse" means the transference of biblical events to another level, whether Hellenic, Hesperian, mythical, or contemporary historical. In this way, what is specifically Christian takes on a new and fresh significance instead of losing itself in the realm of the nonbindingly arbitrary, or in vague generalities. Empedocles tells his

trusted disciple Pausanias: "Now go inside, prepare a meal, that
I may taste once more the fruit of the stalk and the power of the
vine, and my departure may be bright with gratitude." At this
point, the description of the last Passover feast takes on a measure
of historicity and real presence that could never be attained
through direct address, however insistent.

Jesus' saying "The Son of Man has nowhere to lay his head"
now becomes a concrete foreshadowing—far removed from all
religious loftiness—of the complaint uttered by Empedocles, who
has been cursed and hounded out of the city. Until his death,
Empedocles, lonely and abandoned by God, "no longer has a
place where he can find his rest." And how contemporary the
Eucharist—a meal of peace in the here and now—appears in
Hölderlin's interpretation: bread and wine as gifts that man en-
joys, remembering and hoping, in dark days. The grain and the
vine, "durable" provisions for the journey, consumed in the community of the meal, are intended to recall the Host and his disciples: ". . . when they sat together, at the mystery of the vine."

The point here is not to save the Grecophile poet for the sake
of the cause of Christ, nor to do a Jesus-oriented interpretation
of the attempt to reconcile East and West in good Hegelian fashion, which would mean Christ celebrating the bread and Dionysus
the wine. Hölderlin had been striving for this reconciliation, time
after time. From his Master's thesis on, parallels appear between
Hesiod's *Works and Days* and the Proverbs of Solomon, and the
image continues up until his last hymns. I don't mean to pass over
in silence Hölderlin's very personal, occasionally somewhat cryptic speculation about the succession of the gods, from Uranos to
Jesus, the "silent genius." Hölderlin's glorification of Christ is
especially evident in the work of his midcareer. Here we have a
poetic idyll that knows nothing of the passion and the cross, but
refers everything to an ahistorical reconciliation of that festive-
minded Somebody with the world. About this Jesus, he writes
that "one is always for all." No doubt, in Hölderlin there is a
strangely pale figure of Christ "the medium," who functions as
no more than a deputy for a generic divine element.

On the other hand, however, Hölderlin gave the Christ he
evoked a crucial dowry of humanity by including the Greek human
factor. This brings the "Redeemer under the skies" into the modest realm of everyday life, into the historicity of the here and

now. It is the Swabian landscape, meadows and vineyards and
the slopes of the Alb, heaped up like tables, that receive the
prince of the feast, Jesus, the bringer of peace, in the "solemnity
of peace":

And many there are I would invite, but you,
O you that benignly, gravely disposed to men
Down there beneath the Syrian palm tree, where
The town lay near, by the well were glad to be;
Round you the cornfield rustled, quietly coolness breathed
From shadows of the hallowed mountainsides,
And your dear friends, the faithful cloud
Cast shade upon you too, so that the holy, the bold,
The beam through wilderness gently should fall on men, O
    youth.
But oh, more darkly, even as you spoke,
And dreadfully determining a deadly doom overshadowed
    you there.
                        So all
That's heavenly fleets on; but not for nothing;

                                (M. H., trans.)

Here the present is not imposed upon the past. Here the day
and hour—specifically, the Peace of Lunéville in 1801, which was
for Hölderlin a guarantee of reconciliation among the nations—
do not triumph over yesterday. Here, too, a supposedly untouch-
able past is not absolutized—no, here the "once" and "before"
also means the "here and now": Jesus, who spoke to the Samaritan woman under a Syrian palm tree, celebrates along with
his disciples (the "cloud of witnesses" from Heb. 12:1) his entrance into the familiar realm. Distance has become nearness;
there has been transferred to the *here*; the gap between once and
now has been overcome thanks to a descriptive, evocative art that
gives actuality and presence to the quotation, which has been
fused into the context. Sichar could be a village in Württemberg.
The consecrated mountain range, the holy mountain of Gerizim
near Sichar, could lie between Stuttgart and Lake Constance. The
field of grain could be in Swabia as well as in Palestine—in all
those places where the words from the fourth chapter of John's
Gospel serve to give meaning to the familiar everyday domain:

"Do you not say, 'There are yet four months, then comes the harvest?' I tell you, lift up your eyes, and see how the fields are already white for harvest."

Hölderlin employs a very cautious mode of referring to Johannine statements and central concepts that opens up only after precise reading. In this way, he manages, in the "Celebration of Peace," to link together events separated by millennia, and to interpret what is happening now under the sign of a model rich in meanings that casts long shadows from the past. But at the one crucial point, he does not forget the distance that puts an end to the reference game. And in place of friendly softhearted encounters between the mildly beaming (i.e., still bearable for men) youthful Christ, the softly shimmering lightning ray of the Father, and those who suddenly meet him (announced by the exclamation *Ach!*), Hölderlin focuses on that distance that is grounded in the crucifixion. It was the crucifixion, the "darker" overshadowing, no longer a human and kindhearted event, but a deadly disaster, which made the youth all but violently, murderously, and abruptly unrecognizable "in the middle of the word."

Jesus, the Johannine Word, is interpreted in the "Celebration of Peace" as the pure, mildly gleaming light that like a lofty figure of a friend has come to accompany men in the darkness. Jesus is that clear light of one who, if he is recognized in his sovereignty, forces men to bend the knee before him. Men are thankful for his presence in the hour of peace and reconciliation, but they are also full of fear as they recollect Jesus' near disappearance after his execution. Hölderlin calls the place of this disappearance the "hill of wrath," the antipodes of friendliness and familiarity.

Golgotha is the continual threat to a celebration of peace. The author describes the environment with a Johannine vocabulary (or encoded variations on such language) of "clarity," "wellspring," "grain field," "word." In this way, the great phantasmagoria, shaped by the spirit of the young man, takes on a vivid quality. This spirit makes reconciliation triumph over war, dissension, hatred, and rebellion in both life and death.

Thus Hölderlin presents an epiphany of peace, a feast at the end of time, a gathering of friends after "a millennial storm," inner communion in a blessed landscape, a banquet hosted by "the serene, mighty" young man called to be the prince of the feast. In him, those invited to the feast—a bold reversal of the

Johannine material—recognize Jesus because they know the Father. ("And now we recognize him, now, since we know the Father," instead of, "No one comes to the Father except through me.") The great hour of reconciliation, rest, liberating conversation, and release from workaday cares is described in the vision of peace in the last strophes, after "the lofty one, the spirit of the world, has bent down to men, in order to hold days of celebration. The tempest, thunder, and lightning are all bygone. The hope for an era of peace, based on Jesus' coming, has come into its own:

> Winds lightly breathing
> Already announce you,
> The vapor that drifts from the valley
> And the ground still resounding with thunder,
> But hope now flushes our cheeks,
> In front of the door of their house
> Sit mother and child,
> And look upon peace,
> And few now seem to be dying;
> The souls of the oldest even
> Held back by a hint, a promise
> Conveyed by the golden light.

(M. H., trans.)

The pacifist Georg Friedrich Nicolai, as I mentioned before, a friend of Albert Einstein, had planned a "German Peace Library" around the time of the First World War. If anything like this ever came into being, then alongside Andreas Gryphius, alongside Herder ("Seven Convictions of the Great Woman of Peace"), and Kant ("On Perpetual Peace"), Hölderlin would have a place of honor. Hölderlin with his radical "theology of peace," with his utopia of redeemed humanity, was a great champion of peace. However eschatologically he may have formulated his vision, it still remains concrete and oriented to the present: Peace is *now*, revolutionary reason and the Christian communion of love have allied themselves *now*. Freedom, which had been stifled "under the ice-cold zone of despotism"—would flourish *now*; egoism "will bend beneath the holy rule of love and kindness" *now*. These *nows* come from letters to Hölderlin's brother, written between

1793 and 1800. There were good reasons, Hölderlin felt, for believing that "our time is near, that the peace which is now developing will bring precisely what only it could bring; for it will bring much that many hope for, but it will also bring what few imagine."

We hear in this an echo from far, far away of the old seminarist's solution of the "kingdom of God." We can see what peace means as concretized in the moving phrase "And few now seem to be dying." Separation is overcome under the sign of a new oneness ("In front of the door of their house / Sit mother and child": singular, not plural). *Pax mundi* enters into its rights, the peace that guarantees life and salvation, the peace shaped by the thought that the words "Christ" and "peace" belong together. They are bound up with one another here more narrowly, there more broadly, always rather metaphorically: "until out of the mysterious cradle of time the child of heaven, eternal peace, comes forth."

The peace in question may be among men, between men and gods, or among the heavenly ones themselves. In Hölderlin "infinite peace," the "peace of all peace, higher than all reason," always appears as "Being, in the only sense of the word."

It is an amiable picture—with a Christian accent, but taken in a broad and comprehensively religious sense. As always with Hölderlin, it is a Greek perspective that determines the intensification of theological formulas, that transforms comprehensive dogmatic definitions into living contemplation. The "peace of God," expanded to world and universal peace, is identical with Hölderlin's key words, "beauty," "joy," and "desire." "But everything is driven by desire, and everything ends in peace," as the conclusion to *Hyperion* puts it: "Like lovers' quarrels are the dissonances of the world. / Reconciliation is amidst the conflict, and everything separated finds itself again . . . united, eternal, glowing life is All."

Once again, here is an amiable vision that, in the face of broader horizons, brings central Christian ideas into the picture. Poetry as the interpreter of religion vivifies anew what was forgotten and transcends what was historically narrowed through visions that once again reveal the original meaning of free access.

The poetic formula of peace as "Being in the only sense of the word" goes far beyond the church dogma of *pax Christi*. The church's notion of peace is connected with ideas of domination that are precisely what Hölderlin wanted, in his comprehensive thinking about peace, to see done away with. In a letter to his brother, he wrote, "I love the generation of the coming centuries. For this is my most blessed hope, the faith that keeps me strong and active, that our grandchildren will be better than we are, that freedom must eventually come. . . . These seeds of enlightenment, these silent wishes and strivings of individuals to educate the human race will spread and become stronger and bear splendid fruit."

This was written in the fall of 1793. Scarcely a decade later, in the outlines, sketches, and drafts of the latest hymns, the retractions and interpolations, the continually new beginnings, reflections and second thoughts about a few verses, at this time of the gleaning from the very last harvest, immediately before he lost his mind, there was no longer any trace of this enthusiastic confidence, of this trust in the coming era of peace, to which the letter to his sister, written in Hauptweil near St. Gall on 23 February 1801, still attests: "I believe that things will now really go right in the world. Whether I look at the time that is near or long past, everything seems to me to be bringing on rare days, the days of beautiful humanity, the days of secure, fearless kindness and thoughts that are as cheerful as they are holy, as elevated as they are simple."

For contrast, look at the verse of the last creative period. We hear nothing more about the amiability of past days; the hope for the return of the gods in the evening of the workday; the entrance of the festive chorus; the harmonious shift of the heavenly ones from distance to closeness. There will be no reconciling, in a lovely landscape, the many and the Only one, the last and most welcome guest. A demon, Hölderlin says in the hymn "The Only One," rules the world. No mild light falls in the wilderness and night: "For since evil spirit / Has taken possession of happy antiquity, unendingly / Long now one power has prevailed, hostile to song, without resonance, / That perishes in masses, the violence of the mind. But God hates / The unbound" (M. H., trans.).

In ever-new variations, Hölderlin conjures up the revolt of the world against the earth. His voice is inexorable, Junoistically sober, and "patriotic." His paratactic, harsh language revolves around individual words and no longer flows in periodic, harmonic cadences. This rebellion of unchained elements against the forces of subjugation, measure, and prudence draws Christ, too, into its vortex: "For he has had one thing that tore him away, a fate. That is."

Taut sentences, abstract terms, and isolated words harshly juxtaposed make it clear that the broken syntax, shattered by the weight of details, points to a world that is out of joint—and amidst all this is a God who does not love but judges and can destroy: "Yet it is fearful how here and there God scatters all things living."

The oft-quoted phrase from "Patmos" that "all is good" (in the sense of "all is God") has, from this perspective, the character of the "Nevertheless" in an unholy time. What a distance between the last hymns and the earlier works from "Hyperion" to the "Celebration of Peace." How somber in the end is the world picture and therefore how dark and shadowy the figure of Jesus, the Man of Sorrows, who owes his death not to his redemptive will and not to his solicitude, but to the wrath of the Father. It is part of the Father's plan that men should murder the "demigod," not heeding his nature: "Self-willed besides, excessive, boundless, that the hand of man attacks What Lives, more too, than is fitting for a demigod."

Christ, as appears in the late hymns, is no longer the friendly genius and the god traveling heavenward in silent resignation, but the defenseless, the "snow white," distorted by pain and the agony of death: "For suffering colors the purity of this man who is as pure as a sword."

Jesus is characterized now as a *beggar*, no longer as the *prince of the feast*. He is a sober-minded man, subject to be branded as a heretic, whose highest—and most humane—feature is his reflectiveness—the only reliable and constant thing amidst the wild whirlwind about him. It is true that in the early and mature work Hölderlin praises the Promethean spirits who, like Empedocles, take leave of the earth in jubilation so as to be reconciled with the universe in death. It is true that unrestraint and roving about are described as activities of the divinely inspired man, driven by holy ecstasy. Despite this, however, the last verses condemn all the forces pressing people into the realm of the excessive and forbidden. Empedocles' "longing for the abyss," the will "to return . . . to the universe [by] the shortest path," acquires the

character of a revolt against the divine order: "For fearfully mis-
formed it goes, when One is too greedily taken from us, / But
doubtless is the Highest."

It is moving to see how Hölderlin, on the verge of exhaustion
and in danger of falling silent, makes a patriotic turnabout and
bids himself be cautious. Then, voluntarily limiting the given possibilities, he sings in praise of the *true* God, who serves as the
adversary of the wrathful God. In the same way, he praises the
moderate-constant One, who forgoes the hymn to the "wild world
of death" and opposes his constancy to the "longing for the unbound: "For the Heavenly ones are angry" (M. H., trans.), he
writes at the end of the last hymn, "Mnemosyne," "when / Someone has failed to collect his soul, to spare it, for still he must."

In the hour of farewell, the poet talks to himself. He makes a
desperate attempt to keep to the ordered-paved world, by putting
a stop to the decomposition of the soul that threatens. And he
does this while invoking ever more decisively the "demigod,"
who, at the very end, once again becomes more concrete. It is
Jesus in the figure of the servant, denying his origins—bowed
before God and still reminding us, but only from a distance, of
the youth who stood before the chorus of guests.

Hölderlin's Christ, as the late hymns and fragments describe
him—is in a double sense the "last." He is not only, as in "Bread
and Wine" or the "Celebration of Peace," the one who completes
the round dance of Greek gods, sealing their farewell. But he is
also the most modest and humble, who meets on a higher level
with the two other demigods that Hölderlin lets him keep:

> . . . But those three are
> This, they are under the sun
> Like hunters of the hunt or
> A farmer, who breathing from the work
> Bares his head, or beggars.

The three demigods, sons of the same father in Hölderlin's
imagination, are at the same time three modest, indeed humble,
men. Along with the two "worldly" figures, Heracles, the hunter,
and Dionysus, now turned earthward and forced to drudge like
a farmer, they belong together by comparison with the "spiritual"
figure of Christ. While they strive and slave and commit themselves to the world, Christ is the "totally other," removed from

the toilsome souls. He is the image of a humble man who is content, and for that very reason the companion of all those (with Hölderlin in the lead) who are directed to be prudent and to stay away from the danger of losing themselves in ecstasy and bold straying beyond the limits.

In the end, the gods of Hölderlin are small, and close to one another as heralds of the Father who made him, the distant one, accessible to man. They are his "stairs" and see to it that the heavenly element can enter and exit the everyday world.

Hölderlin's pantheon of three little demigods and a distant, raging father has become meager in the late work. It nonetheless wins our confidence. It is a little world in which One, the poorest of all, ultimately stands in the foreground; he is the most beloved and loving and, as such, incomparable.

"I still seek one, whom I love among you." This is an act of faith in the one who, despite all the features shared with the other gods, differs from them on one point. In his helplessness and powerlessness, he awakens love—not through his peculiar gifts, but through *Dasein* ("being there") in the sense of reliably attesting to existence. *I am here. I stand fast. I am silent and help the powerless amid the desolate chatter of the world.* Jesus, the suffering lover, must pay with his death for the light that he has brought. This vision of the reliable companion in a world of unrest and deadly temptations gives Hölderlin's late interpretation of Christ the character of a confession. It is a confession encoded in the laconic, enigmatic language of the late work, a confession whose significance for the theology of our time, the post-Auschwitz understanding of Jesus, is too obvious to need stressing.

> To One alone, whoever,
> Love clings. Anyway is
> Always violent and tries
> To die a wilderness full
> Of faces so that to remain in innocent
> Truth is a pain.

The late Hölderlin does not *sing* the divine world in drunken festivity. He soberly *names* and *interprets* signs, and expounds *principles* (such as the clash between world and earth, between mad ecstasy and the kindness that, having taken shape in Jesus, reduces rage to silence).

Here is one man, one last time, at work, a man reduced to limitation, who clings to the word more than ever. He clings to authentic reports and history, to the letter and the mediate proclaiming of God through the holy Scriptures. The reader never learns so much about Jesus' historicity, about Caphernaum, the slaughter of the innocents, the murder of John the Baptist, about the thoughts of the disciples and the Western tradition that began with Jesus as in Hölderlin's last verses:

> More marvelous.
> More rich to sing. Immeasurable
> The fable ever since. And now
> I wish to sing the journey of the nobles to
> Jerusalem, and anguish wandering at Canossa,
> And Heinrich himself.
>
> (M. H., trans.)

". . . and Heinrich himself": The verses from the "Patmos" hymns are occasionally stamped with the charm of the concrete and an insistent realism unexampled in Hölderlin's poetry. Biblical sources are carried over into the objective, indeed the psychologically plausible, realm: "John lay close to the breast of Jesus," says John 13:25 concerning the beloved disciple. Hölderlin turns this into "But the attentive man saw the face of God" (M. H., trans.).

This is a transposition not into the expansive, but thanks to the use of poetic narrowing, into the genrelike to gain more plausibility. John is the closest one to Jesus because he sees the Lord most exactly. Immediately before succumbing to schizophrenia, Hölderlin (*pace* Pierre Bertaux, from whom I have learned a great deal) was obsessed with details and recognized the whole in the fragmentary. He became enslaved to a realism that blithely ignored the boundaries between the high and low style, the elevated and the biotic, Grünewald's pathos and Dürer's precision. It is no accident that he writes of Jesus that he quenched the sighing of the light as with holy drops. That sighing was like a "thirsty animal" or the "cry of a chicken."

On the one hand, Hölderlin aimed at sanctifying the most in-

significant things and, on the other hand, at a more sober description of legendary events. For orthodox poetics, these were
accessible only to the highest degree of pathos. Hölderlin would
not acknowledge the law of the separation of styles that demands
for every object, according to its valence, an appropriate mode
of representation. Nor would he accept the division of poetry into
secular and spiritual. The secular needed to be spiritualized; the
spiritual needed to be realized in the this-worldly. And he had
to strive for a synthesis, under whose aegis there was nothing that
did not have some meaning.

Hölderlin realized *this* synthesis without a doubt in his late
verses. But his *other* goal was never reached. This was the forging
of an alliance between foreign and national, Greek and Christian,
elements that he tried to imagine once more at the very end,
before he fell silent. This was the synthesis between Cypros,
Aphrodite's island, rich in springs, and the poor, but hospitable
Patmos, John's residence. This *other* synthesis failed: The gap
was too great between the Only One ("My Lord and Master! O
you, my Teacher!") and the many, between Christ, "jewel of the
house," and the chorus of Greek gods; the poet, now become a
realist, could no longer fit these extremes together.

Hölderlin began to take seriously the historical Jesus, inglorious
in his powerlessness and shameful death, trusting the strict word
more then the ambiguous images. At that moment, the art of the
"delightful comparison" was finished. Then the One acquired a
measure of actuality that enabled him to be assimilated by the
evoking ego as a beggar, a porter, a captive eagle (German "Aar,"
the symbol of Christ and John the Evangelist). Meanwhile, the
other gods in this process served more and more as a backdrop.
They illuminated Christ but they were no longer, as previously
with Hölderlin, illuminated in turn by him.

Friedrich Hölderlin was on the way—certainly not to the Christian religion, but to the religion of Christ. By Christ, he meant
the man of sorrows, whom the poet struck by Apollo recognized
in the figure of the brotherly beggar. This may be true, but it
should not be forgotten that the most important statements about
Jesus—"for Christ still lives"—are in the hymn "Patmos."
(Bound up with that is a statement about the Father, "For known
/ To him are all his works from the beginning." M. H., trans.)
"Patmos" is a commissioned work, which Hölderlin took over

from Klopstock and in which he had to pose as someone who was, if possible, more pious, and indeed more pietistic, than he really was. "Patmos," a hymn in the manner of John, the evangelist most prized by Luther for the power of his language, is a model of the art of making old religious formulas nearly invisible for the secular reader through encoding. At the same time, they are recognizable to connoisseurs in the Spirit, men like the Landgrave of Homburg, as encoded dogmas. John has the first word, and Swabia's pious masters, here Brenz, there Bengel, and above all the German-minded Landgrave, must have been satisfied with the incorporation of the Bible and Western history into the realm of patriotism.

Thus the question of Hölderlin as the man who ends up in the house of master carpenter Ernst Zimmer remains open: Was he involved in a continuous Christianization of Hellenic myths? Or did he go back to the antinational—a return to the old gods, to the hunter and farmer, to Jupiter, the "lord of time," and to Saturn, the "spirit of nature?" In any case, what developed in Tübingen over these few years has the nature of a bridge, according to the most ingenious interpreter of Hölderlin, the Romanist and poet Eugen Gottlob Winkler (driven to his death by the Nazis) in his essay on the "late Hölderlin." He describes the period as "this short span of evolution . . . which holds prisoner the builder and all those who use it between this side and beyond. . . . The pagan who steps onto the bridge now understands faith; not completely of course, he only sees the land of faith before him. And the Christian who finds himself on it may well look upon antiquity, but he can never reach it. . . . One and the same god . . . passes over the bridge in disguises of countless shades, most carefully examined; still he does not settle down on it and does not make his nature known."

Or does he? He does at least by hints, in that precise riddling language of poetry, which, by describing what Jesus *could be*, goes far beyond all the scholarly work that tries to present what he *has been* for his own time and for us.

NOVALIS

◇

CHRISTENDOM OR EUROPE

HANS KÜNG

◇

Religion
in the
Mirror of Romantic Poetry

"Hölderlin writes me sometimes from Jena," Hegel announced to his friend Schelling at the end of January 1795. "He listens to Fichte, and speaks enthusiastically of him as a titan fighting for humanity, and a man whose sphere of influence will certainly not remain within the walls of the auditorium" (Lasson-Hoffmeister edition, XXVII, 18). Johann Gottlieb Fichte was eight years older than Hegel and Hölderlin. Like them, he was originally a candidate in theology, then a private tutor, but shortly after they both left Tübingen, he became a professor in Jena at the young age of thirty-two. He thought about God along the lines of the supposedly last, secret, Spinozist ideas of Lessing and the youth Goethe: God as the one-and-all. But then Kant's practical philosophy freed him from this kind of identification and let him see, by stressing morality and duty, the value of the free, responsible, moral personality, of the ego.

May 1795: Fichte and Hölderlin met in Jena, and along with them was a thoroughly congenial person, only two years younger than Hölderlin, of fascinating mind and appearance. His name was Friedrich von Hardenberg; at the time he was an actuary in the county office in nearby Tennstedt. In the future, he would call himself "Novalis," meaning "the one who cultivates new land," after the old Latin byname "de Novali." Novalis would soon become the most important poet of early romanticism in northern Germany. The host of this meeting, a Privatdozent for philosophy named Immanuel Niethammer, a friend of Hölderlin's from Tübingen, notes in his diary about this evening that there was "much talk about religion and revelation, and many questions still remain open here for philosophy" (quoted in Hiebel, 126).

They were a great generation, these young men born around 1770; they included not only Hardenberg, Hölderlin, and Hegel, not only the other early romantics Friedrich Schlegel and Ludwig Tieck, but—along with Beethoven—those two individuals who would shape the history of Europe in the following decades after the French Revolution: Napoleon and Metternich. We can see clearly what a powerful intellectual field of force the young Hardenberg was born into when we reflect that on the narrow ground of Jena and Weimar there sprang up not only the early romantics, but the enlightened Privy Councillor Wieland (who published Hardenberg's first poem), General Superintendent Herder, Associate Professor of History Friedrich Schiller, whose house Hardenberg frequented, and of course the minister and chancellor of the university, Goethe, at whose house Hardenberg dined and who had brought Fichte from Zurich to Jena.

The philosopher Fichte, whom Hölderlin had not idly called a titan, with his advocacy of a lofty way of life, of patriotism, and the rights of man, was nothing less than a challenge. Soft and receptive, closely tied to nature, Hölderlin saw himself at first powerfully drawn and at the same time almost overwhelmed by Fichte. "Philosophy is a tyrant," he wrote a year later (February 1796), "and I endure her compulsion more than I voluntarily subject myself to it" (*Collected Works*, Stuttgart Edition, VI, I, 203).

And what of Hardenberg, whose father, having turned a strict Pietist, had provided financial support for Fichte as a student? Hardenberg was tireless in his "Fichticizing," and saw in philosophy not a tyrant but a beloved mistress. His systematic *study of Fichte*—documented by around seven hundred intelligent entries—took place at exactly the same time as he had his first truly great experience of love. The twenty-two-year-old found in the twelve-year-old Sophie von Kühn his absolute feminine ideal. He was unaware that his "Diotima," to whom he had secretly gotten engaged shortly before he met Fichte and Hölderlin, was destined to be overcome by a deadly disease half a year later. Full of the happiness of love and knowledge, he wrote on 8 July 1796 to Friedrich Schlegel: "My favorite study has basically the same name as my bride: Sophie. Philosophy ["Philosophie" in German] is the soul of my life and the key to my own self. Since making her acquaintance, I have become completely fused with her" (*Schlegel-Novalis Correspondence*, M. Prietz, ed., p. 59).

Like Hölderlin, Hardenberg, too, came from a Pietist home, presided over by a strict father and an empathetic mother, whom the young man ardently loved. Like Hölderlin, he, too, had a great interest in philosophy, poetry, and politics, but in natural science as well. Like Hölderlin, he read Rousseau and was an enthusiast for changing the world through the French Revolution. Patriotically minded in the spirit of Klopstock and the Göttingen Hainbund, Novalis also wrote odes to the enlightened prince (Joseph II) and paid homage to the cult of friendship, which in the eighteenth century was often given a higher place than love between the sexes. For a long time his great model was also Friedrich Schiller, whose supposedly atheistic "Gods of Greece" he defended against "pious types and other enthusiasts" (*Writings*, P. Kluckhohn, ed., II, 90).

So we should avoid drawing up an a priori opposition—as has often been done—between Friedrich Hölderlin and Friedrich von Hardenberg. To be sure, Hardenberg actually studied what Hölderlin would have liked to study—jurisprudence. And instead of taking his final exams in theology he took them in law. Instead of becoming a vicar or private tutor ("Hofmeister"), he became an actuary and then in the same year an almost pedantically dutiful Saxon official in the saltworks near his family's adopted home, Weissenfels. Hardenberg's only original portrait—full of alert intelligence, purposefulness, and strength of will—was unintentionally falsified a few decades later by the widely publicized engraving by Eduard Eichen, which transformed him into a girlishly dreamy "romantic." His extraordinarily vital, brisk, imaginative, and inwardly restless mind was continually struggling to attain steadiness, constancy, and responsibility though strict self-observation and training. And it was precisely through the "titan," Fichte, that he found autonomy. From Fichte, Hölderlin learned the dialectical thinking that moved through contradictions to unity ("thesis," "antithesis," "synthesis" were originally

Fichte's terms; Hegel scarcely ever used them). But the dialectic now led Hardenberg's philosophy to the comprehension of the Absolute: "Spinoza mounted to nature—Fichte to the ego, or the person, and the Ego to the thesis of God," he writes self-consciously in his notes (*Works*, G. Schulz, ed., p. 300). God himself is understood as the great Ego in Hardenberg's poetically framed ego philosophy. In this Ego, every individual ego has its basis for life, and the whole universe has its intellectual-moral foundation and center: That center is God understood entirely along the lines of modernity as God *in* the world, God present in our self, our conscience.

A controversy about atheism broke out over Fichte's philosophy that was no less irritating than the pantheism controversy in connection with Lessing. In the last phase of this dispute, even Fichte's passionate 1799 "Appeal to the Public" ("A writing you are asked to read before confiscating,") could not prevent his resigning his post in Jena. Novalis unequivocally took Fichte's part. He wrote to a friend with reference to the "Appeal": "It is an excellent little piece and familiarizes you with the extremely peculiar *thinking* and *plans* of our *governments* and clerics, with a scheme for the suppression of public opinion that is in part already in the process of being carried out. Hence it calls for the attention of every rational person, to follow these steps and to draw an important conclusion from these premises" (*Writings*, IV, 270). In his "General Sketch," Novalis even says that the founding of an "intellectual knightly order"—which he thought of in thoroughly realistic terms, along the lines of the humanitarian societies of the Enlightenment—would be a "chief occupation" of his life. Isn't someone who talks that way defending the rights of reason? Could it be that in the bottom of his heart Novalis was an *Enlightenment thinker* after all?

From what we have seen, it is already clear how false it would be to look at "the" *Enlightenment* (Lessing) and "the" romantic *movement* as mutually exclusive. That is the direction taken by scholars inclined to equate romanticism with the political restoration of the Metternich era after 1815 (one sign of political restoration was Friedrich Schlegel's entrance into the diplomatic service of Hamburg in 1808–1809). First, the intellectuals of

"Young Germany" (especially Heine), then the liberal literary scholars (Gervinus, for example), and finally even the Marxists (above all Lukács) marshalled the Enlightenment against romanticism, which meant political reaction, as far as they were concerned. By contrast, both the "neo-romantics" around the turn of this century, as well as the students of romantic literature between the two world wars (such as Novalis specialists Rudolf Unger and Paul Kluckhohn) saw in romanticism a pure protest movement against the enlightened eighteenth century.

Yet the Enlightenment and romanticism are no more total contraries than Descartes and Pascal. As has become increasingly clear in research since the 1960s, particularly with respect to Novalis (cf. W. Malsch, H. Schanze, C. Träger, P. Pütz, W. Rasch, K. Peter), the two movements have to be seen *in a refined polarity*. Romanticism develops—as the biographies of Hölderlin and Hegel, Fichte, F. Schlegel, and Novalis show—out of the Enlightenment. Romantic flight from reality is a cheap cliché. The Enlightenment and early romanticism are fully in agreement in their pragmatic opposition to the absolutist rule of princes and clerics, in rejecting prejudices, superstitions, hypocrisy, repression, and burning at the stake. In short, both affirm the liberation of man into selfhood.

In other words, romanticism originally had only an indirect connection with irrationality. It was concerned with mediating between reason and the irrational, which means the domains not yet accessible to consciousness in the human soul, nature, and history. The romantic movement first wished to be understood as a critical continuation and intensification of the Enlightenment. It was—before it turned to reaction and restoration—a further phase of the movement for autonomy *within the paradigm of modernity*.

In November 1799, at an early "meeting of romantics" (the Schlegel brothers and their wives Caroline and Dorothea, Tieck, Schelling, and Ritter), Novalis read a piece, *Christendom or Europe*, that immediately led to considerable controversy among the friends. It provoked Schelling into writing an "irreligious" satirical poem, and when Goethe was called upon to arbitrate, he advised against publishing it. It never appeared in Novalis' lifetime, and was not printed in the first editions of his work. Not until a quarter century after his death was it published by Schlegel, without the knowledge of Tieck, who again excluded it from the following editions. Finally, from the late 1860s on, it was regularly printed and counted among the master's central works. Today, *Christendom or Europe* is considered a first-class religious-political-poetic document of romanticism. How did Novalis come in so short a time to produce this stirring piece?

Novalis' poetic work came into being in only three years between the death of his bride at Easter of 1797 and the outbreak of his own fatal case of tuberculosis in the summer of 1800, although this poetry was, of course, grounded in a long process of development and maturation. Confronted with Sophie's death (and shortly thereafter that of his brother Erasmus), everything at first seemed to Novalis "dead, desolate, deaf, unmoving" (IV, 179): "It is evening around me, while I was still looking into the dawn. My grief is boundless, like my love" (IV, 183). Still, in his loneliness and abandonment, his will to live imposed itself, ultimately, against his every death wish and intention of dying. It was not a will to live exactly, but what he himself called his "vocation to the invisible world": "this lovely approach to God and to the loftiest quality of the human race" (IV, 190). Not until several weeks later did he dare to visit Sophie's grave, but there in "lightninglike moments of enthusiasm" (I, 385) he experienced something like a vision of his bride.

As Diotima did for Hölderlin, the figure of Sophie became the great ideal force of his life for Novalis' poetic activity. Indeed, she became the Christlike mediatrix between this visible world and the invisible one. His new engagement some time later (to Julie von Charpentier) does not contradict this. Like no poet before him, Novalis clung to death, night, and love, with all their countless variations, as *the* theme of his work. Through the connection with Sophie, for whom he now felt not only "love" but "religion," the existence of an invisible realm of harmony and love became a certainty. He, the jurist, now devoted intensive study to "the sciences," to philosophy and natural science (special studies at the mining college of Freiberg). But he approached everything as dialectically as possible and often combined it all in arbitrary-contradictory fashion from the perspective of "higher goals" or "from a higher standpoint," so as to gain from that vantage "views of the invisible world" (IV, 192).

"Higher standpoint," "invisible world": The break with "Fichte's magic" ("he entranced and trapped one in his circle"), from his "fearful whirl of abstractions" (IV, 208), was now more than clear. Under the influence of Friedrich Schlegel, who faulted the absence of the aesthetic, the poetic, the social, and of love in the rigid system of Fichte's "theory of knowledge," Novalis now studied with special intensity the long familiar writings of the Dutch philosopher and theoretician of art Frans Hemsterhuis (d. 1790). Hemsterhuis managed to awaken what Novalis must have missed in Fichte and Kant—the analogy between physical-corporeal basic forces and the unity of the universe, which man can experience only in a knowing-feeling "moral organ" (heart, conscience), located within him, of course. The basic force of this organ is love and its expression is poetry (poetic truth). When the moral organ finds its development, then the golden age awaited by so many will arrive.

"Pollen" (1798) was the first publication of Hardenberg (now labeled with the pseudonym "Novalis") after the poem that came out in 1791. Many of his ideas, inspirations, and themes found expression in the "mixed remarks" that "Pollen" provides as the stimulus for active further thinking, for a common "symphilosophy," a "total philosophizing." Together with the other, more politically oriented thoughts on the ideal state as a poetic state, collected under the title "Belief and Love" (1798), this was the first example of the now popular "romantic fragment" with a clear and *specifically romantic inward turning*: "We dream of trips through the universe: yet isn't the universe *within us*? We do not know the depths of our mind, the mysterious way goes inward. In us or nowhere is eternity with its worlds—the past and future" (*Works*, 326).

———————◆———————

So was Novalis a "romantic dreamer" after all? Was he some-one who brooded and indulged in political illusions about his poetic state, about the king and queen (of Prussia!) as represen-tatives of a monarchical republic or republican monarchy, about the poet as priest, and who now announced his reveries on "Chris-

tendom or Europe" to the public, even though a small one? It
sounds almost like a dream when we hear the first seemingly
smooth, virtuosically simple, extremely melodic sentences from
Europe (that was Novalis' own name for his piece): "They were
beautiful, brilliant times when Europe was a Christian country,
where *one* Christendom inhabited this humanly shaped part of
the world; *one* great common interest bound together the most
distant provinces of this broad spiritual kingdom" (*Works*, p.
326).

The one Christendom—here something unheard of has evidently occurred. We can see this particularly when we compare
Novalis with Hölderlin, who in the end wanted to reconcile antiquity and Christianity by seeking (in vain) to crown his world
of the Greek gods with Christ the returning god. Novalis took a
different tack: He remained unconsciously rooted in the Christian-
Moravian Brethren world, shaped in modern ways by idealistic
philosophy and exact science. But religiously awakened by the
death of his beloved, he now recognized afresh the *opposition
between antiquity and Christianity*, and considered the Greek
world of the gods definitively overcome by Christ. "They have
to see him, because if they read thirty books by him, they will
not understand them as well as they would if they drank tea with
him once," Dorothea Veith, Friedrich Schlegel's companion
wrote to Schleiermacher about Novalis. "Enfin, I have not yet
fallen for him. But he looks like a ghost-seer, and has his own
quite peculiar essence for himself alone, that can't be denied.
Christianity here is à l'ordre du jour . . ." (quoted in G. Schulz,
p. 124). So is Novalis a kind of "Imperator" or "Napoleon" of
romantic intelligence, as the disturbed Goethe mockingly suggests? Novalis himself undoubtedly thought of himself as—to
quote a remark he made to Schlegel—"one of the first-born of
the new age—the *religious* age. With this religion a new world
history begins . . ." (*Letters*, p. 164).

This was an astonishing turn of events: It was a great day for
the high classicism—completely oriented toward Greek antiquity—of Schiller and Goethe, who place themselves at a great
distance from Christianity and look upon it as an antiquated premodern affair. But at the same time, "Christianity is à l'ordre du
jour." Now with Novalis, a surprisingly new, living *synthesis* of
renovated Christianity and extreme modernity has found its literary

expression in *Christendom or Europe*. Quite in keeping with the brothers Schlegel was the watchword that at once completed and shattered classicism: no longer the classical "Back to antiquity," but the romantic "Forward to extremely modern poetry!" This presupposes, of course, a new reflection on the past.

Didn't Schelling miss Novalis' basic intention with his satirical poem, the "Epicurean Confession of Faith"? Whatever one may object to in his *Europe*, Novalis had no notion of pleading for the restoration of the medieval papal church or even of converting to Roman Catholicism, as Goethe himself gossiped, in his irritation at the posthumous Novalis cult. (Tieck had formally to deny this in 1837.) Novalis assumed that—ten years after the outbreak of the French Revolution—"the old papacy will be lying in the grave." For this is dramatic contemporary background of *Europe*: The same Pius VI, who had begun his rule in 1775 with a shameful new edict against the Jews, and who after the Declaration of the Rights of Man in France solemnly condemned all human rights, freedom of religion, freedom of thought, speech, and the press, as "monstrosities," this same pope in November 1798 had to accept his own deposition and removal to France. In August 1799, he died as a prisoner in Valence, an occasion that the French government took to forbid the election of a successor. At the beginning of October, Novalis began, under the impact of Schleiermacher's *Speeches on Religion*, which had just appeared, to write his *Europe*. Then Napoleon returned from Egypt to France to overthrow the Directory in Paris on November 9 (two days later the meeting of the romantics in Jena began) and to take over sole power in the state as the first consul. Napoleon was thus at once the bold completer and realistic-pragmatic conqueror of the revolution.

And so the early romantics, who gathered under such circumstances, were not a pack of nostalgic dreamers. From their standpoint, they were the literary avant garde of modernity. Novalis, too. For all his retrospectiveness, in the final analysis he was forward-looking in *Europe*, which aims to be not a study of historical sources, not a lyrical poem, nor a philosophical essay, but *a speech as highly reflective as it is highly poetic* (W. Malsch calls it a "poetic discourse"). In it, he speaks to his contemporaries about the relevance of religion, of Christianity, for Europe. It has rightly been called "the most compressed self-presentation of the early romantic intellectual legacy . . . everything condensed in the narrowest space, a highly reflective mixed form combining poetry and truth, the metaphysics of history and historiography, rhetorical-edifying mythopoesis in the style of a fairy tale and magical conjuring up of a pan-European order of peace" (H. Timm, p. 114).

Along with Schleiermacher's *Speeches* about the invisible church, Lessing's *Education of the Human Race* also stood as godparent to Novalis' work. Thus, it is a retrospective altogether in the service of a prospective. The past is evoked only with an eye to a better future, to the gospel of a third age. But this is done neither, as with Lessing, by means of crisp philosophical-theological theses, nor, as with the romantic historians, by means of precise tracing of historical processes. Instead, with the help of great poetic *images*, the earlier ages or, as we would say, the various paradigms of Christianity, are brought vividly before our eyes.

With this perspective, Novalis certainly undertakes surprising and sometimes downright daredevilish accentuations and trans-valuations that proved decisive for romanticism. This takes place silently through the fact that he completely ignores the old church, the Hellenistic *ecumene*, which has been preserved, for example, in the Byzantine-Russian Christian world (we shall hear more about this from Dostoyevsky). Without even mentioning the East-West schism, Novalis directly champions the fully developed Western Roman Catholic church of the Middle Ages, which he idealizes at least as much as the Swabian Friedrich Hölderlin does ancient Greece.

A *first image*: "How cheerfully one left the fair gatherings in the mysterious churches, which were adorned with stimulating pictures, filled with sweet scents, and enlivened with holy, uplifting music" (*Works*, 500). What are we to make of this suggestive poetic evocation of the "beautiful, brilliant times when Europe was a Christian country," with a single supreme head, with Rome as the new Jerusalem, a flourishing spiritual life, a zealous clergy, and contented people united in kindness and concord, with relics and pilgrimages, miracles and signs, venerating the saints and trusting in the Virgin with the heavenly child? Anyone reading all this for the first time will find such naiveté—even considering the other options available at the time—altogether grotesque. Can we take seriously so much idealization and mystification, glorification and distortion? Quite needlessly, Novalis shifts the Galileo case to the Middle Ages, and praises the papal measures against the "untimely, dangerous discoveries in the realm of knowledge" at the expense of "infinite faith."

But this piece has to be read carefully before we dismiss it. Is it really so naive, curious, and starry-eyed? We might reflect that this image of "genuinely Catholic or genuinely Christian times" still functions today. Or it is functioning again—for some people— as an ecclesiastical-political guiding image? Don't we find in this piece an archetypal expression of the current ideal notion of the "Christian West," which, needless to say, provided support chiefly for those who were pursuing their own interests with Novalis' vision? Nowadays isn't the cliché-ridden image of the "Christian West" invoked by all sorts of self-styled "Westerners," including church circles in Catholic countries like Poland that have gone through neither a Reformation nor an Enlightenment? Indeed, isn't the Roman church today being led once more by men from Poland, Bavaria, Italy, and Spain, who, despite their clever strategies of adaptation to modern times, are oriented to that medieval, then Counter-Reformation, antimodern model of Christianity? That is why they like to pass over John XXIII in silence and complain not about him but about the "wrongheaded spirit" of Vatican II. In other words, these are the people who ignore and discredit the authorities who finally managed to carry out the paradigm changes of the Reformation and modernity. (Their achievements range from high estimation for the Bible and use of the vernacular in the liturgy all the way to human rights and a new relationship with the non-Christian religions.)

So Novalis is anything but naive and behind the times. These same reactionary Catholic circles would naturally join Novalis in bemoaning the fact that in the late Middle Ages "faith and love" were replaced by "knowing and having" (autonomous science and individual possession). They would regret that self-interest, greed, the laziness of the clergy, covetousness, and the earthly-mindedness of people in general prepared the end for the "first love" of the High Middle Ages. Indeed, according to Novalis, in the sixteenth century the only thing left over from the church was a "ruin" and a "corpse" of the early Christian national system, so that the "actual rule of Rome . . . silently came to an end . . . long before the violent insurrection" (503).

In any case, our Catholic conservative champions of the West would not be willing to go *that* far with Novalis. The infallible papacy, in the final analysis, never ceased to live and rule. And they would certainly not agree with Novalis when, in an unexpected dialectical twist, he begins praising the "firebrand" Martin Luther and "public insurrection against the despotic letter of the earlier system." That is our *second image.* The Protestants, he said, rightly issued a "solemn [protest] against every arrogant seizure of an irksome and wrongful-seeming power." They also proposed, he says, "a host of correct principles, introduced a host of praiseworthy things, and did away with a host of harmful statutes" (503).

Isn't anyone who speaks in this way at once for Rome *and* Luther fence-sitting? Or is he standing in sovereign ecumenical majesty over all religious parties? In any event, Novalis criticized sclerotic orthodox Protestantism even more sharply than he did decadent medieval Catholicism. And with a one-sidedness that can scarcely be justified, historically speaking, he even laid the blame for the split of Europe on Protestantism. But his criticism strikes a nerve (and Lessing and Hölderlin would have agreed with him) when he makes the orthodox Protestant system responsible for the provincialization and desiccation of the Christian world: first, for delivering the church into the hands of the princes and thereby losing "cosmopolitan interest" by making religious peace in accordance with principles hostile to religion; second, for delivering religion into the hands of the paltry dead biblical letter and hence to philology by doctrinaire miseducation in a "religion of antiquarians."

"With the Reformation, Christendom was finished. From now on no such thing existed," Novalis observes in lapidary fashion. In so saying, he takes a stand against Catholics *and* Protestants, both of whom he promptly accuses of "standing further apart in sectarian isolation from one another than from Mohammedans and heathens" (p. 505). That is why powerful princes and national states in Europe had tried to set up their hegemony and "to take possession . . . of the vacant universal see" (p. 505). Novalis had in his head, as we have seen, a plan for an intellectual knightly order, a peacemaking Lodge. And he praised the Jesuits, who were fighting against the downfall of Christianity, even though the order was politically compromised and had been suppressed by the pope in 1770 under pressure from enlightened regimes. He praised the Company of Jesus despite its Counter-Reformation front-line position, as an "exemplary mother of the so-called secret societies" (p. 506). At the time this statement met with a very hostile reception, which was understandable: It was roughly the equivalent nowadays of extolling as a model, not the Jesuits (who aren't a secret society, anyway), but that true secret society, so close to the heart of the Supreme Pontiff, "Opus Dei."

But in the dialectical course of history, the advanced European countries (apart from subcultures) have long since seen the Reformation and Counter-Reformation give way to a new paradigm, *modernity*—and here is our *third image*. Since the end of the wars of religion and the arrival of Europe's new political order, new forces have made a breakthrough: "The sound heads of all nations secretly came of age" (p. 507). This coming of age was an emancipation from churchly Christianity, the Enlightenment as a necessary second Reformation: "The scholar is instinctively hostile to the old-fashioned clergy" (p. 507).

Novalis now considers the Enlightenment with biting irony and radical criticism. And yet he also doesn't want to go back. He was a mining expert, with an outstanding education in law, philosophy, and science. He was living in the age that discovered the steam engine, the steamship, the lightning rod, new mining methods, the first paper money in Germany, Cook's second circumnavigation of the world, and the Kant-Laplace world system; and he explicitly praised scientific, technological, and political progress. It was the "radicalness of his position, his morality" (abolition of social classes) "that prevented Novalis from becoming politically active" (K. Peter, p. 138).

But what then is his decisive criticism of the evolution of modernity? Novalis objects to the fact that it has become a "history of modern unbelief." This was "the key to all the monstrous phenomena of modern times" (p. 509). "The result of the modern way of thinking" is that knowledge and faith are fully separated, and the earlier spiritual garden of Europe has been made desolate and turned into a wilderness of the understanding. Through internal consistency, the falling away from the church was followed by the falling away from Christ, and then by the falling away from God. Thus the path leads from hatred of the church to hatred of the Bible to hatred of religion pure and simple. Indeed, contempt for religion brought with it contempt for the imagination, feeling, the love of art, morality, earlier times, and the future. Man? A merely natural creature. The cosmos? A gigantic mill without a miller, clacking emptily away. God? The idle spectator of a melodramatic show put on by the learned. Priests and monks? Relieved of their post by this new guild of Enlightenment thinkers and lovers of mankind. And finally we have a revolution that leads to the Reign of Terror, and revolutionary wars that conjure up chaos pure and simple. Novalis' sharp-eyed, pointed analysis was adopted as part of the arsenal of Roman Catholic apologetics, and advanced as a devolutionary theory against the modern Protestant celebration of progress. But does that make Novalis' ideas false, entirely false? No, nor are they in any sense culturally pessimistic.

For the anarchistic-chaotic situation of the present shows that after a nadir of irreligiosity, "the time of resurrection has come" (p. 510). From Germany, we can already point with certainty to what will come in the other European countries only with peace: "the traces of a new world: 'a new, higher religious life [begins] . . . to pulsate' " (pp. 511–12).

And so now Novalis presents us, *fourthly*, with an overwhelming *final image*: the utopia of a reconciled, peaceful humanity that recalls the concluding scene of Lessing's *Nathan*. This image makes it clear that the political reactionaries and antiecumenical, Roman agents of restoration do not have Novalis on their side. Who does he think is the exemplary poet for a "new history, a new human race"? Dante, perhaps, or Calderón? No, it's Goethe, because Goethe was also a great physicist. And who does he think is the theological pioneer amid this powerful ferment of science, literature, and art in transition toward "a higher epoch of culture" in Europe? Thomas Aquinas? Martin Luther? No, he opts for the theologian who succeeded in talking about religion in a timely manner to "its cultured despisers" and who would be *the* theologian of modernity: Friedrich Schleiermacher.

Like Schleiermacher, Novalis was convinced that without the gravitational attraction of heaven all the efforts of those political leaders or revolutionaries to counter the forces pulling downward were a Sisyphean task, peace was only an armed truce. *Without religion, no united Europe*, which the other parts of the world were waiting so eagerly for. *Without Christianity, no peace in the world.* The poet's words now become prophetic and visionary:

> Blood will flow across Europe until the nations become aware of their terrible madness, which drives them around in circles, until, moved by sacred music and rendered meek they approach their former altars, mingling colorfully together, until they undertake works of peace, and a great banquet of love is celebrated on the smoking battlefields as a feast of peace, with hot tears. Only religion can reawaken Europe and bring the peoples security, can make Christendom visible on earth, installing it in its old office of peace-making. (p. 516).

Is all this only the religion of art? That is the appeal Novalis issues, and in making it he calls for a European council. Modernity's "sleep of religion" must cease; the "rule of ghosts" ("where there are no gods, ghosts rule," p. 513) must end. As Enlightenment thinkers like Lessing demand the reconciliation of religions, Novalis the romantic demands the reconciliation of denominations and ideologies—including the Freemasons. Is it sheer syncretism when Novalis calls for the reconciliation of Catholic universalism, which stands for the old values, and Protestantism's "permanent revolutionary regime," which has become pointless in the face of the prostrate condition of the papacy? Or when he calls for the reconciliation of tradition-minded conservatives and freedom-minded democratic progressives, of believing Christians and enlightened "philanthropists"? "No one will protest anymore against Christian and secular compulsion, for the essence of the church will be genuine freedom . . ." (pp. 517–18). But when—and this is the big question—when will this happen? Like Lessing, Novalis answers: "Just have patience, it will, it must come, the holy time of eternal peace . . . and till then be cheerful and bold amid the dangers of the time, my fellow believers . . ." (p. 518).

The enormous longing for earthly peace—we recall Gryphius, Lessing, Kant, Hölderlin—was picked up by Novalis. But it was not fulfilled. The longing for superterrestrial peace, the yearning for the blue flower, the infinite, and hence for a final home also remained. "Where then are we going?" asks Novalis in *Heinrich von Ofterdingen*, his last work, begun after the meeting in Jena. And the answer is: "Always homeward" (p. 267). But Novalis couldn't finish this work (conceived as a *Bildungsroman*) either. His health rapidly worsened in the following year, and he succumbed to tuberculosis on March 25, 1801, age twenty-nine.

Can we imagine Schleiermacher dying at the same age? How would we judge him? And Novalis? Of course, from the literary viewpoint, many objections can be raised against the poetry and the poet, this most romantic of the romantics (Walter Jens will give a clear formulation of this), and the same can be done from the theological standpoint. Especially with their eye on his private sketches, novels, hymns, and spiritual songs (which are not my topic here)—theologians criticize the glamorous-dubious elements in Novalis' understanding of religion and the ambiguity in his concept of God. They criticize the vague Christology, the cosmology and anthropology that in the final analysis were influenced by Jacob Böhme; they criticize his "Catholic fantasy religion," his "skeptical relativism," his "subjectivism and individualism" (E. Hirsch), which were often only the consequences of the romantic urge toward the universal, the cosmopolitan, the humane, indeed the infinite.

Karl Barth, who clearly sees in Novalis the danger of the Christian element dissolving into the generically religious—into the human love, eroticism, sexuality—issues a much kinder judgment, with a view to the Spiritual Songs. "There is a life behind them that managed to know enough of the 'terrible fear,' that seems to have known enough so that for all the misgivings it may cause us we must in any case respect his confession of faith. Thousands and thousands of people have thought for the last hundred years that they were hearing the most genuine witness here. Who wants to argue with them and claim that they didn't really hear it?" (pp. 340–41).

But all this affects *Europe* only in a marginal way, and no reaction to this great speech would be so inappropriate as small-minded theological scolding and squabbling. This romanticism, as it is embodied in Novalis (according to Nietzsche "one of the authorities on questions of holiness through experience and instinct," *Human, All Too Human*, n. 142), can in any event not be mocked because of a "naive" belief in the poetic transformation of the world, cannot be reviled because of exotic artfulness in creating moods, or gotten rid of because of the consequences that ideologies of different colors have drawn from it.

On the contrary, we can ask instead: What would the world have been spared if more people had let themselves be moved and changed by the gentle power of Novalis' poetry, if his romantic dream of peace had become political reality, if his dream of a church in freedom had come true? Novalis could have declared his agreement with an ecumenical-Catholic papacy in the spirit of John XXIV, but never with a Roman Catholic papacy ruled by a Pius XIII. Neither the narrow-minded Roman nor the provincial Protestant church, but the truly catholic, universal church, the European ecumene, was his ideal. And on this score we seem to have made only a little progress since then.

Novalis did not live to see the transition from romanticism to the political restoration, which naturally stood in sharp contrast to the Enlightenment. He had poetically prefigured not a reactionary paradigm but something like a *postmodern paradigm*. In it faith would not be, as it was in the Middle Ages, placed above reason nor, as in the Reformation, placed over against reason nor, as in the modern period, opposed to reason. Instead, against all unbelief, *faith would find its enlightenment in reason*.

Christendom or Europe: Truly, Europe doesn't need the return of a Christendom where religion (as in the High Middle Ages) dominates society in an altogether totalitarian manner, from sexual morality to the law of the state. Nor, secondly, does Europe need a Christendom in which religion and the church on the one hand and society, politics, and the state on the other (as Luther would have it) form two parallel kingdoms. Nor, thirdly, does Europe need—after Auschwitz, Hiroshima, and the Gulag Archipelago—a system where (as in modernity) a society without religion—and then de facto for the most part without morality—is proclaimed. What remains of romanticism is the vision of a great synthesis of society and religion. Unless all appearances are deceiving, even today many citizens of Europe are still longing for a religion credibly realized in society and hence at the same time for a society rooted in religion in a manner worthy of reason. Or to say it one last time poetically with Friedrich von Hardenberg: "a new golden age with dark infinite eyes, a prophetic wonder-working and wound-healing, comforting time that sparks eternal life—a great time of reconciliation . . ." (pp. 512–13).

WALTER JENS

◆

A Great Festival
of Peace
on the Smoking Battlefields

"C hristendom must again become living and effective. . . . It must again pour the old cornucopia of blessings over the nations. . . . From the holy womb of a venerable European council Christendom will arise. No one will protest any longer, (but) all necessary reforms will be made under the direction (of the church) as peaceful . . . processes of the state. . . . It must come, the holy time of eternal peace." Novalis' treatise *Christendom or Europe*—it cannot be said often enough—is not a carefully calculated partisan piece, shaped by precise interpretation of historical facts, written in favor of the one, holy, saving church. It is not a divinatory anticipation of the Holy Alliance (Metternich anointed by Novalis the Herrnhuter as part of higher Christian strategy). *Christendom* is rather a masterpiece of religious eloquence, punctuated by prophecies, commands, and imperative visions. As an allegorical exercise and a fairy tale pregnant with ideas, it allows for practically any interpretation. The one thing it can't be taken for is a document of conversion.

Novalis was interested in producing an example of enthusiastic eloquence, an example of the great rhetoric that needed "magnificent materials" in order to present itself effectively on stage. No wonder, then, that he was planning to combine *Europe* in slightly altered form with other public speeches, with addresses "to the princes, to the European people, for poetry, against morality, to the new century."

This was a proclamation to the new century, stamped by the spirit of religion. Novalis had the confidence, in 1799, to stand up to Schleiermacher's *Speeches on Religion*, which appeared in the same year. Hardenberg the preacher enters the lists against Schleiermacher the preacher, to teach the people (and not just the "cultured") what religion was—from a different perspective. On the threshold of the new century, the golden era at the end of the still ongoing "central age" (Friedrich Schlegel), two Protestants, a theologian and a saltworks assessor, set out to restore the "catholic" (that is, all-embracing) religion to its rights.

Schleiermacher and Novalis, two men with a Herrnhuter education (Kant makes a third with his book on *Religion Within the Limits of Reason Alone*), were two pioneers of the romantic movement. The one was a preacher at the Charité, the other an inspector of the salt mines in the Electorate of Saxony. Both proclaim in ecstatic discourse the emerging kingdom of peace, of religion and freedom (as Friedrich Schlegel said, "In the Golden Age and in the Kingdom of God there is no controversy!"). Both had an appellative obligation to an imaginary community: "Don't forbid us to adore the God that is in you," we read at the end of Schleiermacher's rhetorical treatise, *On Religion: Speeches to Its Cultured Despiser*, while Novalis ends his sermon on the secret meaning of history and its God-determined dialectic with the words: "Be cheerful and bold amid the dangers of the time. My fellow believers, preach the divine gospel with word and deed, and remain faithful till death to the true, infinite faith."

In both cases we hear the ecstatic language of the spiritual orator. In both, we see the vision of a religion not dogmatically fixed, whose workings are as clearly manifested in nature as in history, just as much in human civilization as in the feelings of the individual. A (supposed) Catholic, Novalis, follows in the traces of a (supposed) advocate of natural religion. This was the homage of a Herrnhuter to his older predecessors: "I wish to lead you to a brother," Novalis says in *Europe*,

> who is to speak with you, so that your hearts may be
> warmed, and you may clothe your dead, beloved revenge
> with a new body, may again grasp and know what you were

thinking of and what ponderous earthly understanding . . .
you could not get hold of. This brother is the heartbeat of
the new age. Anyone who has felt him will no longer have
doubts about its coming, will come forward with sweet pride
to join the band of his contemporaries, leaving the crowd for
the new flock of disciples. He has made a new veil for the
Holy One that fits snugly and reveals her heavenly
shape. . . .

Schleiermacher in the service of the Madonna passes to her a
fabric, behind whose folds lips open to sing of the birth of a new
century ("let everyone make himself ready"). The Protestant
preacher is in league with the Virgin Mary, whose appearance,
evoked by Schleiermacher, lets Novalis hear the "wingbeat of an
angelic herald passing overhead"). In fact this is more a boldly
syncretistic than a Catholic vision. Here everything fits in with
everything, the *primal gathering* with *birth*, the *coded music* with
the first *birthpangs* of the new age . . . and as for the church that
Novalis dreamed up in *Europe*, it is a Catholic cathedral just as
it is a *peacemaking lodge*, a house for Freemasons of Lessing's
stamp, in which *lovers of humanity* and *encyclopedists* will be
welcomed by their grand master, Friedrich Ernst Daniel Schleiermacher, as a sign of their reception into the church of peace:
"And receive the brotherly kiss."
    Was *Europe* a hymn to catholicity? Well, it is, if catholicity
means "lodge and church," "peaceable kingdom of reason," and
a "world of liberated sensuousness," in other words, a great synthesis, reconciliation, and conjunction of what had been previously separated in history. Then, but only then, is Hardenberg's
spiritual discourse *actually* a catholic discourse. But it was *not* an
elaborate treatise in the fashion of enlightened or pious-
authoritarian writers like Burke or de Maistre. Rather it was a
Herrnhuter's song. It sought, à la Schleiermacher, to bring religion back to the center of all things, and it makes use of a lofty
cadence in order to blaze up in the sermon "Associations of
Divine Inspirations, of Heavenly Contemplations."
    Seen from these aspects, *Europe* is not least of all a story of
the sort the brothers and sisters told one another in those *gatherings for worship* that Novalis refers to at the time of his intense
involvement in Christianity and religion, 1799–1800, when he

stresses the enthusiastic, inspired, and spirit-filled character of rhetoric. *Music* had to be the highly poetic proclamation from the pulpit, which knew that rhetoric belonged to the *psychological science of creating moods*. "Religious attention to the sunny side of the other world" would be aroused in the hearts of the listeners not through the sterile word, not by means of fixed letters, terms, and numbers, not through the language of the *auditorium*, but thanks to *theatrical conjuring*: "The purpose of every sermon"— as far back as the *General Sketches* of 1798–1799 Novalis often uses Schleiermacher's diction—"is to awaken religion—to present religious truths. It is the highest thing that a person can deliver. Sermons contain God's meditations—and God's experiments. Every sermon is the effect of an inspiration—a sermon can only be, must be, the result of genius."

Had sentences like these been published, people in the Charité, seeing so much religious enthusiasm, would have clapped their hands. This, of course, does not exclude the fact that Schleiermacher was not altogether comfortable in reading what his Catholic admirer had finally accomplished in *Christendom or Europe*. *This* apotheosis of an imaginary papacy was too much for the ingrained papist as well because it glossed over evil. Embarrassment spread. The letter-writing authorities met. Doubts whether it was advisable to print the speech grew from week to week. Finally the question was put to—who else?—Goethe, and he said no.

General sighs of relief. Had everybody always been against the idea? "Long live Goethe," wrote Caroline Schlegel—and the addressee of her letter, Schleiermacher, is said to have expressed *his* relief to Ms. Ilm. The public speech of an acolyte demanding that he wrap the head of the Madonna in a precious cloth would remain unpublished. Long live Goethe: Caroline (Madame Lucifer, as she was called) was quite right.

The only really troubled person in all these quarrels was, therefore, Hardenberg himself. Not because his own work was eliminated (he bore that with understanding, already having in mind a new use for the speech). No, the problem was that his sermon could not, as Schlegel had planned, appear together with Schelling's parody of the whole Schleiermacher and Hardenberger *shtick*, the cult of the Madonna and religion, worship of women and heavenly ecstasies. *That* pained Novalis. First *Christendom or Europe* and then a Swabian-materialistic production of irreligious thinking, Schelling's "Epicurean Profession of Faith by Hans Widerporsten," a sometimes blunt, sometimes allusive pamphlet in the style of Hans Sachs . . . hymnic testimony countered by the blustering speech of the old Tübingen seminarian disgruntled by some far too ethereal statements: This was altogether in keeping with Novalis' taste, but unfortunately not at all with Goethe's.

And so a religious dispute was never settled. Had it ever been published (with Hardenberg's public support), the suspicion would absolutely never have arisen that *Europe* might be a papist fervorino, begotten in Rome and delivered in the Electorate of Saxony. Friedrich Wilhelm Josef Schelling had already seen to that with his transmogrification of Novalis' medieval enthusiasm. Catholicism (said Schelling)—by all means, why not? But, if you please, make it the right kind of Catholicism: earthly, solid, realistic, and bouncing. It was concretely and joyfully averse to all the spiritual element of the Schleiermachers and their retinue:

> I think nothing of the invisible,
> I cling only to what is evident,
> What I can smell, taste, and feel,
> What I can wallow in with all my senses.
> My only religion is this,
> That I love a pretty knee,
> Full breasts and slim hips,
> And flowers with sweet smells,
> Full nourishment of all pleasure,
> Sweet allowance of all love.

Greetings from Heinrich Heine—and Novalis lavishes applause on verses that he would not like to see banned under any circumstances. Friedrich Hardenberg met the reproach that materialistic atheism was being preached here with the thesis: *And the gods of Greece?* Did people perhaps wish to forbid them, too—and Schiller with them? And so, go on, Schelling, let your Swabian seminarian's humor have free play:

> Hence, if there still has to be religion
> (Though I can just as well live without one),
> Of all the others only the Catholic sort can satisfy me,

As it was in the old days.
Then there were neither squabbles nor disputes,
Everything was cakes and ale,
They wouldn't go off on wild goose chases,
Nor gawk at heaven.
They had a living ape of God,
Thought the earth the center of the universe,
And Rome the center of the earth,
. . .
And the laymen and the clerics lived
Together as in the land of Cockaigne.
And besides in the lofty house of heaven
They lived high on the hog,
They had a wedding feast every day
Between the Virgin and the Old Man.

Novalis in no way felt that *this* text, bristling with wit, impudence, and occasional obscenity, was blasphemous. On the contrary, dialectician that he was even *in theologicis*, he wanted at all cost to see it printed *together* with his vision in his friend Schlegel's *Athenäum*. Romantic irony, ah, how humane and unfanatical it was. How intent on balance, the play of allusions and reciprocal illumination of theses. How useful if the idea was to realize the planetary visions of the poets, philosophers, and founders of religions, as they had established themselves under the heavens after the failure of the French Revolution. Since on earth there was obviously nothing more to be gotten, how useful to bring down to earth the great promises of salvation, *absolute* revolution in art, the *true* church, the total *world* of poetry, the rational kingdom of the Golden Age. And, as Heine and Büchner later did, how useful to raise "the great soup question," where idealistic minds go about compensating for earthly misery with their effusive conceptions.

But the point is not *just* compensating. The sad here and now, where the poor man had no chicken in the pot on Sunday, was not *just* to be veiled through references to a (supposedly) soon-to-be-arriving kingdom of peace, which in truth, as the following period showed, would take place on St. Nevercome's Day.

The bolder Schiller's, Fichte's, and Novalis' dreams of the absolute and transcendental turned out to be, the more clearly if indirectly was the real alienation of people brought into view. How wretched seemed the reality of Germany around 1800, distorted into recognizability through heavenly visions. I think it speaks for Novalis that in his work the discrepancies between the era's great dreams and prosaic everyday facts come right into focus.

Dreams first and foremost! Novalis was the chief advocate of the magical idealism that wanted to make poetry religion and religion poetry, so as to restore to the poets their old priestly dignity. Then poetry was celebrated as the science of salvation and reconciliation, the poet, in Schleiermacher's footsteps, as a mediator between two worlds. (Fragment 73 of the collection called "Pollen" looks like an anticipatory explanation of the "mediator figure" in the *Speeches on Religion*.) Here the poet acquires the dignity of a godlike being who reconciles man and nature, the spiritual and the animal, with one another—the mediator: a "transcendental physician." Here the inspired poet succeeds in doing what remains prohibited to the philosopher—to redeem man, leading him out beyond himself and making visible to him, in the likeness of poetry, the universal world, not dismembered but once again come to itself in art. "The poet," we read in Hardenberg's novel *Heinrich von Ofterdingen*, "fills the inner sanctuary of the mind with new, wonderful, and pleasant thoughts. He knows how to excite at will those secret powers in us, and lets us perceive an unknown, splendid world through words. As if out of deep caves old and future times arise in us, countless men and women, wonderful regions and the strangest circumstances, and tear us from the familiar present."

Tear us from the familiar present: This was poetry as a drug to enchant people—as a stimulant for those dreaming themselves away from the world in the feeling of mystic union, in the intoxication of night and death. These are the people whom Novalis, in the second "Hymn to the Night," which celebrates the great sleep, has participating in an oblivion, a lostness to the world, which the *golden flood of the grape* and the *brown juice of the poppy* help to achieve.

Alcohol, opium, and, in addition, sex (Novalis celebrates a holy sleep that "hovers over the tender maiden's bosom and makes her womb into heaven") are used as vehicles for becoming one with the universe.

There can be no doubt that in the "Hymns" and *Ofterdingen*, the "Spiritual Songs," and the "Apprentices at Sais," we see the anticipation of drunken modes of initiation that will acquire central importance more than a hundred years later in the poetry— Hesse's *Steppenwolf*—and the reality of our time. Consider the note sounded in Goethe's *Werther* and in the youth movements, with different accents, and projected from 1910 till today: nature, mysticism and glorification of the Absolute, the cult of the mother, ecstatic religiosity, and allusions to the brotherly ties between Eros and Thanatos. We find all this spelled out in Novalis. He presents the visions, pantheistic as well as decidedly Christian ones, ever the prophet, preacher, lawgiver, and bard. Hardenberg is concerned not with history as historiographical fact, but with history as gospel, as the sum of countless human lives shaped by pains and dreams, emphases, transports, and ecstasies. He paints the simultaneous vision of all time and space, to which he was predestined by personal experience as well as by his capacity to visualize ideas in images, to mirror the universal in the private realm and the absolute in the individual.

"The history of each person should be a Bible—aims to be a Bible," is a key line by Novalis, in form and content. When the poet wishes something to happen—think of the conclusion of *Europe*—then it *will* happen, without regard to the resistance points of history. What counts for Hardenberg is not the fact itself, but the spirit apportioned to this fact by the inspired ego, the freely chosen, self-determined mediator. It is not *reality*, but *possibility*, not the factual but what is believed to be probable, meaningful, consoling, and necessary by millions of people, here in this way, there in that, which defines in the eyes of the romantic poet-priest true history, the kind that promotes the awareness of salvation and the creation of meaning.

"There is more truth in the fairy tales (of the poets)," declares Count von Hohenzollern in *Ofterdingen*, "than in learned chronicles. If their characters and their fates are invented, the meaning in which they are invented is nonetheless true and natural. It is to a certain extent all the same for our pleasure and instruction whether the persons in whose fates we can trace our own really lived at one time or not. We long for the intuition of the great simple soul into temporal phenomena, and if we find this wish granted, we do not care about the accidental existence of the external figures."

This is a personal confession, I think, that shows the greatness and the limitations of Hardenberg's poetry. Visions and prophecies, however eloquently they may unfold, are stamped by a sort of ahistorical quality. This means, for example, that once in *Europe* the Middle Ages have to serve for the long ago Golden Age, another time in *Ofterdingen* this job falls to Atlantis, and a third time, in the fifth "Hymn to the Night," to antiquity. This means that Christ can be at home in Jerusalem as well as in India or at Sais; that the blue flower is to be found not in Thuringia, but in the no man's land of poetry; that, by contrast to Gryphius, Lessing, or Hölderlin, no shimmer of reality legitimizes the pathetic surges. It means above all that the private realm has become too weightless to be able to bear the powerful burdens that Hardenberg saddles it with: Sophie Kühn as Mary, the dead mistress as Savior, the one grave as the grave of all graves.

Transitions are missing between here and there, precise references, unifying connections that realize the matter of legend and faith in the here and now. Symbols are abruptly coupled with symbols, and metaphorical namings fitted together that refer to no actuality, no specific this-way-and-not-otherwise. In the end, the night of Grüningen and the night of Golgatha are lost in one and the same fog, since, in both cases, it can never be ten o'clock at night and six o'clock in the morning.

While Gryphius' night is at once the darkness of the Thirty Years War and the light-filled night of Bethlehem, while Hölderlin's evening, in the "Celebration of Peace," unfolds like a quite ordinary Swabian night off, Novalis' visions of darkness remain an artifact of a poetry that poses as metaphysics without first having penetrated reality. And it was just this that aroused Schelling's anger. In comparing Hardenberg and E. T. A. Hoffmann, Heine sounded a rather pensive note on the subect of Novalis' poetry:

Frankly, Hoffmann was much more important as a poet than Novalis. For the latter, with his idealist figures, was always hovering in the blue air, while Hoffmann . . . always clings tightly to earthly reality. But just as the giant Antaeus re-

mained invincibly strong when he was touching Mother
Earth with his feet, and lost his strength as soon as Hercules
lifted him up, so the poet too is strong and mighty, as long
as he doesn't leave the ground of reality. He becomes powerless as soon as he floats through the blue air in pious
ecstasy.

Considering Heine's gift for invective, this is an almost gentle
way of distancing himself from Novalis' muse, whom the author
of *The Romantic School* calls "a slender, fair-skinned girl with
earnest blue eyes, golden hyacinthine locks, laughing lips, and a
little red birthmark on the left side of her chin." A gentle and
accurate distancing, all in all, as far as the songs and novel chapters
go (not parts of the "Hymns to the Night"). At the same time
this *is* invective, and its problematic nature can be seen immediately, if we reflect that poetic work constitutes only a fragment,
and by no means the most important one, of Novalis' *oeuvre*. But
the *real* Hardenberg is someone else, I mean the real Novalis,
even though he is still misunderstood as much as ever (exceptions,
such as the editors of the *Opera omnia*, principally Mähl, Schulz,
and Samuel, prove the rule). The unmistakable Novalis, the man
who insisted on the dialectic of the great dream and the little
reality, the man who was matched by nobody, not even his *alter
ego* Fritz Schlegel—this is the writer who found in the fragment
the form that suited him. Hardenberg was a "snapshot thinker"
and a "punctualist," a man of the quick note and the telling,
lightninglike formulation. He did not fill in his sketches or complete what he had earlier thought up in the fragment. What was
perfect in the nutshell, because it was essentially unsurpassable,
became increasingly problematic with every expansion.

Fritz Schlegel was right on target when he said of his friend
Hardenberg: "He thinks in an elementary manner. His thoughts
are atoms." It makes no difference whether Novalis, in an act of
thinking out loud, formulates "fragments of a continual conversation with himself," shorthand reports of never-ending, fascinating monologues, or fashions together splinters of thoughts into
a polished, literary point. In any case, as the author of the "Soul
Journal," writing practically like an epigrammatist, he interprets
the perceptual mode of the modern ego. He speaks of an individuality that knows how to view the world both soberly and

lyrically, at once with scientific precision and religious enthusiasm. We should not forget that the same man who wrote the "Hymns to the Night" also meditated on the problems of gravity, on the theory of heat machines, on blast techniques, wine factories, potash, and essential oils. Novalis' writing bristles with clipped sentences, substantives strung together, abbreviations half divided, half connected by diagonal strokes, formulae that have the effect of synthetic concentrates of infinite connections, interdependencies and oppositions. In articulating his fragments, Novalis measured them against the Schlegelian ideal of the thought-hedgehog ("A fragment," reads Friedrich Schlegel's famous Athenäum fragment, "must, like a little art work, be entirely separated from the world around it and be complete in itself like a hedgehog"). But however he articulated his fragments, here as aids to memory à la Pascal, there as pointed maxims, it is undoubtably true—and this bears repetition—that *sub specie religionis* the briefest, most unassuming, most modest note is far superior in urgency and pithiness to the pretentious amplification. The sketch outdoes the watercolor; the watercolor beats the oil painting.

An example: "Thursday. *Sophie got fatally sick.* . . . Friday, *This morning I saw her for the last time.*" Once again, "Friday. *Tonight Francke returned with very sad news. It was exactly her birthday.* . . . Sunday. *This morning at nine thirty she died. Fifteen years and two days old.*" One could not imagine a more gripping chronicle. Here we have words that, to echo Walter Benjamin, are steeped in the acid of tears. This is terseness on the edge of silence; these are communications that manage with the help of a few sober words to illustrate a universe of suffering, everyday terms that, thanks to the context, become particles in which a scarcely speakable measure of despair finds expression *in extremis: It was exactly her birthday. Fifteen years and two days old.*

That was the description of the death of a beloved, uniquely beloved person. Here is the description, later in the *Journal* of the deathwatch at the grave: "In the evening, I could not get to my place of rest until late. There were so many people going there. . . . Much noise and bustle in the house. . . . Yesterday evening I was at the grave and had some wild moments of joy. . . . We sat in the big room . . . and quietly sang the melody— how they rest so gently."

Again—interrupted by a single, paradoxical phrase ("wild moments of joy at the grave")—we get the mention of suffering through objective correlatives (grave, room, song). Again there is elucidation of the worst torment by noting the situations that indirectly show how one man is suffering here and how great his loneliness is.

In contrast to that, consider the poetry. Here we find an ambitious interpretation of the event at the grave, presented in the third "Hymn to the Night": "Once when I shed bitter tears, when my hope dissolved in sorrow melted away, and stood in loneliness at the barren hill, which in narrow dark space concealed the form of my life—lonely as no lonely man has yet been . . . powerless, no more now than a thought of misery. As I looked around there for help, could not go forward nor backward, and clung with infinite longing to fleeting, extinguished life:—then out of the blue distance—from the heights of my old bliss came a shiver of twilight. . . ."

Doesn't every extra word here make the impression that much weaker? Isn't the language talked out, chattered away, expressed, killed by adjectives, stifled by empty formulas? ("dissolved in pain," "hope melted away," "lonely as no lonely man has yet been," "could not go forward nor backward"). And then the idyll at the end—shaped by the use of prefabricated "mood" words from the arsenal of trivial poetry, religious clichés, and solemn-sounding set pieces from the literature of death, graveyards, and hope. Yet that much, unfortunately, is not enough: Driven by the poetic furor of the grave, Novalis in the fourth Spiritual Song transforms his vision still more, into a chorale, in whose second to fourth strophe we read:

> My world was shattered,
> As if stung by a worm
> My heart and bloom withered;
> All that my life owned,
> My every wish lay in the grave,
> And I was still here to be tormented.
>
> Since I thus grew sick in silence,
> Cried ever and hankered away,
> And remained only from fear and madness:
> Suddenly the gravestone was lifted

Off me from above,
And my innards were laid open.

No one asked whom I saw
And whom I caught sight of at his hand,
Forever will I see only this;
And of all the hours of life
Only this one will, like my wounds,
Forever bright, stand open.

Here the heartrending notes end up turning into edifying religious verse. Here, as vocabulary, word position, and rhymes (in the German original) show, the elements of the Protestant hymn take on an independent existence. Hardenberg the poet is content with a routine collection of the available image material.

The primordial experience at Sophie's grave has transformed itself into a religious educational experience, within which the dead bride, like a heavenly Virgin Mary, can walk at Jesus' side over the grave, and the wound of the mourner points to the wound of the risen Christ. No doubt, the more directly—or, as we can confidently say, the more indecently—Novalis "Christianizes" his texts and generalizes them into the realm of the religiously meaningful, the more striking becomes his failure as a religious writer. We see this failure in the description, which idyllically transforms everything unique and concrete into something atmospheric and sentimental, of the life and death of Christ. We see it in the transfiguration of the Madonna who has ceased to be the Mater Dolorosa. We see it, too, in the intimate description of heavenly events as well as in the manner with which Novalis, in the tradition of religious love literature, from the Song of Songs to Zinzendorf, subjectivizes Christian traditions. As a result, the only thing remaining in the end is a bold spectacle stamped by the mystique of death and pansexuality. In this spectacle the Last Supper takes on the character of a lustful copulation, in which the physically united pair swims in heavenly blood, and the feast of Passover finds itself transformed into an orgiastic celebration lasting from eternity to eternity. "The sweet meal never ends, love never grows sated, never can it have the Beloved ardently enough or to itself enough. What has been tasted is transformed more fervently and more closely by ever more tender lips. Hotter lust quivers through the soul. The heart becomes more hungry and thirsty."

This is no Lutheran Last Supper, nor is it an incense-filled Eucharist levitating in pious ecstasy. Here, in the spirit of the kabala and pansophy, a black mass of love is celebrated, in the course of which the seas pass away into blood and the mountains into flesh. Sexuality triumphs at the banquet of love and—union of man and woman—the heavens as well: "O! that the world's ocean was already crimson, and the rock was swelling up into perfumed flesh!"

Only those who know the mystery of love, Novalis' maxim runs, those who know the mysteries of sexuality, and still more, those who have experienced what orgasm means—the quieting of infinite hunger and thirst—will, by grasping the analogy of earthly and heavenly in-corporation, understand the meaning of the Last Supper. They will see it as the great communion between God and man—the act of love on the threshold of death:

> But who ever
> sucked from hot, beloved lips
> the breath of life,
> whose holy fervor
> melted into trembling waves of the heart,
> whose eye opened,
> so that he could measure unfathomable depths,
> Will eat from his body
> And drink from his blood
> Unendingly.

When we read verses like these, lines from the dithyramb "Hymn," Novalis' boldest, but also most macabre, religious poem, we can understand the disgust that engulfed the poet with his great vatic dream in the face of Protestant belief in the letter.

But was he Catholic just because the Madonna seemed more sensual to him than Mary in the garment of his Dürerlike mother at home? Was Lavater Catholic because he knew how to give an evocative description of the thoughts of a Protestant in a Catholic church? Was Kleist a Catholic because he confessed in Dresden: "I never found myself . . . more deeply touched in my innards than in the Catholic church, where the greatest, most elevated music was added to the other arts of powerfully moving the heart. Ah . . . our worship is none at all. It speaks only to the cold understanding, but a Catholic feast speaks to all senses. . . . Ah, only a drop of oblivion, and I would become Catholic with voluptuousness."

Now, as we know, Heinrich von Kleist did not convert, nor did Friedrich von Hardenberg—least of all Hardenberg who in his youthful poems, celebrating Joseph II, wrote invectives against the monastic "brood of pious raving" and the "fearful papist holiness."

And, nevertheless, though he could *believe* in Protestant fashion, he could *write poetry* productively (and not just do Herrnhuter copies) only where sensuality came into play, where there was eroticism and vitality—that is, where woman could be looked upon simultaneously as mother and mistress, bride and queen of heaven, where sensual gestures, embraces, genuflections, and kisses attested to the fact that the most pious and most elevated things could be mirrored in the ecstasies of the lower kind of love. That was where the child pointed to the dialectical tension between bright early times and their return in the coming dream realm of peace, the tension that Novalis, bound to the thought of the triadic system of history, tried again and again to put into images. ("Where children are, there is a golden age.")

But the same man who, like so many after him, held the Catholic interpretation of Christian religious truths to be the only artistically fruitful one, still was and remained an arch-Protestant. He was a liberal Protestant, to be sure. He sided with Herder and Schleiermacher instead of with the pious souls from Herrnhut and Gnadenfrei, and counted Lessing, whose *Education of the Human Race* he wished to continue, as one of his patron saints. Friedrich Hardenberg and his friend Schlegel were intent on varying the linear model of Enlightenment concepts of history so that the mysterious primal state would be preserved on a higher level instead of being overcome, and nature, having become reason, could return in the same way to its ancestral rights as the community of the gods. Hardenberg, secretly agreeing with Hölderlin, wanted this community not to be *gotten rid of* by Christ but *redeemed*: "An apotheosis of the future, of this actual, better world, this is the core of Christianity's commands. . . . At this point it connects with the religion of the antiquarians, the divinity of the ancient world, the restoration of antiquity, as the second main wing: Together they keep the universe, like the body of the angel, in eternal suspension."

Which would bring us back again to Hölderlin, to the idea of the great reconciliation under the sign of peace. It would also bring us back, once again, to Lessing, whose bourgeois apotheosis at the end of *Nathan* returns in Novalis' vision of the family. The unity of the family symbolizes the agreement between the separated religions that shapes Schleiermacher's *Speeches on Religion* as well as the (planned) sequel to Schlegel's *Lucinde*, and Eichendorff's examination piece with its postulate that the denominations should interpenetrate and interanimate one another. And not least of all it shapes Hardenberg's materials for the second part of *Heinrich von Ofterdingen*: "The book closes . . . *with a simple family*. [Everything] becomes more silent, simple, and human. . . . It is the primeval world, the golden time at the end."

The family celebration at the end of the days: It's strange to see how in Jena, Berlin, and Dresden, in the circle of the religious lodge brothers, people keep returning to the thought of Lessing, the secret interlocutor, in all disputes—in solidarity and opposition to him.

In *solidarity*, because Novalis as well as Schlegel considered the thought of the divine plan of education indispensable. *In opposition*, because Lessing's idea that it was possible in the coming age of reason to do without not just the Old Testament but the New Testament, too, had been replaced by a new thesis. This envisioned a springtime for humanity that had to be preserved at all cost, with its sunniness, its charm, and its unfolding under the aegis of a nature that had not yet been usurped, not put into service, not forced into exploitation.

So then is Friedrich von Hardenberg a writer to teach us how someone serious about religion can present traditional testimony to revelation in an enlightened age with the help of poetic discourse? I think he is. Novalis may have come to grief through conjuring up a religion of art. He may have come to grief too in his attempt to transform, through radical subjectivizing, the Bible, tradition, and Western history into a romantic *Gesamtkunstwerk* where Eros and Thanatos function as fundamental principles of the universe. Despite that, as a fragment writer and philosophical artist he left behind, on thousands of pages, a "religious journal" that was supposed to be the first "scientific Bible" of modern times. Volumes of notes and studies, fragments and sketches prove that he tried to continue composing the Bible (Novalis declared it was unfinished) in the age of science.

Was all this no more than speculation? Just a crazy notion? A mad prank, planned and already forgotten? A jest along the lines of Schlegel's proposal to found a new religion? (That, too, came under Lessing's aegis: "If [he] was still alive, then I wouldn't need to begin the work. The beginning would then be quickly completed. No one had divined more about the true religion than he.")

The scientific Bible as an attempt to reconcile faith and reason within the framework of an encyclopedia filled with the spirit of religion. Is this really just the absurd plan of an artist manipulating references, a verbal magician at whom even Fritz Schlegel sometimes shook his head? ("Hardenberg," he said in a letter to Schleiermacher in 1798, "is on the point of mixing together religion and physics. It will be an interesting plate of scrambled eggs.")

Just scrambled eggs? *If* Schlegel deserved our credence! But who can really trust a man who mistreated his closest intimate in the realm of art, philosophy, and religion: "Your mind stood closest to me among the images of the uncomprehended truth," he said, even while exposing him to mockery with the remark, "The only reason I don't believe Hardenberg is killing himself, is that he definitely wants to and considers it the beginning of all philosophy.")

Or did Hardenberg himself in the end give up on his great plan of supporting the age of peace and concord among the nations by a kind of *Organum Novissimum*, namely the scientific Bible as an expression of a religious encyclopedism? "To wish to write a Bible is an inclination to madness, of the sort that every rational man must have in order to be complete": In this note to Schlegel's *Ideas*, has the failure of the project of the century been figured in? We don't know. The question remains open, like the documents about a writer who is perhaps the most puzzling among the many ambiguous authors in our portrait galley. A utopian who had to hold out for the legitimation of the darkest kind of clericalism, a conservative in whose name Thomas Mann based his move toward democracy and republicanism in 1921, an apolitical person who—as consolation in the darkness of the present day—sought to unite memory of the Garden of Eden with hope for the millennial kingdom of the Golden Age: "The Bible begins splendidly with Paradise, the symbol of youth, and ends with the eternal kingdom, with the holy city."

Friedrich Hardenberg, who has been made here into the pioneer of Metternich, and there into the star witness for Bloch's principle of hope, the Janus-faced Novalis has nevertheless, and not least of all, managed one thing: to serve as the key witness for the liberation of humanity, which he saw as always possible, at a moment when this humanity's existence was threatened as never before.

"Blood will flow over Europe until the nations become aware of their madness and . . . a great love feast will be celebrated with hot tears in the name of peace on the smoking battlefields. Only religion can reawaken Europe and visibly install Christendom with new splendor on earth in its old peacemaking office." This was written in 1799, with a view toward an age of universal emancipation, centered around a church of peace. It was quoted in 1942, under the banner of the Nazi politics of extermination, by the conspirators from the circle of the "White Rose."

Christendom or Europe was a signal for freedom under the gallows. The religion conjured up by poetry was an element of human refractoriness. And so Novalis was a writer whom a handful of young people invoked as their helper in time of need almost sixty years ago before being led, some months later, to the scaffold.

The chiliastic sermon of a Christian became, under the sign of the cross, a challenge to barbarism. In this way it fulfilled its most secret goal, as it pointed to emancipation from a force that aimed at the cancellation of both reason and faith.

SØREN KIERKEGAARD

◆

TRAINING IN CHRISTIANITY

HANS KÜNG

◆

Religion
as a Contradiction
of the Existing Order

If we are asked where the modern period in Europe, which set in around the middle of the seventeenth century, reached its zenith, where would we look to? To revolutionary, then Napoleonic, France? Hardly—that was the triumph of Mars, politics carried out with the help of the army and the police. But we may look to Germany, which was so politically impotent at the time. Between Lessing's death, Kant's *Critique of Pure Reason*, Schiller's *Robbers*, and Mozart's journey to Vienna to see Haydn, all in the year 1781, and the deaths of Beethoven and Schubert, in 1827–1828, then of Hegel and Goethe, in 1831–1832, the country experienced an unparalleled epoch of brilliance in philosophy, poetry, and music.

Again, if asked who succeeded in conceptualizing this modernity, in getting an intellectual grasp on this era, and thereby bringing on the Golden Age, at least in philosophy, we shall have to name the third and originally the slowest of the friends from Tübingen, Georg Friedrich Wilhelm *Hegel*.

Hegel incorporated many strands into his tremendously patient conceptual work: the foundations that had been laid by the *Copernican* revolution and the liquidation of the traditional notion of heaven; the philosophical beginnings made by *Descartes'* concentration on man and human reason; the further developments by *Spinoza* with his all-embracing unity of God and the world; *Leibnitz* with his theodicy; *Lessing* with his program for transferring accidental historical truths of Christianity into necessary truths of reason; the territory secured by *Kant* with his religion within the limits of reason alone; the translations into a new metaphysics made by *Fichte*, moving beyond all epistemological criticism with his philosophy of ego; and the young *Schelling* with his philosophy of the identity of subject and object, what *Hölderlin* came to grief on and what *Novalis* had anticipated only in his poetry.

Yet Hegel did more than merely incorporate these diverse strands. He also relativized them, and integrated them into a higher synthesis. Or, as he liked to say, he "sublated them" (*aufgehoben*), a triple-decker word that means at once conserved, abrogated, and transcended. Philosophy was supposed to comprehend everything that existed, every individual thing in an all-embracing, dynamically dialectical *universal system*, as a moment of the unified development of the Whole, the Absolute, God himself. Thus Hegel tried in a "speculative" ("looking at"), reflective fashion to describe *"God's career."* This was the self-divesting course followed by God into worldliness (in natural philosophy) and through worldliness back to the complete coming-to-oneself of mind. All this took place in Hegel's philosophy of mind, which embraces an anthropology (cum psychology), a philosophy of law and of world history, and finally a philosophy of art, religion, and philosophy itself (the history of philosophy).

This was really an ontotheology, of a sort never before available to Christianity, a universal Summa of absolute knowledge and thus a summa theologica of mind itself. For that is how many theologians perceived it then. What a miracle it seemed in an age of faithless philosophy, so hostile to revelation, when Jean Paul (pseudonym of Johann Paul Friedrich Richter, German novelist, d. 1825), anticipating Nietzsche's visions, dreamt the somber dream of a speech by the dead Christ, declaring that in the empty spaces which had already terrified Pascal there was no God. Hegel presented an ontotheological system in which Christianity was neither polemically dismissed nor indifferently disregarded, but accepted in a profound, sympathetic way, ideally "aufgehoben." This was a system that not only, as earlier systems did, unified antiquity and Christianity, but the Renaissance and Reformation as well. It fused the Enlightenment and romanticism, the revolution and restoration, indeed reason and reality. It was a system that basically mediated all imaginable oppositions, and reconciled reason and reality in absolute Mind. And for all this it aimed simply to be a knowing, philosophical religion—Christianity knowing and thinking itself. In the dispute between Enlightenment thinkers and the purely emotive psychologists, and finally in the mortal struggle against the onstorming forces of modernity, the question was: Should Christendom greet this saving Christian system with enthusiasm?

Karl Barth was right to ask: Why didn't Hegel become for Protestant theology what Thomas Aquinas was for Catholic theology? That is to say, the *Doctor communis*, the "common teacher," who sifted the material accumulated by history both inside and especially outside the walls of Christendom. Why wasn't he the one who gave it a new conceptual structure, and worked out in a scholarly, creative fashion the new comprehensive, philosophical-theological synthesis that had now become necessary, the new paradigm of the Christian world?

Hegel died in 1831 at the height of his scholarly reputation. Yet just ten years later everything was completely changed.

1841: In this year, *The Essence of Christianity* was published by a former student of theology, then a Hegelian, finally an atheist, Ludwig *Feuerbach*. He rejected any absolutizing of either the Hegelian system or Christianity. He thought he had discovered that the secret of theology was anthropology: God was just a projection of man. In this way, he became the critic of religion, the atheistic schoolmaster, for the whole Hegelian left, especially for Marx and Engels. In the middle of the 1830s, the critical *Life of Christ* by the Tübingen Seminary tutor, David Strauss, split the Hegelian school into right- and left-wing Hegelians.

1841: In the same year, another student of theology, twenty-eight years old, came to Berlin. In his understanding of Hegel, he was influenced primarily by the right wing, and early on he had taken a hostile stance toward the Hegelian system. Having just been awarded his doctorate for a dissertation on the irony of Socrates, he now wished to solve his problems by studying both

Hegel and Wilhelm Josef Schelling, who had developed into Hegel's opponent and hence had been called to Berlin, despite his age of sixty-two, to stem the Hegelian tide. This was the delicate, introverted, at once coldly and wittily analytic Søren *Kierkegaard*, Denmark's most important prose writer, philosopher, and theologian. He would have only a good twelve years to carry out his unique literary work.

What was Kierkegaard concerned with? In the boundless expanse of the literature on Kierkegaard, which even specialists can no longer keep track of, the Norwegian Per Lönning has demonstrated that some of his philosophical-theological interpreters (Petersen, Bohlin, Hirsch, Lindström) view him more from the standpoint of Schleiermacher, others (Diem, Olesen-Larsen) more from the perspective of dialectical theology, and still others (Haecker, Przywara, Dempf, Fabro) from a Catholic theological position. Niels Thulstrup, director of the Kierkegaard Institute in Copenhagen, provides an excellent overview of the history of research on Kierkegaard's relationship to Hegel and a helpful historical and analytical guide for investigating the earlier periods of the writer's life. What, then, was Kierkegaard concerned with, the man whose voice so much reminds us of Pascal, and who confesses that in his generation no one doubted so deeply as he?

"What is actually lacking to me is to make up my mind about *what I should do*, not about what I should know—except insofar as knowing has to precede all action." In this, his famous first intellectual inventory, six years before his trip to Berlin, he made the programmatic determination that: "Everything depends on understanding my destiny, on seeing what the deity actually wants *me* to do. The thing is to find a truth that is truth *for me*, to find *the idea that I wish to live and die for*. And how would I be any closer to that if I worked my way through the systems of the philosophers and could hold a military review of them, if asked?" On Christianity, he observes: "What good would it do me if I could elaborate the meaning of Christianity and explain many individual phenomena, if it had no deeper meaning *for myself and my life*? (*Collected Works*, Diedrichs-Ausgabe, *Diaries*, I, 16–17).

The contrast to Hegel could not be greater. Where Hegel is speculative and meditative, Kierkegaard, who at that time scarcely knew Hegel in the original, is active and existentially engaged. Kierkegaard is convinced that *Philosophy and Christianity can never be united* (I, 23). Why not? Because in Christianity the infinite difference between the holy, merciful God and guilty, sinful man is given expression. This difference cannot be overcome through any kind of harmonizing or leveling philosophical mediation. Hence both fields will always be incompatible.

Quite in keeping with the down-to-earth approach of *Pascal* (whom he quotes only once and then indirectly through Feuerbach), Kierkegaard thinks from the angle of the distress impinging on his own existence. He could not be satisfied by any objective-impartial knowledge of reality in the spirit of *Descartes*. A purely methodical-experimental doubt struck him as itself dubious (see his very early, unfinished piece *Johannes Climacus or De omnibus dubitandum est*, presumably from 1842–1843): When man doubts in earnest, when he doubts completely, practically and existentially, when he looks to his contradictory self (and it was this kind of doubt that Christianity brought into the world), doesn't his doubting then turn into despair? And from such despair there is no intellectual escape, not even through Hegelian speculation.

> Thus the philosophers are worse than the Pharisees, of whom we read that they bind heavy burdens on people and will not lift a finger to remove them. For it comes down to the same thing, if they themselves don't remove them when they can after all be removed. The philosophers, however, demand the impossible. And if there is a young person who thinks that philosophizing does not mean to chatter or to write, but to do uprightly and carefully the things that the philosopher says should be done, then they make him waste several years of his life. And then it turns out that it is impossible, he has been so deeply caught up in it that liberating him may become impossible. (p. 162)

Are such statements far removed from the real world today, especially in the universities? Kierkegaard himself presses ahead from analysis to decision; every person in his concrete life faces an *inevitable choice—either/or*. This was also the title of a book basically written for his ex-fiancée, Regina Olsen, in which Kierkegaard—hoping for a *Repetition* (1843) of the failed relationship on a higher level—develops the alternatives under the pseudonym Victor Eremita. "Either" the person chooses an "aesthetic" (oriented to sensual pleasure) attitude to life (in the first part, we find the famous "Diary of a Seducer"), "Or" an "ethical," consciously responsible one (in agreement with the demands of society). Either—or! Nevertheless this second part ends with a surprising Neither—nor. For, in a brief "Ultimatum," Kierkegaard presents a third possibility—the *religious* attitude. He would develop this *tertium quid* and describe it as his own mode of life, shaped by suffering, as opposed to the aesthetic and ethical modes. This development would occur only in the following years—after exploring the *Concept of Dread* (1844)—in the presentation of the three stages of life (*Stages on Life's Way*, 1845). Walter Jens will make clear how much behind all this Kierkegaard's wholly personal life story—love affair, guilt complex, and sexuality—finds expression.

1846: Five years after getting his doctorate, breaking his engagement, and traveling to Berlin, the ten-year process of clarification was concluded and with that, as he understood it, the "turning point" from "aesthetic" to "exclusively religious" writing was reached. This was marked by the large-scale, two-volume *Concluding Unscientific Postscript* (to his dogmatic magnum opus, *Philosophical Fragments*, 1844). He now bade a definitive farewell to all idealistic speculation and particularly to the Hegelian system, with an illuminating image: "The relation of most systematic thinkers to their systems is as if a man built an enormous castle and lived in a shed alongside it. They themselves do not live in the enormous systematic structure they build. But in matters of the spirit this is and remains a crucial objection. Spiritually understood, a man's thoughts must be the building that he lives in—otherwise it is perverse" (*Diaries* II, 42).

It is clear enough; Kierkegaard continually brings charges against Hegel's enormous intellectual "castle," citing the distress of the *individual's concrete existence*. He is concerned with the individual person in his contradictoriness, torn between anxiety and hope, guilt and repentance, despair and bliss. But under no circumstances can this individual be "aufgehoben" into a system, either philosophical-speculative or ecclesiastical-dogmatic system.

Existence versus system—this means at the same time that Kierkegaard boldly enters the lists against the first great power of modernity, *"modern science,"* which Hegel uniquely embodies. Kierkegaard makes his entrance with a piece provocatively called "unscientific," full of irony, wit, and humor. He cries out his great "Stop!" and calls for a change of thinking. Much as objective knowledge (logic, history) has its meaning, it also has its limits. In any case, "modern science" can in no way give an answer to the meaning of life and how it is to be lived. Kierkegaard's pseudonym, Johannes Climacus (who according to him is a humanist, humorist, and experimenter, but not a Christian) is not interested in either philosophy or theology. He is concerned purely and simply with the basic human problem—being a Christian, or rather becoming a Christian. And on this score not only does he develop a speculative teaching but he proclaims an absolute existential communication, a message (*kerygma*) that, unlike science, always includes an ethic: "Putting it as simply as possible (so as to make experimental use of my own person): 'I, Johannes Climacus, born here in the city, now thirty years old and, after a fashion, a human being, like most people, assume that I, as well as a maidservant or a professor, have a chance of obtaining what is called eternal happiness. I have heard that Christianity provides you with this benefit. Now I ask: How do I enter into a relationship with this teaching?' " (*Postscript*, p. 14).

But whom can Kierkegaard invoke as an ally? Schelling the philosopher? Like Hegel, Schelling had presented himself as a great idealistic-speculative constructor of systems. He offered no help. Another thinker, however, took on a surprising importance for Kierkegaard—Gotthold Ephraim *Lessing*. In the *Postscript*, Kierkegaard directs a subtly emphatic word of thanks to Lessing— needless to say, not only to Lessing as a scholar, poet, aesthetician, and sage. No, Kierkegaard's gratitude goes out primarily to Lessing as the type of subjective thinker who produced neither a "system" nor finished "results." He was grateful that Lessing, "from the religious point of view did not let himself be led astray like a fool into becoming world-historical and systematic. Lessing understood—and held on to the fact—that religion concerned Lessing, and Lessing alone, as it concerns every person in this way. He understood that he had infinite business to do with God, not purely and simply with a human being" (p. 57). At least, that's how it might be, although for Kierkegaard, too, Lessing's ultimate attitude toward Christianity ("Did he accept Christianity? Did he defend it, did he attack it?" p. 58) remained ambiguous.

In brief, Lessing—he, too, was nothing but a "freelancer" without office or commission—was Kierkegaard's ideal ally. He, too, had no supposedly complete system of truth. God alone, and only God, is the truth. He, too, affirmed only pure striving for truth, which includes an ethic. He had already taken a penetrating look at the "vile broad ditch." By that, Kierkegaard meant the 1,800-year historical distance separating the Christ event of the origins and the men and women of today, along with the break this implies with the basic experiences of the first disciples. Kierkegaard had already declared that a direct transition from accidental historical facts to religious certainty was impossible. He had insinuated the necessity of a leap as the only way to establish the necessary simultaneity with the experiences of the earlier time.

So Kierkegaard was familiar with Lessing. But he did not know another great figure who was already at work—Karl *Marx*. In 1848, in the wake of the democratic revolution, the kingdom of Denmark, impoverished after the Napoleonic wars and still under absolutist rule, saw nationally minded young people coming to the fore. This was the year in which Kierkegaard wrote his last great work, *Training in Christianity*, while Marx and Engels were publishing *The Communist Manifesto* in several languages.

Attempts have been made to play both works off against one another. While Marx and Engels, the socialists, were concerned with the *economic misery of the masses*, Kierkegaard reduced the problem to the *religious misery of the individual*. Arguing this way overlooks the fact that agrarian Denmark had a capital that, for all its intellectual vitality, was still quite provincial. And despite the struggle between conservative and progressive forces, it had never known, as Paris had, the "army of industrial reservists" called up by economic, social, and demographic evolution. Hence, it had no experience with a workers' movement, social protest, or socialism.

As for Kierkegaard personally, he was no doubt interested more by questions of aesthetics and literature, philosophy and theology, than by questions of current politics (revolution, war) or science. And as he was by nature not an old Hegelian idealist (E. Hirsch), neither was he a new Hegelian revolutionary (K. Löwith). But on the other hand he protested no less than Marx against Hegel's supposed reconciliation ("mediation") of thought and being, rationality and reality, of the kind the political restoration seemed to confirm, and in this sense he was a pronounced anti-Hegelian (N. Thulstrupp). Nor was there anyone even far beyond the confines of Denmark who would attack, as radically as Kierkegaard did, the popular political-religious paradigm of state, church, and society, thereby risking the ultimate, even his own personal existence.

Kierkegaard the writer and theologian was in many ways a contradictory and yet in the final analysis a consistent man. He was much too passionate in his battle against the indifference and characterlessness of his age not to feel sympathy for the revolution, the time of passions and ideas. But at the same time he kept up his mistrust toward the crowd, the majority, the shaping of opinion by an accumulation of anonymous votes; and so he opposed any sort of parliamentarianism. He had scarcely any awareness of the characteristically nineteenth-century problems of industrialization, capitalism, and imperialism. He was convinced that all questions, even the political and social ones, were ultimately peripheral in comparison with the central religious question. This he addressed in his *Training*, a book as controversial as it is reflective, much more existentially than in the more analytical/philosophical *Concluding Unscientific Postscript: What does it mean to exist, to really be a person?* This is a question that is identical for him to the other: *What does it mean to become a Christian?* Isn't it the Christian's most important responsibility to become a Christian?

No one has raised the question of the relation between the Christian and the human as clearly and acutely as Kierkegaard did. In an age of growing skepticism vis-à-vis pure reason this question has overshadowed the traditional theological question of the relationship between reason and faith. Like Marx, Kierkegaard launches a violent assault on Christianity, but only because he takes average Christianity to be pseudo-Christianity. For him, true Christianity is the kind that can be legitimized by a connection with Christ. And being a Christian, becoming a Christian, does *not* mean for him accepting a specific doctrine, a philosophical or theological system, but committing oneself existentially to this concrete Jesus Christ, who makes up Christianity in its essence. In this respect, Christianity is for Kierkegaard an unquestioned standard of comparison, a spiritual homeland, a critical battleground. He is not concerned in some detached way with a theoretical "introduction" *to*, but with practical "training" *in*, Christianity.

This is Kierkegaard's central reproach: Current Christen*dom* has de facto done away with Christian*ity*. It doesn't even think about a serious commitment to this Jesus Christ—now anymore than it did then. What then are the well-fed burghers, above all the *ministers*, expecting from this Christ—that he will "recognize the status quo as authoritative, convoke all the clergy to a synod, present to the synod his findings as well as his certification. And then, should he get a majority in the secret ballot, he will be accepted and greeted for what he is: the Longed-for-One" (p. 46).

And the Christian *politicians*? As they see it, doesn't this Christ hover in the air, as it were? What does he want? "Does he wish to struggle for the idea of nationality, or does he aim at a communistic overthrow? Does he want a republic or a monarchy? With which party will he make common cause, and against which party? Or does he look to be in good standing with all parties, or will he combat all parties? To commit myself to him—no, that would be the last thing I would want. I'll do even more, I'll take every possible security measure against him" (p. 49). Indeed, this is how the Christian politician thinks: "This person is dangerous, in a certain sense enormously dangerous. But my calculation aims at getting hold of him precisely by doing nothing at all. For he must be overthrown—and the safest way is by making him do it to himself, by tripping over his own feet" (p. 49).

In fact, "Christendom has done away with Christianity, without itself properly noticing this. Consequently, if one wishes to accomplish anything, one must try to introduce Christianity into Christendom once more" (p. 34). But how? Unlike his procedure in the earlier revivalist sermons, which still dealt wholly with a churchly context, Kierkegaard is less interested in the renewal and reform of the institutional church than in the personal Christianity of the individual. Christianity is reintroduced into Christendom through the individual who becomes a Christian. And becoming a Christian means, according to Kierkegaard, *becoming*

contemporary with Jesus—as contemporary as his own contemporaries were with him, as contemporary as someone living at just the same time. What is Christian should take place for us as if it were happening today.

Contemporaneousness is a fundamental category for Kierkegaard, developed as early as the *Philosophical Fragments*. It is the central idea of his life, as he himself confessed, not without pride, in his confrontation with the official church exactly two months before his death:

> I may also say in truth that I have had the honor to suffer in order to bring this thought to light. For this reason, I die gaily, infinitely thankful for the guidance that was given me to become attentive in this way to this idea and to draw others' attention to it. Not that I discovered it, God forbid that I should be guilty of such presumption. No, the invention is old, it goes back to the New Testament. But still I was allowed, in my suffering, to recall this thought to mind, this idea that, like rat powder, is poison for the professors. (*The Moment*, p. 283).

Contemporaneousness is Kierkegaard's answer to the world historical-professorial speculation of Hegel and to Lessing's basic difficulty with the "nasty wide ditch." The temporal distance has to be overcome through the simultaneity of the disciple, which leaves myth and history behind it. Typically mixing piety and polemics as early as the *Invocation*, Kierkegaard presents this simultaneity in the form of a prayer to the Lord: "Lord Jesus Christ, may we too become contemporary with you; may we see you in your true form, wrapped about with reality, just as you went about here on earth, not in the form to which an empty and insignificant or a thoughtlessly enthusiastic or a world-historically chattering thought has mistakenly assigned you. For it is not the form of the humiliation in which the believer sees you, and it cannot possibly be that of the glory in which no one has yet seen you" (p. 5).

Contemporaneousness is the active ferment of the Christian element in Christendom. It reveals what is truly Christian and at the same time unmasks the pseudo-Christian. Training in contemporaneousness is therefore the purpose of all three meditations. Jesus' words open the three parts (originally planned as three autonomous writings). Before all the biblical, conceptual, and existential discussions, right at the beginning, after the "Invocation" of Jesus Christ, they become the "Invitation": "Come to me, all who labor and are heavy laden, and you will find rest." Every individual word is now brought home to the reader with the greatest urgency.

But who will ever accept this invitation? Who will let himself be helped when it becomes clear that the one issuing the invitation has a very different notion of human misery from humans themselves, that for him the actual misery of mankind is not hunger, sickness, and pain, but *guilty alienation from God*? The actual misery, therefore, is the misery of sin. This is not (as for Hegel) a necessary evil, a transitional stage for the good that will triumph in any event, but the untruthfulness of the existing person. It cannot come to light simply through human self-knowledge, but only through divine revelation. And under circumstances like these who would wish to accept the invitation of one who is humiliated and despised, who is a sign of offense for all his contemporaries? No, the actual difficulty of becoming a contemporary of Christ is not the temporal distance, but something else.

"Stop!" suddenly rings out here. This cry aims to prevent any false drawing near to Jesus Christ, or any drawing near to the false Jesus Christ. It aims to return Christianity to its original basis. The "enormous halt," which goes out from the inviter himself, is the "stop that is the condition for faith's coming into existence: You are bidden to stop before the possibility of scandal" (p. 38).

This *stop* applies to the historian's research, which never gets beyond an uncertain approximation. But it also applies to the understanding of the orthodox theologian or the reason of the speculative philosopher, which claim to "prove, and hence to know something," about God. To be sure, the one issuing the invitation is a specific historical person, but none of the "proofs" from the history of philosophy so beloved in the Hegelian school, no speculative knowledge, can be deduced concerning him from history. Indeed, not even from Scripture—its prophecies, miracles, and signs, including the resurrection—can any "proofs," in the strict sense, be adduced for Christ.

This Christ implies for human beings—and here we have, along with contemporaneousness, another key word that Kierkegaard introduced into theology—a *paradox*. Such a paradox must appear to objective thought as the absurd, something that can be accepted only on *faith*. The code of paradox in this process is not to serve as a justification for all possible mysteries of faith fabricated by the theologians, which are only obstacles to an authentic faith decision. No, Kierkegaard means here paradox pure and simple—Jesus Christ as an "object of faith, there only for faith." He means "scandal pure and simple," which consists in the fact *that an individual person is God, i.e., says he is God* (p. 23). Amid all that is historically conditioned Christianity is "the unconditioned" (p. 61), because God himself, Christ, is the unconditioned: eternity breaking into time, God in the form of a servant under the signature of unrecognizability, of the incognito (cf. H. Gerdes, H. Fischer). This had not become evident even to Jesus' contemporaries. And today, too, one can become contemporary to Jesus only in faith.

All these thoughts are pressed further and sharpened in the second and third part of the *Training*, beginning with Jesus words, "Blessed is he who is not scandalized in me," as well as, "And I, when I am lifted up from the earth, will draw all men to myself." These remarks are directed at both the church as an institution and its teaching, which aim to deprive the individual of personal decision, while presenting themselves as divine. Here Kierkegaard develops a third famous concept, *the existing order*. This phrase made history and even then was the prime reason why the primate of the Danish church considered Kierkegaard's book written against him, the bishop (with the other half written against Martensen, the professor of theology).

The existing order in the general sense is the totality of things standing outside decision, what Heidegger later called "das Man." At the time of Jesus the existing order was Judaism, which "precisely because of the Pharisees and the scribes had become a complacent, self-deifing existing order" (p. 83). But at the time of Kierkegaard the existing order was *Christendom*, which, with its bourgeois self-satisfaction and state support, is represented by the hierarchy and theology, by the bishop, behind whom stands the clergy, and by the professor, behind whom stand the students. The existing order prides itself on being objective reality, higher than any individual, than all subjectivity. Indeed, it boasts of being the whole, which knows nothing over itself and has the right to give orders to every individual. As at the time of Jesus the existing order, which posits itself as absolute, again takes offense at the individual witness to truth. "What does this individual then imagine; does he perhaps imagine that he is God, or that he has an immediate relationship to God, or even that he is more than human?" (p. 80).

But, according to Kierkegaard, this is a "mishearing." In fact the situation is exactly the opposite. "The existing order secretly tells itself that *it* is the divine" (p. 82). But the fact that the existing order *wishes to be something divine* and wishes to be taken for divine is, according to Kierkegaard, a falsification and a denial of that order's actual origin. It is self-deification, permanent insurrection against God. In fact in the existing order of Christendom custom and usage, laws and ceremonies, have become an end in themselves, articles of faith—everything equally important, everything divinized. This, says Kierkegaard, is a fear of God that is de facto a contempt for God, a divinization that is de facto a secularization.

Indeed, what has become of this church of Christ?

First of all, has the *Church Militant* of the beginnings, which, far from its goal, saw itself as only on the way, in conflict with a society that was not Christian? Has not this Church Militant turned into a *Church Triumphant* that understands itself as the possessor of the all-conquering truth of Christ, that fancies itself already at the goal, that appeals to its great history? But it is fully adapted to the world and has become reconciled with bourgeois society, in which all persons are presumably Christians.

Secondly, what of *Christian preaching*, that great act of daring in the presence of an invisible hearer, God himself, in which what is at stake is quite personally the ego of the preacher and of the audience? Hasn't this preaching turned into *pious meditations* and artful lectures on a subject, a topic, in which along with the I the Thou has also gotten lost?

Thirdly, haven't the *practical followers* of the humiliated Christ, who is himself the model for individuals and the whole community, turned into *adoring admirers* of the exalted Christ? Whether detached or involved, they applaud Christ as if in a theater, from the perspective of observers. And yet they give up nothing. Rather, if they have not fully laid the Christian life aside, they have nonetheless shifted it into constricted interiority where it has no consequences.

————————◆————————

In truth, Søren Kierkegaard is a challenge even today, and by no means only because of this critique of the church, but in the first instance because of his understanding of God and Christ. To be sure, we can also raise serious theological *objections* against him (the downplaying of politics and science in his work has already been spoken of). Taking Lessing's perspective, we can raise three objections:

1. Kierkegaard considers anyone who doubts Christian reve-lation—an unquestionable, nondiscussable fact, as he sees it—as ipso facto a sinner. He uses the category of contemporaneousness to obscure completely the historicocritical questions (though he did know about them). These issues are posed by altogether sin-cere scholars who in the New Testament itself distinguish between the words of the historical Jesus and those of the community, and who above all find they cannot come right out and ascribe the words of the Johannine Christ (which Kierkegaard loves to quote) to the Jesus of history.

2. In particular, Kierkegaard overlooks the fact that the Jesus of history never called himself "God," the "God-man," and prob-ably not the "Son of God" either. Indeed, Jesus did not even want to be called "good master," because only one is good, God himself.

3. Kierkegaard shifts the "scandal," as it were, from Good Friday to Christmas. But, according to Paul, the "skandalon" in the strict sense does not consist simply (to speak in Greek-Platonic terms) in the fact that "a man is God" (the Eternal in time), but that (to speak in Jewish, Old Testament terms) the Messiah, the Christ, the Son of the one God (and for Paul, too, the Father alone is God) is to be the crucified one. For Jews, this is a stum-bling block, for pagans a true folly, and only for believers the power and wisdom of God (cf. 1 Cor. 1:24).

Nevertheless, for all the possible and necessary historicocritical distinctions we have to concede this to Kierkegaard: In the face of modern evolution in the church and theology, he established

in a powerful and original way what all of New Testament tradition agreed in proclaiming as crucial, what nineteenth-century
modern liberal theology increasingly lost sight of, and what Karl
Barth and the "theology of crisis" were the first to bring back
into focus after the First World War, the breakdown of cultural
Protestantism and liberal theology: the *distinctively Christian* or,
as Kierkegaard himself says, *Christianity "as the unconditioned"*
(p. 61). This means that for all the modern God-being-in-the-
world and world-being-in-God there remains an infinite qualitative difference between God and the world, between God and
man; that for all the possible revelations of God in other religions
the one God is revealed, spoke, and acted in this one person,
Jesus, in a unique way; that this revelation of God took place
under the sign of unrecognizability, that the Lord is found only
in the incognito of the servant; and that man, therefore—without
being compelled by any proofs from Scripture and history—is
faced with an either/or: either to take offense or to believe, either
to remain a heathen or essentially, sincerely, to become a Christian. Nevertheless, Kierkegaard admits that "No one can tell a
person to what extent he will succeed in essentially becoming a
Christian. But dread and fear and desperation are of no use.
Uprightness before God is the first and last thing, to confess one's
condition sincerely, uprightly before God, continually keeping
one's responsibility in view—however slowly one may go, even
if one only creeps forward" (pp. 65–66).

Training in Christianity is Kierkegaard's great legacy in which
the foundations were laid for the conflict that would soon break
out with his church, and which ended with Kierkegaard's complete
physical exhaustion, his collapse in the street, and his peaceful,
happy death at the age of forty-two (on November 11, 1855). He
lived to be three years older than Pascal, with whom he had till
the very end so much in common. His church gave him a solemn
funeral, against his will and with his nephew protesting at the
grave against this coopting. But it did not accept his legacy, and
it did not consider confessing its failure vis-à-vis the message of
the New Testament. Apart from exceptions in Scandinavia, the
theologians ignored Kierkegaard the outsider. Instead, it was a
handful of writers such as Ibsen, Jacobsen, and Strindberg who
listened to his voice.

In Europe, the church and theology would remain for a long

time stuck in the romantic vein. In the history of modern literature, romanticism represents the last movement in which religion still played a key role. But after the phase of political restoration basically came to an end in 1848, the year of revolution, not only science, history, and philosophy, but in the second half of the century literature, too, increasingly developed without any sort of religious frame of reference. Indeed, this evolution often occurred under the sign of naturalism, positivism, and atheism. This was a late phase within the modern paradigm, all of whose ambivalence we have not been able to appreciate till today, when the euphoria of progress has faded away in the transition to postmodernity.

Kierkegaard, the warner of the first half of the century, had tried to call attention in a timely fashion to the crucial fact that alongside the aesthetic dimension there is also an ethical dimension, and alongside the ethical there is the religious; that in all, the conditioned man has to deal with the unconditioned; that the individual in the presence of God—even in the face of the leveling, collectivist tendencies of early mass society—has an irreplaceable, irreversible, sacrosanct value; and that the individual and society can find an unconditional standard for the ultimate and primary questions of orientation in life—not, of course, in the existing order, but in true, original Christianity, in Jesus Christ himself.

To be sure, in his *Training*, as he observed in his three forewords (which, in the end, he retracted) to the three individual parts, Kierkegaard did "raise the requirements for being a Christian to their highest level of idealism." To be sure, in his last year when he was driven by the struggle with the church into complete isolation, Kierkegaard was all too ready to make his own "exceptional existence" the general norm. To be sure, with his critique of the bourgeois national, established church, Kierkegaard—as a "man of the spirit"—also poured contempt on marriage, women, and sexuality.

But from the beginning Kierkegaard was a highly sensitive, complicated, pathologically burdened, and overreflective "exceptional existence," long before Dostoyevsky and Kafka, who will occupy us later. And precisely because of this he showed a brilliant psychological flair for everything beneath and behind the scene. It is no wonder, then, that modernity first had to plunge into a crisis with the First World War and the breakdown of bourgeois culture and the state church in Europe before people would pay any attention to Kierkegaard. He got a hearing, first of all, from theologians and philosophers, above all from Barth, Bultmann, and Tillich; and he found a broad echo not just in Heidegger, Jaspers, Marcel, and Sartre, but also in Adorno and, in a subterranean fashion, in Marcuse, Bloch, and Wittgenstein.

To be sure, Kierkegaard the Protestant is himself what he called Protestantism in general, *not the norm but a corrective*. And as a corrective, as the precursor of a new theology, church, and Christendom, he got more support than anyone could have assumed he would in the Christian world at the time.

For, from Europe to North and South America we find nowadays a double development that he foresaw: on the one hand, the apparently unstoppable breakup of the existing state and national churches of Protestant (or Catholic) provenance; on the other hand, (despite all resistance from above) the decisive Christianization of countless individuals as well as new groups and communities, from the foundations upward. In short, we are witnessing *a reintroduction of Christianity into Christendom from the bottom up*.

WALTER JENS

◆

Now,
When We Need
Martyrs by the Thousands

Come unto me, all you who labor and are heavy burdened,
and I will give you rest. . . . You disdained and overlooked,
whose existence no one, no one at all looks after, not so
much as they do for a house pet, which has more value!—
You sick, lame, deaf, blind, cripples, come here! You lepers!
. . . The invitation blasts away all distinctions, so as to unite
all. It aims at repairing the damange done by drawing distinctions: by directing the one to his place as lord over millions along with the possession of all the blessings of
happiness, and sending the other out into the wilderness.
. . . All you victims of malice and betrayal and slander and
envy, you whom vileness has chosen for itself, whom cow-
ardice has left in the lurch, though you may now fall by the
wayside and alone as victims, after you have stepped aside to
die, or are trampled on in the press of people, where no one
asks what right you have, no one asks what injustice you are
suffering, no one asks how it . . . can hurt, when the crowd
treads you down into the dust: Come here! The invitation
stands at the crossroads, where death draws the line between
death and life. Come here, all you who bear your suffering
. . . (and) vainly struggle under the burden!

It is moving to see how Søren Kierkegaard, the role-player and playactor (ever new masks, pseudonyms, characters, and costumes) now at the end of his life reflects insistently and consistently on a *single figure*. It is moving to see how this inventive, chameleonlike writer leaves his imaginary stage and says farewell to his beloved shadow images of yesterday, his Don Juan and Faust, his Job and Abraham, his Abraham, and Donna Elvira. And from 1848 on, after canceling his borrowed names at the end of the *Concluding Unscientific Postscript*, he carries on his great dialogue with the single *alter ego* left him, Jesus of Nazareth. Jesus is a figure he tries to secure with the help of the pseudonym Anti-Climacus. In contrast to the other names he took on, Eremita or Constantius or Buchbinder, this one stands *over* him. This is no theatrical role, therefore, into which a sovereign subject can slip. It is a fictitious figure that has the author at its disposition and makes him its servant, while the author dares to approach it only in parables, only poetically and allusively.

Anti-Climacus is a masculine Beatrice with a Danish twist who accompanies the hesitating Virgil (alias Søren Kierkegaard) from Inferno to Paradiso. The name Anti-Climacus was not supposed to be a symbol of the sovereignty of an omnipotent magician, but a sign of voluntary limitation for the author of *Sickness unto Death* and *Training in Christianity*. In Kierkegaard's report on his "activity as a writer," we read that (my) "whole earlier pseudonymity has a lower position than the 'edifying writer.' The new pseudonym is a higher pseudonymity . . . [now] 'a halt has been called': Something higher is presented that forces me back into my limits, passing judgment on me, because my life does not correspond to such a lofty challenge. And hence the piece is too literary."

Anti-Climacus, Kierkegaard's last mask, is different from all the rest. It is the sign of a penitent who knows that he is no apostle, no martyr, and no witness to God, who lets himself be struck dead for the truth's sake. He knows that as a religious writer his is a genius whose task it is—without an apostolic mandate, but nevertheless sure of the way—to restore what is Christian to its rights by attention-grabbing discourse. This means to bring Christianity back to Christendom, which has fallen away from the Nazarene. In this way, Kierkegaard would have us follow the Jesus who, more anti-Hegelian than a figure of flesh and blood, flared up in the *Philosophical Fragments*. Shortly there-

after, this Jesus made an appearance in sermons, spiritual discourses (which Kierkegaard basically wrote under his own name),
in the meditations of the repentant genius, Anti-Climacus, and
finally in the accusations where he played the part of the great
counterfigure to the whole existing order (at once its witness and
judge). Jesus was the star witness for the prosecution, called in
by the author of the *Moment* against a church. By this, Kierkegaard meant the church in the sign of the Antichrist, a church
that was neither his own, nor, as Kierkegaard maintained with
an increasingly histrionic, even grotesque shrillness, the church
of Christ.

On the one hand, Jesus of Nazareth always was—and remained—the figure of *art*. Kierkegaard decked this Jesus out with
his old, favorite (because highly personal) set pieces. He gave
him the incognito and coded way of speaking of a religious genius,
to whom direct communication was denied, since he lived in an
unrecognizable condition. On the other hand, however, after 1848
Kierkegaard's Jesus began to step out of the Socratic darkness.
He moved out of the charmed circle of the wise man who would
bring the truth to light by playing the part of the midwife-artist,
and took on some unmistakable features of his own.

The paradox of the minor servant who brings the light could
be documented not just with Christ, but also with Socrates. This
paradox is completed by reference to Jesus' discourses and actions, to his origin and environment, to his teaching, offensive as
it was, to his followers beneath the cross, and his opponents, then
and today, on the judgment seat and in the church pew.

With a realism and a precision that can be found nowhere else
in religious literature after 1830 (the fading years of romanticism),
Kierkegaard makes the *historical* Jesus visible in the humiliated
and contemporary Jesus, the one who is *always* coming (not returning) and determining the moment (not history). Jesus is a
man who remains present across the ages, not because of his
ubiquitousness and his interchangeable typology, but because of
his "this way and no other." His *peculiarity*, Kierkegaard says,
is what makes Jesus not timeless, but present, wherever someone
believes. For that very reason (a preview of Dostoyevsky's Grand
Inquisitor) Jesus is so dangerous for some Christian-minded persons. If the Nazarene appeared here and now in Copenhagen with
his retinue of marginal figures, all the failures and outsiders, such

"Christians" might not execute the Messiah (they wouldn't take him seriously enough for that), but they would wrinkle their noses and give him a dressing-down.

Get rid of him, cover him with gossip and contempt! In a grandiose scene, Kierkegaard invites Copenhagen society for a grand review, has the Christian burgher becoming incensed at the child born out of wedlock, has the churchman articulating his dignitary's misgivings: Can one really approve Jesus' attempt at wide-ranging church reform without the sanction of the authorities?

With one panther leap, Kierkegaard dashes from Palestine to Denmark, from Herod's palace to the Strøget. The "then" becomes "now," and the Pharisees slip into the suits of Danish bourgeois, who, without noticing it, have stripped off their Christianity. Kierkegaard makes this clear through the lament that the churchly Christians settled between the North Sea and the Baltic intone upon the emergence of the *contemporary* Jesus: Clergyman and philosophers, statesmen and honest citizens (along with mockers and charitable Maecenases) are one and all filled with blank incomprehension. They can't get over the fact

that a person who looks like that, . . . whose company everyone flees, provided he has the tiniest bit of brains in his skull, or has the tiniest bit of property to lose in the world; the fact that—and this is the most absurd and craziest thing of all, one doesn't know whether to laugh or cry about it— that he, yes, this is absolutely the very last word that one would have expected to hear from him (for if he had said, come here and help me, or leave me alone, or spare me, or [proudly] I despise you all—*that* one could understand)—that he (however) says: come to me! Yes indeed, this certainly looks inviting. And then, later, all you who labor and are heavy laden—this is just as if such persons didn't already have more than enough misfortune to drag around with them, that in addition they should now be exposed to all the consequences that commitment to him brings with it. And then last of all, I will give you rest. That was the only thing lacking—*he'll* help them. . . . Trying to help others when oneself is in such a state. That is just as if a beggar were to report to the police that he'd been robbed.

This passage makes it suddenly evident that even the late Kierkegaard ("late" in quotation marks, a man not yet forty years old) was as much in command of his old art of slipping into masks, of opening up brain pans, analyzing thoughts, shedding light on moods, as he had been in his playful phase.

But during *Either/Or* and the *Concluding Unscientific Postscript* Kierkegaard had rushed out, so to speak, under the stars and into the world kingdom of legend (What did Nero, what did Nebuchadnezzar do? What was Abraham thinking as he went to Mount Moriah, both companions at his side, the beloved son and the murderous knife, which God had thrust into his hand? And what was Isaac thinking, when he recognized the Angel of Death silently going alongside him? What did the marked and the seduced think, the unhappy ones, emigrants from the regions of normalcy? These were characters whom Kierkegaard edged up to with an experimental, psychological art that spilled over into the paradoxical, in a way that of his successors only Kafka mastered). And then there were Victor Eremita, Frater Taciturnus, Vigilius Haufniensis, Nicholas Notabene, and *tutti quanti*, the great exceptional figures, demons, unhappy and desperate souls. They sought to trace out ever new variations, continual retractions, shifts of accent and perspective (Here! See what I make out of Job! There! Abraham with the knife! See what a modern Solomon looks like, or a Sarah who knows how to reflect). By contrast, Anti-Climacus and Kierkegaard, the author of the edifying, pious, and Christian discourses, placed all the emphasis on the psychoanalysis of the *One and Only*—and on the thoughts of the Christians, the robust meditations of the pastors, the careful calculations of the churchgoers in the front pews, the strategic evaluations of the press, and the cynicism of the so-called men of the people.

Kierkegaard's radius had grown smaller. Measured against the artful interlocking complexities of the early work, where author, editor, collector of quotations, and writer sometimes engaged in four-tiered games of concealment, the theatrical productions of the last works look modest. Kierkegaard himself said that his early technique helped to make his position so complicated that "the one author ultimately lies inside the other like the boxes in a Chinese box game."

But after all he remained the old mirror artist, romanticist and director of an inner—his own inner—theater. He was always intent on mirroring reality in significant play, in a world of thoughts and—like the Musilian *Monsieur le Vivisecteur* that he was—on mirroring his own perceptions, dreams, fears, and despair in the fears and nonfears, the despairs and self-certainties, of others.

With the exception of the *Writings About Himself*, which were not published until after his death and then only in the most mutilated condition possible, between his debut as Victor Eremita and his swan song as Anti-Climacus Kierkegaard *never* spoke about himself. And yet he *always* did. He said not a word about Michael Pedersen Kierkegaard, his father, who wanted to sacrifice his son Søren to God. And yet this Michael Pedersen, in his ruthlessness, his religious fanaticism, and his remorse, which made him worthy of compassion, was present in the thoughts running through Abraham's head, and in the speech where Solomon protests against Yahweh. He was present in the here and now.

Kierkegaard spoke no word either, in *Either/Or* and *Repetition*, about Regine Olsen, the young woman he broke his engagement to, because he didn't want to impose on her his melancholy and religious despondency. He sacrificed Regine, presumably in God's name (just as Abraham had to sacrifice his dearest possession, his son, at Yahweh's command), publicly exposed her, and put her on stage by transforming life into play. He mimicked the seducer and aesthetic demon (something he was not), signed a pact with Hell *in effigie* ("I had to go to Hell in order to learn how a devil looks"), and used the sacrifice of a woman to establish himself as a writer who made artistic documents out of love letters. He did this by inserting the notes, originally directed to Regine, into a romantic diary, the "Painful History" of Quidam. (Goethe treated his erstwhile beloved, Frau von Stein, no less despicably, by using letters meant for her in the *Italian Journey*.)

Here we see reality transformed on paper into a thousand possibilities by a brilliant role-player. The one indicative is reworked into countless subjunctives placed with calligraphic accuracy. Here a man, praising occasionalism, pours out a never-ending stream of reflections. He is encouraged to do so by promptings from the realm of the Living One (insofar as he has not long since anticipated them in poetry). Here, on the soul stage of Søren Kierkegaard, new troops keep on marching in, and in Copenhagen an aesthetic cynic celebrates his triumphs. This was a person whom one of Kierkegaard's beloved romantics, Jean Paul, crystallized in the figure of Roquairol (from the *Titan*). Roquairol was

> a child and victim of the century. . . . All the splendid conditions of humanity, all movements, to which love and friendship and nature lift the heart, he experienced all these things sooner in poetry than in life, sooner as an actor and dramatic poet than as a person, sooner on the sunny side of fantasy than on the stormy side of reality. Hence when they finally appeared alive in his bosom, he was able to grasp them calmly, kill them, and stuff them well for the ice cave of future memory.

Ice cave of future memory: It was under the sign of this definition, a lightninglike, illuminating description of the artist that both Nietzsche and Thomas Mann would have approved—it was under the sign of this maxim of Jean Paul that Kierkegaard tried to exist. He tried to exist in dialogue, first of all, with his imaginary figures. He sought to describe their transcendence of limits in parables and artistic exercises, the masterpieces of his poetry. (It was no accident that Kafka later did a variation on the meditation on Abraham and Isaac.) He tried to exist in dialogue, secondly, with his dead father and his abandoned bride, his sacrifice, for whom during all his life he stored in the cupboard a second copy from the shelf of his *opera omnia*. He tried to exist in dialogue, finally, at the end of his life, with Jesus of Nazareth, into the folds of whose mantle he slipped, so that in his name (better, as his echo) he could admonish the Christian world. Kierkegaard wanted to warn Christians about holding to a course that was heading directly to the little white point he describes in his parable of the luxury liner. This was a sort of dream anticipation of the *Titanic*, with one thousand passengers who, thanks to the "music, song, and conversation," forget the night and the danger around them.

Already marked out for death, a few weeks before his end, Kierkegaard asked what would happen, if not even the captain recognized the white point on the horizon. What if the only one to recognize it was a passenger to whom no one, least of all the captain, paid any attention; what if the captain would let himself

be brought out on deck only against his will? And that isn't all:
The captain has to be grabbed by the sleeve, as he pretends to
be deaf, and by the same token, immerses himself in the "noisy,
rollicksome joy of the company in the cabin, where amid general
jubilation his health is toasted, for which he politely thanks
everyone."

The ship is Christendom—on the way to destruction. The
helmsmen, bishops, pastors, theologians—under the spell of a
world to whose amusements ("noise and rattling of plates and
dishes, champagne corks pop, people drink to the captain's
health") they have sacrificed the only important thing, the eternal
salvation of their souls. For the sake of their salvation, they are
obliged to "die to" the world, instead of being at its service. The
only man awake amidst the sleepers and dreamers—a man without authority or the power to command—is one Søren Kierkegaard, who, when he says "I," lets it be known "that, from the
Christian point of view, the white point on the horizon is visible.
It means that a terrible storm is threatening—I knew that, but I
am and was only a passenger."

An artist full of puzzles and contradictoriness, this Kierkegaard.
He, too, like Pascal or Novalis, was a double being: a romantic
aesthete and a Christian warner, a prefiguration of Tonio Kröger,
who despises and nonetheless longs for the joys of habit. He was
a monomaniacal loner who sings the praises of marriage; a *path-
ological egoist*, on the order of Lichtenberg, who unlike his model
from Göttingen could never have broken through to that gripping
song for the dead, the way Lichtenberg sang to his beloved, little
Stechardin. But Søren Kierkegaard was nonetheless a man who
experienced his isolation not only as a distinction—because God-
given—but also as guilt. He thought he had to issue warnings
about himself, and played before his readers the role of Simon
the leper who had the salve to make his abcesses invisible, but
avoided using it. He wanted no one to get infected by him, this
Victor Eremita (who was in truth a *Victus*), and catch his
melancholy.

Can we imagine Søren Kierkegaard married, in a comfortable
situation, the father of a family? A pedagogue surrounded by his
nearest and dearest? Johannes Climacus, alias Hilarius Buchbinder, highly decorated, frequenting the court, and respected as
a sort of shining example of bourgeois society? It's unthinkable.

If anyone was lonely among the writers of his century (when eccentrics were not exactly in short supply), then Søren Kierkegaard was. He was lonely as Proust would be after him, playing the part of the flâneur. He was lonely amidst the people, thanks to a press campaign against him, undertaken by the liberal freebooter magazine *The Corsair*. Cartoons pictured him as the crank with the cane, the humpback, his hat shoved back down onto his neck, so that even old friends no longer dared to greet the butt of mockery.

Kierkegaard was lonely in his study and lonely in the theater. There, hidden in the dusk of his loge, he made the great parade pass by him on the stage, as was his wont. There he played something like the part of Adam, watching the deployment of the people and animals gathered for the grand march. He felt bored and ultimately even vexed, because, as Kierkegaard says, referring to the Progenitor of humanity, "among them all he doesn't find one who really satisifes him; and so he gives them their walking papers."

No, Kierkegaard, the author of *Either/Or* and *Training in Christianity*, didn't like people. He annihilated some (Paul Ludvig Møller, for example, his opponent in the *Corsair* controversy). He was a man who could acknowledge only individuals, only "exceptions," but no groups acting in solidarity. He despised the public, Christendom, the anonymity of the many, in brief, human beings so long as they apeared in troops. The manner in which Kierkegaard—in one of his most fascinating descriptions, a showpiece from *Repetition*—describes the ambience of the theater, the happiness of isolation and the fear of the "perspiration of the audience of art enthusiasts," betrays the snob and passionate aesthete, who mixed with the people only once. This was not during the revolution, of course; there he remained a spectator on the fringes. It was in Berlin, when Schelling held the lectures that the cultivated world hastened to attend. Some, like Kierkegaard, came by ship (via Stralsund); others, like the subsequently famous Marxist Friedrich Engels, came by coach (from Lichterfelde, where he was doing his military service). In letters that the twenty-four-year-old student wrote from Denmark to Peter Johannes Spang and Friedrich Sibbern in the fall of 1841, Kierkegaard notes, "Schelling has begun, but amid such a ruckus and din, whistles, and pounding on the window panes by those who couldn't get in, with an audience so crammed together that if it keeps up this way, one would almost like to renounce listening to him. Externally Schelling is an extremely insignificant man, he looks like a tax collector. . . . In the meantime I have put my trust in him and I wish to take the chance of hearing him once again, though I risk my life."

This already sounds a bit self-satisfied and self-mocking, like everything else Kierkegaard did up to the second great conversion, at which point he began to understand himself as a "religious writer." (The first "rebirth" took place ten years earlier and was written down in Pascalian fashion: "There is an indescribable joy," Kierkegaard wrote in his diary, "that shines through us as inexplicably as the unfounded outburst of the Apostle: Rejoice . . . a joy that like a breath of wind cools and refreshes, a breeze that blows from the grove of Mamre to the everlasting huts. 19 May, 10:30 in the morning."

Did this mean, then, that the artist, psychologist, and literary dialectician, operating on the lowest level of Kierkegaard's world structure, abruptly leaps over the middle stage (home of the ethicians and administrators of the universal), and is catapulted to the highest step? From here—saved now!—he surveys a period in which the great and celebrated seducers, monomaniacs with a metaphysical tic like the dissector of souls, Constantin Constantius, or the merman from the *Painful History*, carried out their experiments, described with horror and admiration.

The phase of aestheticizing playacting, presented before a crowd of readers blinded by Chinese puzzles and philosophical fireworks, had passed. Was it to be replaced by strict instruction that dispensed with artistic sleight of hand, and dealt in preaching, treatises, and pious meditation?

Was this the once-and-for-all reduction of the aesthetic to the absurd? Had Kierkegaard's poetic operations, with the sketch of ever new pairs of opposites, reached their goal at the end of a "gradually progressive literary effectiveness"? Such a course, as the foreword to the "Two Discourses at Center Aisle on Friday" puts it, "started off with *Either/Or* and seeks its decisive point of rest at the foot of the altar."

Was the reconciliation of religion and poetry—under the sign of Anti-Climacus—labeled once and for all as madness? Was the realm of the poetic, in Kierkegaard's view, to be overcome, "like a joke"? Was poetry incapable of presenting the ultimate and most actual of all things—the person standing before God in repentance, believing certitude, and responsibility? There can be no doubt that Kierkegaard, after 1848, actually thought so and was determined to sacrifice the aesthetic to the religious. As he once had with Regine, now he would abandon art. But this abandonment would come from the one who had (all too long) been the seduced one, no longer, as once before, from the sovereign seducer.

This was Kierkegaard imitating Pascal: In both cases the diabolical pact with aestheticism was to be dismissed, and the artist posing as autonomous was to be put in his place. This was the figure whom the Magister from Copenhagen sought to dispose of in that grand image of the printing error that refuses to be corrected, and so brings the pitiableness of its writer to light.

It is a moving drama: Two writers, Pascal and Kierkegaard, each in his own way, wish to sacrifice themselves—and neither can do it. Both *write* about the sacrifice instead of *making* it. Both say farewell to the world, but in high poetic fashion. Both attack the devil, the heretics, their spiritual adversaries, but with a journalistic brio, in the *Provincial Letters*, or in the *Moment*, Kierkegaard's last and most bitter attack—with a verve that makes the heart of all the gourmets in Inferno, all the aestheticizing agnostics, beat faster. What refinement in the struggle against the subtleties of the Evil One!

Thus the later Kierkegaard was blinded by an idealistic theory that wished to give the aesthetic first place among the arts of understanding (blinded besides by the romantic axiom that "to live poetically means to live truthfully"). And blinded in this way he tried to devalue the poetic, but he would not *give it up*. At least as a means to his end, pressed into service by belief, it had to have its justification for the religious writer, too. Even if it could not transmit truth itself, poetry was nonetheless useful in luring people into this very truth by cunning adaptation to the world.

Kierkegaard saw poetry as an art of insinuation, which "in rapport" with those in need of redemption can strengthen faith *per negationem* by showing the sensory delusion of this world.

Literature was a midwifery of the one, holy truth. Poetry was a maieutics within the world, practiced by a band of poeticizing secret police who—with the author of the posthumous treatise "The Viewpoint for My Literary Activity" at their head—try to find their way as "God's spies." In fact Søren Kierkegaard had to pull out all the stops on his dialectic to get literature back in through the back door, having just chased it out the front. Reversing the Kantian dictum, he declared that it was no longer suitable for carrying the torch before theology, but of holding its train behind.

This was an attempt, in other words, at an act of castration. It was an attempt to deprive of its power the aesthetic realm that Kierkegaard the romantic, even at the end of his life, continued to view as evil and antireligious. But was this really that sort of deprivation? Or was it rather a secret homage to the omnipotence of the poetry without whose support even—and especially—the religious writer would not make it?

Kierkegaard might disparage the poet ("A poet now!" he wrote in his diaries in 1849, "Now when we need, if possible, martyrs by the thousands, the real rescue team!"). Weary with speech, he might glorify the silence of the lilies and the birds. Still, he was rhapsodically disparaging and glorifying silence with the help of a rhetoric that intoxicates and entrances the listener. With every sentence that Kierkegaard the religious writer in his last phase uses to damn poetry, he testifies at the same time that he cannot live without it. Because even the witness of the pious—the speech of Christ's follower—has no other way to work except poetically, ironically, with images, an aggressively pamphleteering and rhetorical style.

One need only read *Training in Christianity* and note how—and this bears repeating—the old role-player and imitator has his Danes argue about Jesus, his contemporary, how he brings his troops up onto the stage and gives his actors monologues that with their witty retorts could be taken from a farce by Nestroy rather than from a theological treatise. "The honorable burgher"—assuming he met Jesus in Copenhagen—"would probably repeat his family's ruling maxim: *No, leave us humans alone.*" As the parrot in Andersen's fairy tale, "The Galoshes of Happiness," remarks so pointedly, "everything in moderation":

and I heard the French proverb from a traveling salesman: Whatever aims too high ends up on its face—and this person (this Jesus), really his downfall is as good as certain. I too have seriously taken my son to task, admonished him, and warned him that he won't get that past me . . . and join up with this person, and why? Just because everybody is running after him. Indeed, who are they all? . . . idlers and vagrants, who can't give up riding around. But not a whole lot of settled people, and not a single one of those prudent and respected people by whom I . . . set my watch, neither state councillor Jeppesen, nor conference councillor Marcus, nor the rich agent Christophersen, no, no, *those* people know already what something is and what it isn't. And then let's pay attention only to the clergy, who (after all) understand best how things are. As Pastor Grönvald said yesterday evening in the club: "*This* life will end in horror"; and the lad can do more than just preach, you have to hear him, not on Sundays in the church but Mondays in the club. . . . He said quite rightly, the words could have come from my own heart: "It's only unstable, idle people who run after him. And why do they chase after him? Because he can do a few miracles."

And yet some critics say that the author of *Training in Christianity* is a lesser writer, measured against the author of *Either/Or*. This is surely false. The description of the lowly Jesus and the dubious company around him, a parade of notorious, crazy, despised figures is, thanks to the combination of pathos and precision, no less a showpiece of mysterious beatification than the presentation of the bookkeeper who lives in wretchedness and dies in isolation in the parable, "A Possibility" (from the *Painful Story*, Brother Taciturn's psychological experiment).

Kierkegaard writes with all sorts of nuances, when he tries to approach Jesus, via Anti-Climacus, from the perspective of the witness beneath the cross. He writes with great levelheadedness, despite his anger, so long as he remains in the shadow of that One whose life he wished—like Pascal, like Dostoyevsky—to present in a comprehensive, not just epigrammatic fashion.

Nevertheless, his diction become noticeably shrill when, falling all over himself in self-assurance and insistence on always being right, he attacks the church for falling away from Christ and has his Climacus, with whom he ultimately identifies himself, sit in judgment on Christendom.

I know what Christianity is: With this motto Kierkegaard delivers a stern lecture to the "junk and nonsense church." This was a church in which the martyrs were few in number and the "honored and revered councillors" were all the more plentiful. It was a hypocritically pious church that had made the spat-upon, crucified one into a "great man," who stood for solvency and reputability. "I prefer to gamble, drink, go whoring, steal, and murder," Kierkegaard wrote in *The Moment*,

> than consider God a fool. I would rather spend my days at bowling alleys and in billiard rooms, my nights at the roulette table or masquerades, than share in that seriousness that Bishop Martensen calls Christian. Indeed, I would rather take God for a complete fool, climb up some elevated place, or go out into open country, where I would be alone with him and there say straight out: "You're a good-for-nothing God, of no use except to be taken for a fool." Better that than take him for a fool by solemnly putting on the pious act that my life is all industry and zeal for Christianity.

As soon as Kierkegaard begins to shout—against the Christian states, the Christian nations, the Christian provinces, against the "silk-and-satin pastors," the spiritual-worldly chancellors, the Christian murderers and Christian pimps, the soul-murdering pastors, the comedians bellowing in the pulpits—he gets short of breath, his language turns monotonous, the argumentation stereotyped. But then suddenly there is the old flash of caustic wit and grandiose satire, when the bartender, who gives alcohol to youths, appears as a venial sinner in comparison to the priest who cheats confirmands out of their salvation. The wit flashes again, when, in the aphorisms "Brief and Pointed," the most malicious thing Kierkegaard wrote against the leaders of Christendom, the gap between church ideology and Christian truth is sharply defined: "In the splendid cathedral church the Honorable, Reverend

Privy General Head Preacher appears, the chosen favorite of the fashionable world. He appears before a select group of select individuals and preaches, deeply moved, on the text he himself has picked: 'God has chosen things low and contemptible'—and nobody laughs."

Here we have an individual addressing the world. Nietzsche, who was likewise filled with the sense of mission of a man of spirit in a herd of mass men, would philosophize in 1888 with the same pathos of a "genius without authority." He would try, "seven thousand feet above sea level," to shout down his isolation by preaching, not an encoded message of Jesus, filled with poetry and secret refractoriness, but, on the contrary, a stiff, legalistic gospel. Here Kierkegaard's discourse, instead of making the most of the iridescent ambiguity of crazy provocations—as would have befitted someone who secretly rivaled Shakespeare—slips into the simplicity of a theatrical countersermon. It still has sarcasm and wit, but no dialectic, no doubt, and no opening up and questioning of issues—even if only sentence by sentence.

Instead of the interplay between the positions and the abundance of references, the power of allusion and poetic transparency, the only thing left in the end is rigid antitheses and harsh confrontations between salvation and apostasy. Only in the 1850s does the formula either/or, which had never been definitively accepted before, become the motto of Kierkegaard's writing—and not to its advantage. What had once been great religious poetry—presentation of the doubting, erring, overbearing, repenting man before God—became in the end dogmatic discourse. It turned into the confession of a passenger, pronouncing *ex cathedra* in the most extreme isolation, as he watched a ship without a helmsman sail into the storm. Meanwhile, he, the only sighted person on board (Cassandra in Copenhagen), was crowded in among the blind.

Kierkegaard asks the question "With the help of which technique is it possible for a poet to speak of the presence of humanity in a world in which there might be a God and in which Jesus lived?" In this regard, it is strange to see how far direct statements in favor of Christianity remain artistically *and* theologically behind the encoded discourse in which Kierkegaard, serving as a prelude to Kafka, showed how *sub specie metaphysicae* man looks in a world whose divine shape is guaranteed by doubts and questions, rather than by prerecorded answers. Precisely because he himself was no perfect Christian, Kierkegaard could *describe* the perfect Christian. The absence of ultimate certainty, which he longed for but didn't have, made him eloquent. It gave credibility to his productions on the "stage of the inner man," and it provided the imaginative artist with his insight into the twilight realm between despair and hope that marks out the true religious writer, the man who understands his either/or as a postulate but not as a description of reality, as an optative and not as an indicative.

It is strange to think, one last time, that Kierkegaard ceased to be a religious writer (in the same class with Dostoyevsky or Kafka) to the exact degree that he declared himself to be one. And, on the contrary, he *was* such a writer when, in keeping with his own later conviction, he would let himself be called only an "aestheticizing psychologist," "only" a poet. To be sure, he remained a poet, as at least the diaries show, despite the harsh pamphleteering, until the end of his life. He was a poet, whose parables, seen from today's perspective, look like sketches for Franz Kafka's religious paradoxes.

Søren Kierkegaard was more than half a century ahead of his time in his search for a transcendence realized in paradox. In the year 1838, in Copenhagen, Kafka's parable "Before the Law" sounded like this:

> Suppose a man had a letter about which he knew or believed that it contained information concerning what he must look upon as his life's bliss, but the characters were fine and pale, the handwriting nearly unreadable. In that case he would likely read and reread it with fear and unrest, quite passionately, and at one moment get a certain meaning out of it and another in the next, according as he, if he thought he had definitely deciphered a word, explained everything in accordance with this word; but what would he go on to, except to the same uncertainty with which he began. He would stare, more anxiously and ever more anxiously. But the more he stared, the less he would see. His eyes would sometimes fill with tears, but the more often this happened, the less he would see. In the course of time the writing would grow paler and more indistinct, finally the paper itself would

molder, and he would have nothing left but an eye blinded by tears.

In the ideal case, secular discourse about God might look like this. We might call it nonreligious language on the horizon of the Absolute.

FYODOR MIKHAILOVICH DOSTOYEVSKY

◆

THE BROTHERS KARAMAZOV

HANS KÜNG

◈

Religion
in the
Controversy over the End of Religion

In the Foreword to his *Letter to the Romans* (1921), which like no other book draws the line against modern programs and ideologies and thus signals the transition in theology from the modern to a postmodern paradigm, the *Protestant theologian Karl Barth* unexpectedly stresses two names: *Kierkegaard* and *Dostoyevsky*. They had, he said, given him crucial inspiration in his rethinking: "If I have a 'system,' then it consists in keeping my eye as unwaveringly as possible on what Kierkegaard called the 'infinite qualitative difference' between time and eternity. 'God is in heaven and on earth' " (vii, xiii). And, prompted by Eduard Thurneysen, Barth quotes Dostoyevsky more than anyone else on the "impenetrably problematic nature of life" (p. 489), on the critical situation of humanity, and on the liberating grace of the hidden God. Thus, with the two most important early critics of modernity, Kierkegaard and Dostoyevsky, we have a "dialectical" theology of crisis for a world in crisis. In fact, the "impenetrably problematic nature of life" is Dostoyevsky's central theme.

Holy Week in Tübingen, 1945, at the end of the Second World War: the *Catholic moral theologian Theodor Steinbüchel* gave five lectures on this Russian thinker, writer, and Christian amid the newly dawned "crisis of the West": "What moved Dostoyevsky moves us too, across the ages: the question that man always raises when he has become questionable to himself, the question of his being and meaning" (p. 15).

In Western Europe, people for the most part never developed a sense of the immensity of this author and his work until the times of crisis. There was nothing comparable to him in his age. And it is no accident that to *represent the second half of the nineteenth century* we have chosen not a German, an English, or a French author, but this one Russian writer. He wrote his great works a whole generation after Kierkegaard, at a period when the forces of modernity—science, technology, industry, and democracy—had begun to overtake one another in a "dialectic of enlightenment"; when the bourgeois-feudal world, driven by reckless capitalism and nationalism, was plunging ahead in an apparently unstoppable course toward the catastrophe of world war; and when the great modern visions of the eighteenth century had paled into chimeras.

Indeed, after scarcely one hundred years, what had become of the visions of the Enlightenment, of Lessing's dream of a third age of complete clarification, of a time of fulfillment, and peace among the religions as a prerequisite for peace among nations?

What was left of the vision of German classicism, of Hölderlin's vision, of mankind, education, art, and religion renewed through the Greek ideal of humanity?

What had happened to the vision of romanticism, to Novalis' vision, of a medievally oriented reconciliation of religion and society, of a higher cultural epoch, a holy time of eternal peace?

All these utopias remained unfulfilled, and thus they pointed far beyond modern times. But early on, those two great "noncontemporaries" from Copenhagen and Moscow saw through the ambivalence of modernity. They were both men of terrifying personal complexity and yet of forward-pointing spirituality. Imprisoned in their age and yet analyzing its contradictions, splits, and abysses, they described this ambivalence. Different as they were from one another, the Dane was representative of the first half, the Russian of the second half, of the nineteenth century.

Born on November 11, 1821, Dostoyevsky was eight years younger than Kierkegaard, the son of a doctor and the grandson of a Russian Orthodox priest. Like Kierkegaard, Dostoyevsky came from a strictly religious home. He, too, was a hypersensitive individualist, and became involved with literature early in his life.

In the upper classes of Russia—the stronghold of counterrevolution—he found himself confronting a decadent Christian world. But Dostoyevsky, the man from the big city, who went from Moscow to Petersburg, where he attended the Engineering School of the Military Academy, later entered the Ministry of War, and proved to be much more *socially and politically committed* than Kierkegaard. He was increasingly open to the influence of French utopian socialists, to the criticism of religion by Feuerbach, Strauss, and the pioneering Russian thinker Visarion Belinsky. In 1846, when Kierkegaard published his *Concluding Unscientific Postscript* in Copenhagen, Dostoyevsky had already had a giant success with his novel *Poor Folk*. Together with *The Double*, published in the same year, this established him as a writer of some stature, a sharply analytic critic of society and an advocate of humanity threatened by the metropolis. He wanted to write not "landowner" literature," à la Turgenev and Tolstoy, but social novels about the lower classes, and he called himself a "literary proletarian."

In 1847, Dostoyevsky came into contact with a philosophical-political circle gathered around Petrashevsky, which gave rise to a small, radical, conspiratorial group to which Dostoyevsky also belonged. This had crucial consequences. Two years later, the entire group (thirty-four youthful idealists) was arrested, and twenty-one of them were condemned to death. They were led to the execution site, dressed for burial, and had the death sentence read to them. Then, as they stood there on the scaffold, they were pardoned, literally at the last second. Dostoyevsky was sentenced to four years of *hard labor in Siberia*, with accompanying military service. In 1850, when Kierkegaard published his last great work, *Training in Christianity*, Dostoyevsky found himself in the nineteenth-century version of the Gulag Archipelago, without connections, writing materials, or books—except for a New Testament.

Nine years later, almost forty years old, Dostoyevsky returned from Siberia to St. Petersburg. He was a changed man. For the rest of his life, he could never get out of his head those terrible moments of awaiting immediate death, of terror followed by an explosive joy at the new gift of life. Nor could he forget, naturally enough, those four dreadful years in the work camp—recorded in *The House of the Dead*—and the four years of military service in Siberia. All in all, it brought about an upheaval in his view of life and his concept of faith.

But how are we to judge this upheaval? Did the "good," progressive, humanitarian Dostoyevsky (up to and including *Crime and Punishment*) turn into the "bad," reactionary, religious Dostoyevsky? Did Dostoyevsky abandon his freedom-loving political dreams in favor of religious notions from the illiterate Russian peasantry? This is the argument of Leonid Grossmann (1922, 1964), one of the most important Soviet interpreters of Dostoyevsky.

Hardly. One key to understanding his new basic attitude is what Dostoyevsky expressed in a letter written in February 1854 from Omsk (Siberia), when he was completely cut off from correspondence with relatives and friends, and yet never alone for a moment: "I wish to tell you about myself that I am a child of this time, a child of unbelief and doubt and will probably (I'm sure of it) remain so till the end of my life. How terribly this longing for faith tormented me (and torments me even now). It becomes stronger the more counterproofs I get." This was to Mrs. Fonvizin, who sent him the New Testament in Siberia. And yet, Dostoyevsky continues, God sometimes sends him moments of perfect rest. At such moments, he loves and believes he is loved. At these moments he made his *profession of faith*, in which everything was clear and holy to him: "Here it is: I believe that there is nothing more beautiful, more profound, more sympathetic, more masculine, and perfect than the Savior. I tell myself with jealous love that not only is there no one like him, but there cannot he anyone like him. I will say even more: If someone proved to me that Christ stood outside the truth, and if truth *in fact* lay outside Christ, I would prefer to stay with Christ and not with the truth" (*Letters*, 86–87).

Thus, we cannot read Dostoyevsky, the careful analyst of St. Petersburg slum life and passionate spokesman for the "insulted and the injured" (1861), without taking into account his *deeply skeptical, but authentic religious faith*. It cannot be ignored as it has so often been among the Western bourgeoisie and existentialists, or denounced as "irrationalism" and "mysticism," as it has been in Soviet criticism (in Stalin's time *The Possessed* and *The Brothers Karamazov* were scarcely obtainable). Ludolf Müller, the Tübingen Slavicist, could be said to have the consen-

sus of unbiased scholarship behind him when he responds to Soviet critic Leonid Grossmann that the religion of this "child of
unbelief and skepticism" in his second period (after his release
from the house of correction) was anything but a superficially
adopted ecclesiastical-religious system; that it had instead gone
through the Enlightenment, Kant's critique of the proofs for the
existence of God, and Feuerbach's atheism; that the transformation was less a matter of theoretical convictions than of a basic
attitude toward the problems of life; and that (and here Dostoyevsky reminds us of Pascal) along with the work of the *head*, of
critical understanding, and Euclidian thought there is the power
of the *heart*, of other levels in man, of lived life, which is more
than the rational sense of life.

"Life had come in place of the dialectic," we read à propos of
the transformation of the student Rodion Raskolnikov in the
epilogue to *Crime and Punishment*. And, though it is not my task
here, Ludolf Müller can document this notion of Dostoyevsky's
religion, especially from Dostoyevsky's third phase, the period of
the *great novels* (along with *Crime and Punishment*, 1866, *The
Idiot*, 1868, *The Possessed*, 1871, *A Raw Youth*, 1875, up until
The Brothers Karamazov, 1878–1880). In so doing, Müller has
support from the excellent study on Dostoyevsky's religion by the
American A. Boyce Gibson (1973) and the major new biography
by Joseph Frank (1976–1984)—all works that steer clear of the
anathemas earlier launched by Maxim Gorki or Georg Lukács on
the left and the idealizations of Nikolai Berdayeff or Vyacheslav
Ivanov on the right.

------------◆------------

Here we have to concentrate entirely on Dostoyevsky's last and
greatest work, *The Brothers Karamazov*, written over a century
ago. In itself, it justifies all the considerable posthumous attention
paid to Dostoyevsky by writers as diverse as Friedrich Nietzsche
and Sigmund Freud, André Gide and Hermann Hesse, Ortega y
Gasset and Thomas Mann. It is a work that came into being in
the years of *Russia's ongoing social crisis*, that fatal alliance between autocracy and orthodoxy that made the church so hateful
to the people. It was published immediately before the assassi-
nation of the initially liberal, then reactionary, tsar Alexander II
(1881). The book was contemporary with Tolstoy's *Anna Kar-*

enina, Ibsen's *A Doll's House*, Fontane's *Before the Storm*, and Emile Zola's *Nana*. It appeared (and this is an important fact in understanding the Grand Inquisitor) less than ten years after Vatican I and its definition of the primacy and infallibility of the pope (1870).

At this time, Russia was the most socially and politically backward country in Europe. Not until 1861 were the mostly poor, illiterate peasants (ca. eighty percent of the entire population) set free, at least legally, from slavery. But, unlike the Papal States, Russia in the decades after the victory over Napoleon did have enough intellectual freedom for a liberal intelligentsia; and, for the first time in history, a Russian literature of European caliber could come into being. In the novels of Dostoyevsky that literature took on reality in an incomparably more radical and more universal fashion than, for example, in the mildly idealized, conciliatory proletarians and outsiders of German novelists such as Gottfried Keller or Theodor Fontane.

In dealing with such a psychologically and intellectually complex work, the theologian is doubtless tempted simply to elaborate the *ideas*. Philosopher Reinhard Lauth did a meritorious job of this for Dostoyevsky's work as a whole in his *Systematic Presentation of Dostoyevsky's Philosophy* (1950). But this method makes it easy to overlook the specific features of Dostoyevsky, because many religious philosophers and political prophets have presented their ideas in articles and monographs. Dostoyevsky did it in *novels*. This cultivated engineer understood himself not as a philosopher, but as a writer and artist. His novels are dominated not by ideas but by concrete human beings of the most varied origin, character, bias, and worldview. They have a genius for observing themselves and others (similar to Kierkegaard in this) with unexampled psychological empathy and sympathy.

In fact, Dostoyevsky created a type of completely new "polyphonic" novel. This many-voiced narrative is characterized by plots that run in several parallel skeins and are reflected in the consciousness of the various characters, who are dialectically-antithetically opposed to one another. But does this mean, as the Russian critic Bachtin concludes, that the author himself identifies with none of his voices and that in his view all standpoints are simultaneously possible? Does this mean that in Dostoyevsky there is no last word? By no means. Dostoyevsky's letters and

Diary, his essays and speeches speak a different language. But so do the novels themselves; they clearly reveal the author's position by the way the action is conducted and in particular by its outcome. Where, then, in this novel, for all the numberless narrative threads, do the decisive lines run? Where are not so much the external focal points of the action, but the basic intellectual-ideological antagonism in this novel, for which "antithesis constitutes the fundamental architectontic principle" (Leonid Grossmann)?

Anyone who begins to read an edition of *The Brothers Karamazov* lacking the author's Foreword runs immediately into the polarity between the father and his eldest son Dmitri and, indirectly, the other two sons from a second marriage, Ivan and Alyosha (all in their twenties)—not to forget, on the margin, the illegitimate son Smerdyakov. This *constellation of persons* reveals the writer's own complex personality, divided up among the very different brothers: We have the wily old landowner Fyodor Pavlovich Karamazov, addicted to unbridled libertinism, alcohol, and women, a debauchee who has never cared about either of his wives or any of his children. He finds himself confronting, literally at knife point, his son Dmitri. As his mother's heir, Dmitri demands three thousand rubles so he can marry the seductively beautiful Grushenka, the very femme fatale whom his father has promised exactly three thousand rubles for a single night.

The Oedipus complex, no doubt, can explain many things here, but not everything: Dmitri (twenty-eight), whose libidinous urges are no less powerful than his father's, is also moved by an honorable and humane generosity. He is engaged to the proud beauty Katerina Ivanovna, but he has fallen in love with Grushenka. And with his unbridled passion he takes the initiative in almost all the action in the novel. His challenge begins the dramatic tale, which ends with his condemnation as a murderer to hard labor in Siberia and his planned escape. There can be no question that with his "Confessions of a Passionate Heart" in verse and stories Dmitri is the most colorful and original figure in this novel, without precedent in previous novels. Does that mean that he is Dostoyevsky's hero? Not at all.

For the author himself makes it clear in the very first sentence of his Foreword that his hero is not the eldest, but the youngest, Alexei Fyodorovich Karamazov, *Alyosha*. This is surprising, and has given rise to many discussions among commentators. For, even in comparison with Ivan, isn't Alyosha rather a marginal figure? Isn't he an observer, messenger, and mediator? He is a scarcely twenty-year-old novice of a monastery outside of town. With his religious intuitiveness, he is the only one among the brothers who is not at odds with anyone. He is the friend and confidant of almost everyone in the novel, of his elder brothers, Katerina, and then Grushenka, too. He has no long monologues, and for that very reason strikes us at first as paler than the other two. A pure soul, apparently, but no hero.

This can be explained by reflecting that Dostoyevsky had a long-term "investment" in this character. That is, the straightforward unheroic nature of the youngest Karamazov has a precisely justified function in the overall structure of the book. *The Brothers* was to be only the first part of the "main novel," whose second part was never written (and this announcement in the Foreword is too specific to be a literary ruse). Thus we should have something more to expect from Alyosha, namely: "the activity of my hero (Alyosha) in *our* time, in *this* contemporary world."

What does Alyosha embody? What position does he have in the structure of the novel? Alyosha is the crucial counterfigure to the middle brother, *Ivan* (twenty-four), who shares the Karamazov thirst for life, but is a brilliantly rationalistic and yet ultimately impenetrable and mysterious intellectual and "clever atheist" from Moscow. Ivan now, for whatever reasons, lives with his father, whom he nevertheless despises as much as he despises Dmitri.

Dostoyevsky's *Brothers Karamazov* is not only polyphonic, but multilayered, a fact that not only Soviet critics but Nietzsche, Freud, Gide, and Thomas Mann overlooked, or tried to. We must observe not just the external, constantly shifting patterns of the detective story, nor simply the internal, dramatically changing patterns of the different types and characters on the psychological scene. Instead, we must look to the dynamically evolving intellectual-ethical-religious basic positions of this novel. *The Brothers Karamazov* aims to be not just a whodunit or psychological thriller, but a book about its era, about society and ideas.

When we see this we cannot help noticing a *fundamental ideological antagonism* between Ivan's modern, enlightened Western nonreligiousness (his lackey and henchman is the contemned, disowned half-brother Smerdyakov, whom nature and education have made an incarnation of primal mistrust) and the enlightened Christian piety of Alyosha, whose spokesman and spiritual father (starets) is Zossima. In analyzing this basic tension, I acknowledge the contribution of *The Brothers* to the key question of this book: What happens to religion in the modern period and what happens to modernity because of religion?

But as a theologian am I perhaps projecting my own problems onto Dostoyevsky's novel? Hardly, for "Why have we met here? To talk of my love for Katerina, of father and Dmitri? Of travel abroad? Of the fatal position of Russia? Of the emperor Napoleon? Is that it?" This is how Ivan speaks to Alyosha in the central conversation of the novel, which Dostoyevsky himself marks as its high point. "No, not for that" is Alyosha's laconic answer. "We in our green youth have to settle the eternal questions first of all. That's what we care about," says Ivan; all of young Russia is talking today about the "eternal questions": "the existence of God and immortality. And those who do not believe in God talk of socialism and anarchism, of the transformation of all humanity on a new pattern, so that it all comes to the same. They're the same questions turned inside out" (p. 216, this and all subsequent citations from Constance Garnett, trans., Signet Classics).

Thus, the skeptic Ivan defends the position of a dazzling *rejection of religion*: "No, there is no God!" Ivan at first appears the type of the cynic, when after the terrible scene where the eldest son batters his father and threatens to strike him down, he says, "The first vermin will swallow up the other vermin, and it will serve them both right." Cain's answer about "my brother's keeper" is Ivan's answer, too.

As early as 1871, Dostoyevsky's novel *The Possessed*—his first realization of a great "novel of atheism"—contained a passionate confrontation with the sinister consequences of atheistic nihilism (anarchism) for the individual and society. Dostoyevsky was profoundly alarmed by terrorist murders, and he wanted to use all his power to show the Russian people, especially the intellectuals and the students, that terrorism—immediate, violent action without a practical, constructive program for the future—was a symptom of a mortally sick society. A prophet in many areas, Dostoyevsky had recognized the causes that would make Russian society ripe for revolution. These included the rapidly spreading rejection of religion, the breakdown of values and the social background of that breakdown—a parasitical upper class, alienated from the people; a backward church; a modern Western intelligentsia, primarily students, who in losing their faith in God had also lost their standards of good and evil; and finally the poverty-stricken, disoriented masses who had no idea what they could hold onto.

We have to focus on this background in reading *The Brothers Karamazov*. Here, as in no other work, the whole poetic world of Dostoyevsky is mirrored, his message is comprehensively proclaimed, and thus *the problem of modern man without God* is raised to the most dramatic heights. For Dostoyevsky, as for Nietzsche, the question of God is always bound up with the question of ethics, morality, conscience, and conduct. The loss of God, the religious connection, necessarily leads to the loss of an obligatory moral law. Dostoyevsky sees here the weakness, indeed the abysmal misery, of modern times, as it was elaborated at the end of the Second World War by Horkheimer and Adorno in the too often ignored chapter "Juliet or Enlightenment and Morality" from *The Dialectic of Enlightenment* (1944). Referring to the "dark writers of the bourgeoisie," de Sade and Nietzsche, they write: "The fact that they did not gloss over, but shouted from the rooftops, the impossibility of deriving from reason a fundamental argument against murder sparked the hatred with which even today progressives (especially progressives) pursue Sade and Nietzsche" (p. 107).

All this is cruelly demonstrated by Dostoyevsky in the figure of Ivan. There is *one* negative principle than runs through the whole novel: *"If God does not exist, all things are permitted."* In the early chapters, Ivan is characterized by principles like this one, and I would like to cite one longish passage to illustrate the complexity of the position:

> He solemnly declared in argument that there was nothing in
> the whole world to make men love their neighbors. That
> there was no law of nature that men should love mankind,
> and that, if there had been any love on earth before this, it

was not owing to a natural law, but simply because men have believed in immortality. Ivan added in parenthesis that the whole natural law lies in that faith, and that if you were to destroy in mankind the belief in immortality, not only love but every living force maintaining the life of the world would at once be dried up. Moreover, nothing then would be immoral, everything would be lawful, even cannibalism. That's not all. He ended by asserting that for every individual who does not believe in God or immortality, the moral law of nature must immediately be changed into the exact contrary of the former religious law. He said that egoism, even to crime, must become, not only lawful but recognized as the inevitable, the most rational, even honorable outcome. (p. 72)

Notice that Dmitri, the witness of such remarks, "recalls" them, although not he but Smerdyakov ultimately commits the crime against the father. In so doing Smerdyakov merely translates Ivan's wishful thinking into reality. And since this atheistic-nihilistic ideology of the Moscow intellectual provides the logical justification for the parricide, in the final analysis *the principal committer of the crime* is none other than Ivan. Smerdyakov says to Ivan: "*You* murdered him. You are the murderer! I was only your instrument, your faithful servant, and it was following your words I did it" (p. 565)

After this, Ivan experiences his nadir, immediately before the beginning of the trial, his public confession and the outbreak of his madness, in the sinister comedy of the *conversations with the devil*, who (quite differently from Father Ferapont's mythological devil) is Ivan's projected alter ego. The devil's arguments prove to be the same as Ivan's claim that "everyone who recognizes the truth now may legitimately order his life as he pleases, on the new principle. In that sense, 'all things are lawful' for him" (p. 589). It comes as a bitter commentary by the author on this triumphal ideology, when, at the end of the conversation, Alyosha delivers the lapidary report that "Smerdyakov hanged himself an hour ago."

But however self-assured the presentation of Ivan's position may be, it is ambivalent in practice. For Ivan, skeptical even vis-à-vis his own skepticism, manifests the ambiguousness, double-bottomedness, and uncertainty of the atheist struggling for belief in God. When speaking with his father, he flatly denies God in public (without belief in God there would be no culture, and no cognac either). But in the great Fifth Book, "Pro and Contra," in a conversation with Alyosha that reveals extreme intellectual intensity, Ivan now privately and confidentially confesses a "perhaps" ("perhaps I too acknowledge God") and the unprovability of the Feuerbachian "hypothesis" (which is curiously an "axiom" for "Russian lads" and "our professors"): "I have long resolved not to think whether man created God or God man." So Ivan says, "I accept God and am glad to," his "wisdom and his purpose—which is completely beyond our knowledge," which transcend Ivan's "Euclidian understanding." But Ivan accepts God only so he can argue all the more effectively, not against the God of this world but against *the world of this God* (pp. 216–18).

"Yet would you believe it, in the final result I don't accept this world of God's" (p. 217). Long, long stories about the suffering of humanity, no, actually only about the suffering of *innocent children*, outrageously cruel stories, not invented but authentic (Dostoyevsky had collected many newspaper clippings on this), whose "bestial" cruelty according to Ivan was an insult to the beasts, since they could never be so ingeniously, artistically cruel as human beings. Theodicy, cosmodicy, future eternal harmony? All that collapses in the face of those "little martyrs." Such harmony "is not worth the tears of that one tortured child who beats itself on the breast with its little fist, and prays in its stinking outhouse, with its tears to 'dear, kind God.' It's not worth it, because those tears are unatoned for. . . . And so I give back my entrance ticket, and if I am an honest man I give it back as soon as possible. And that I am doing. It's not God that I don't accept, Alyosha, only I most respectfully return my ticket to Him" (p. 227).

Here lies the secret of Ivan's atheism, the basis for his "rebellion." The modern rejection of religion seems to have a rock solid foundation. "Why do I suffer? That is the rock of atheism," Georg Büchner had already written in *Danton's Death* (III, 1). And this means: In suffering, especially in that of the innocent, man comes up against his extreme limit, comes to the decisive question of his identity, of the sense and nonsense of his living and dying, indeed, of reality pure and simple. Given the overwhelming reality of suffering in the life and history of humanity does the suffering, doubting, despairing person really have any other choice? What alternative is there to the rebellion of an Ivan Karamazov against this world of God that he finds so unacceptable, or to the revolt against the "absurd world" of an Albert Camus, who follows Dostoyevsky in pointing to the sufferings of innocent creatures?

Yes, *this* world is absurd, and Dostoyevsky has no intention of prettifying it, of minimizing its evil or justifying it. In all his descriptions of the negative, he is not less sober than the naturalists, than, say, his contemporary Emile Zola. And yet Dostoyevsky stands in contrast to Zola, who in his "scientific" fashion perceives, with deliberate bias, only a part of reality. Zola sees above all what is animalistic, hateful, and immoral (read the justifying Foreword, written afterward, to his novel *Thérèse Raquin*, 1868). Dostoyevsky knew all this, but he always had a counter-image, a counterworld, the domain of ethics, humanism, indeed, of *Christian faith*.

The specifically Dostoyevskian feature is now, of course, that both worlds are not mediated *by argument*. Ivan's world is neither refuted on the philosophical level nor given a moralizing censure on the ethical level, nor explained away apologetically on the Christian level. According to Dostoyevsky (*Diary*, p. 613), "the answer" is given not by a single argument, but by "the whole book." No, we cannot get around Ivan either by philosophy or simply by faith. And we must avoid, as interpreters of Dostoyevsky have often done, meeting Ivan's atheism with sermons. Alyosha, Dostoyevsky himself, renounces cheap solutions: shifting the guilt from the children to the parents, consoling oneself with otherworldly rewards or by dividing people into good and evil. "Ivan is deep," Dostoyevsky writes in his diary, "he's not one of the contemporary atheists, who with their unbelief simply demonstrate the dullness of their tiny brains. . . . In Europe too there is no atheistic *expression* of such force, nor has there *ever been*" (*Diary*, pp. 613, 620).

But this world of Ivan, so subtly portrayed, is now contrasted, in serenity and great inner freedom, with an *alternative world* that has its own plausibility. While Ivan primarily talks, Alyosha acts. Dostoyevsky was convinced that on the ultimate theological issues rational argumentation was impotent. "That is why Alyosha does not argue with Ivan, starets Zossima does not argue with old Karamazov, nor Christ with the Grand Inquisitor. In each case they answer with the sign or the act of love. It is not arguments that are not set off against each other, but ways of being" (L. Müller, p. 88).

What, then, remains to counter Ivan's arguments? There is, in the final analysis, only the reference to Another. "You've forgotten him," Alyosha responds, as we know (and we recall Dostoyevsky's confession of faith that he made while in the Gulag), to Ivan's accusation against God's world and the unexpiated suffering of innocent children. Can't he, the innocently slaughtered One, forgive all guilt? He stands for God, who in Dostoyevsky always remains very much in the background, often never mentioned at all. And Ivan? Doesn't he indirectly agree, when he goes on to tell the legend of the Grand Inquisitor, whose "whole secret" (p. 241) is that he doesn't believe in God? According to Alyosha, in fact, this legend is a wonderful "praise of Jesus" (p. 240). But at the same time it is also an enormous challenge for the Christendom that thinks of itself as exalted above the godless world and doesn't even notice that it has long been a Christendom without Christ. This is the most potent critique to date of the freedom-hating, humanity-despising Roman system (not identical with the Catholic church) and of every totalitarian ideology of whatever sort.

There can be no doubt that, like Kierkegaard, Dostoyevsky is less concerned with theory than with practice, with the reintroduction of Christianity into Christendom. But how different was the Christianity of the Russian. Dostoyevsky was shaped not by Protestantism, which he sees, in the nineteenth century anyway, as on the way to atheism, nor by Roman Catholicism, which he views as the source of totalitarian socialism, but by Eastern orthodoxy, by the piety of "holy Russia." Dostoyevsky understands this "holy Russia" as a hope for all of Europe. Even in his later political statements he all too often combines this with a Russian nationalism, populism, and imperialism (against the Turks). Kierkegaard's forced idealizing, rigor, and gloominess is in any case foreign to Dostoyevsky's Christianity. And in the central figures of this other, alternative world, in the starets, the representative of the older generation, and in Alyosha, prefiguring the lifestyle of a coming generation, there gleams something like the *portrait of a new, more joyful Christianity.*

How should we imagine Alyosha as a Christian? As a "sickly, ecstatic, poorly developed creature, a pale, consumptive dreamer? On the contrary, he was at this time a well-grown, clear-eyed young man of nineteen," blooming with health, with Karamazov "earth force." He trusts people and yet he's not naive; he's bitterly disturbed about many things and yet—this was extremely important for Dostoyevsky—he doesn't stand in judgment over people. Neither a fanatic nor a mystic, he is "more of a realist than anyone. . . . Add to that that he was to some extent a youth of our past generation—that is, honest in nature, desiring the truth, seeking for it and believing in it, and seeking to serve it at once with all the strength of his soul" (p. 34). In this sense, he is a modern and, intellectually, an altogether honest Christian.

As a matter of fact, Dostoyevsky's main figures are as a group *far from traditional Orthodox piety*—stamped by the Old Church/ Hellenistic paradigm. For the solemn Byzantine Russian liturgy, the center of the official church, rites, feasts, processions, etc.— in contrast with prayer and "contact with other worlds"—play practically no role here. Dostoyevsky had very little to do with the Orthodox clergy, and he was not a churchgoer. He had positive feelings about monasticism, which stood as a sign in a world full of the desire for pleasure, possession, and domination (the three temptations of Jesus in "The Grand Inquisitor"). But the monastic way is not the higher way. Asceticism, which in Christianity goes back not to the Nazarene but rather to Hellenistic influences, and is perhaps indirectly derived from India, gets rejected and treated ironically in the figure of the great practitioner of silence, the fanatical faster and candle-lighting venerator of saints, Father Ferapont. In contrast to Russian folk piety, here the love of miracles is kept within limits. Owing to the unexpected stench of corruption from the dead Father Zossima, the "almost always cheerful" monk so criticized by his conservative brethren—veneration of the saints is directed, even for Alyosha himself, along the more sober lines of the imitation of Christ.

Dostoyevsky stresses the importance of Holy Scripture for children (especially the story of Job on the question of theodicy). On the whole, this is rather an *enlightened Christian piety*, with Russian coloring. Both starets Zossima and his disciple radiate an unforced and unaffected *humanity*. For Christianity naturally presupposes the preservation of the human element, the "keeping of the commandments," as found in all religions. Thus the starets remonstrates with the old debauchee Karamazov for his drunkenness, lust, and worship of money: ". . . And don't tell lies" (p. 51).

But Christianity, in its essence, means more than mere "keeping the commandments": God, eternal life—"There's no proving it, though you can be convinced of it," says the starets to the mother of Alyosha's friend Lisa. "How? By the experience of active love. Strive to love your neighbor actively and constantly. In so far as you advance in love you will grow surer of the reality of God and of the immortality of your soul" (p. 60). This attitude stands in direct contrast to the doctor who sadly joked: "I love humanity, but I wonder at myself. The more I love humanity in general, the less I love man in particular" (p. 61).

Kierkegaard, too, might have argued in this ironic fashion. But in answer to the question, "What can one do in such a case? Must one despair?" the starets gives a reply that Anti-Climacus, always aiming at the unconditioned, would never have given: "No. It is enough that you are distressed. Do what you can and it will be reckoned unto you" (p. 61). To his brother Dmitri, speaking about the choice between flight and Siberia, Alyosha says: "Listen, you are not ready, and such a cross is not for you" (p. 689). Astonishingly, what the author of *Either/Or* had scarcely any respect for—measure, modesty—shows up in the author of *The Brothers*. Owing to his turbulent, dramatic career—long tied up with compulsive gambling, permanent debts, torn between two women—Dostoyevsky had fewer grounds for feelings of superiority than Kierkegaard.

No, in Dostoyevsky the *life* of Christians is not "thrust upward" to "the level of the ideal." He wrote *The Brothers Karamazov* only in order to force people to recognize that a pure, ideal Christian is not an abstract thing, but is visibly, really possible" (W. Komarowitsch, *Dostojewski, Die Urgestalt der Brüder Karamasoff*, p. 563). The prerequisite for viable Christian existence is, to be sure, the starets's basic confession, which he shares with the monks as the "crown of the way: "*Everyone of us is un-*

doubtedly responsible for all men and everything on earth"
(p. 155). And in fact the novel makes it palpably clear that each
one of the four brothers, even Alyosha, has his share of guilt in
the death of their father (who is himself not innocent). Everyone
at the trial (women and judges included) is directed to show
forgiveness and compassion. The starets's conclusion: "Hate not
the atheists, the teachers of evil, the materialists—and I mean
not only the good ones—for there are many good ones among
them, especially in our day—hate not even the wicked ones" (p.
155). Such an effort to take guilt and responsibility seriously
makes it clear, of course, how wrong anyone is to demand a
reckoning from God for this unjust world. Instead, we are bidden
(as Alyosha and his group of schoolboys do so exemplarily) to
oppose the man-made injustice in this world through active love
here and now in the solidarity of everyone with everyone else
(*sobornost*). This is not a new theological apologetics or theodicy.
Rather, Dostoyevsky calls for a basic new Christian attitude and
practice.

————◆————

Indeed, Dostoyevsky's Christianity is programmatic—an active, busy Christianity: "He (Alyosha) was incapable of passive
love. If he loved anyone, he wanted at once to help him"
(p. 176). Opposed to destructive egocentricity, oriented to Jesus,
it is an attitude of mutual helping, giving, serving, sparing, forgiving. This Christianity of active love changes people. It has not
only an individual dimension, but a political-social one as well,
although Dostoyevsky (unlike Tolstoy) offers no political and
educational pat solutions. The discourses by Father Zossima
preach freedom, equality, fraternity, but a freedom that leads
neither to new slavery nor to suicide, an equality based on the
spiritual dignity of each person, and a fraternity that overcomes
modern isolation.

This Christianity even has a *cosmic* dimension. To be sure,
Dostoyevsky himself, as he once wrote, would have spoken in a
more modern language than his starets. And yet he stands
squarely behind the message of the old monk, the "Pater Sera-
phicus," whose love embraces, in Franciscan fashion, every living
thing. God, for Dostoyevsky, too, is *in* this world. God's mystery
is *in* all things: "Love every leaf, every ray of God's light. . . .

Love animals: God has given them the rudiments of thought and joy untroubled. Do not trouble their joy, don't harass them, don't deprive them of their happiness, don't work against God's intent. . . . Love children especially, for they too are sinless like the angels; they live to soften and purify our hearts, and as it were to guide us. Woe to him who offends a child!" (p. 294).

Among all the countless little stories by Dostoyevsky within the larger story of the Karamazovs, the ones about Alyosha and the children and again the ones about little Ilyushka and the dog Shushchka belong to the most moving, literarily and humanly. The whole novel ends with Alyosha and the group of schoolboys, the model of an alternative society, who after the death of little Ilyushka go happily to a funeral meal—in hopes of a new life from death: "And always so, all our lives hand in hand! Hurrah for Karamazov!" (p. 701).

There is no denying that all the wretchedness, ugliness, shame, and shock of this measure-shattering tragedy, where Dostoyevsky the incomparable psychologist dissects certain attitudes down to the last consequence, are confronted by truly glad tidings: a message of joy in life and universal hope, which in the end also includes Dmitri and Ivan, Katerina and Grushenka. The ethic presented here is not ascetical or world-denying. Instead, in an altogether Russian fashion, it is a world-shaping ethic that integrates eros and sexuality, understanding and feeling, heart and head. For binding oneself to God means freedom in the world. Inner freedom is matched by the outer freedom to act creatively in the world (and the church).

At the very beginning of the novel, Zossima predicts Alyosha's future—and thereby demonstrates not just the capacity to look into people's souls but also the strength to relativize his own lifestyle. After Zossima's upcoming death, Alyosha is to leave the monastery for his "great service in the world": "Yours will be a long pilgrimage. And you will have to take a wife, too. You will have to bear *all* before you come back. There will be much to do. But I have trust in you, and so I send you forth. Christ is with you. Do not abandon him, and he will not abandon you. You will see great sorrow, and in that sorrow you will be happy. This is my last message to you: in sorrow seek happiness" (p. 78). As Zossima says, over Alyosha's life, work, and sorrow—

a story Dostoyevsky never lived to tell—stand Christ's words from the Gospel of John, as they stand as a motto over the entire novel: The grain of wheat must die, in order to bear much fruit. These same words would very shortly be inscribed on Dostoyevsky's gravestone in the Alexander Nevsky Cemetery.

———————◈———————

"Yours will be a long pilgrimage": We have no authentic statements about how Dostoyevsky concretely imagined he would continue his novel. All considerations on this score remain speculation. This one thing, however, is certain: In Dostoyevsky's mind, the conclusion of the novel was bound up with his certainty "of living and writing for another twenty years. So don't get the funeral repast ready just yet," he wrote to N. Lyubimov, the editor of the *Russian Messenger*, when he sent him the Epilogue to *The Brothers Karamazov* (*Letters*, p. 506). This was on November 8, 1880. Less than three months later, Fyodor Dostoyevsky, not yet sixty years old, died of a stroke on January 28, 1881.

In the months before, he had been busy defending his famous Pushkin memorial speech (June 1880), with which he had stirred enthusiastic agreement among the public, thanks to his combining Christian and Slavophile views, while he drew skeptical commentaries from the liberal press. There is much to criticize in Dostoyevsky's political and theological notions—from Slavophilism and Russian popular messianism through anti-Semitism to eschatology. But, like every writer, he must be understood not primarily as a politician or a theologian, but as a writer.

This speech by Dostoyevsky the writer conjures up the vision of a different Russia. A hundred years later, especially in the face of contemporary Russia, so greatly changed, it can move us in another way: Dostoyevsky was convinced that the Europe of Western science, technology, and democracy needed Russia's spirituality and conciliating power in order to find its way to a new, free unity. This was "not a unity wrested with the sword," but a "unity realized through the power of brotherly love and our brotherly striving to reunite people."

Indeed, that was the great utopia of the greatest Russian writer, his testament as it were:

I am working on the firm conviction that in the future we—
that is, of course, not we, but the Russians of the future—
will all, without exception, readily grasp that to be an authentic Russian means nothing else but to strive definitively
to reconcile in oneself the European contradictions, to show
how the longings of Europe may find a way out in the all-
human and all-denying Russian soul. It means to accept
them all in this soul, in brotherly love, and thus perhaps to
speak the last word of the great, universal harmony, of
brotherly concord of all peoples in keeping with the evangeli-
cal law of Christ. I know, I know only too well, that my
words, spoken in enthusiasm as they are, may seem ecstatic,
exaggerated, and fantastic. Very well, they may be, but I
don't regret having spoken them. (*Diary of a Writer*,
pp. 504–5)

WALTER JENS

◆

But I Want to See with My Own Eyes . . . the Victim Rise Up and Embrace His Murderer

Ivan Karamazov . . . studied math, lost an arm in the Second World War, was arrested at the end of the war because he declared that the way Germany was occupied and conquered, and the people humiliated, was unsocialistic. He spent years in the camps, but after his rehabilitation he took up his studies again. He has a little income, is very frugal, given to silence, and occasionally makes some money on the side as a reader in a music publishing house. Some people take him to be an informer; he smiles a rather tortured smile when someone reads out loud from the Bible.

This is Dostoyevsky's Ivan Karamazov translated into the reality of our time by Heinrich Böll. The man of possibility from the realm of poetry is here transposed into a figure of reality. Ivan, the intellectual and the poet, the bitter-end thinker and challenger of the devil (his twin brother) has been transformed into a laconic fellow—a humble person who listens to music and has long since forgotten his powerful charges against God's corrupt world, the misery of children, and the Luciferian practices of the Roman Catholic church.

If we are to believe Heinrich Böll, then in the Soviet Union Ivan has to be reconciled with his brother in the spirit, Alyosha. (Except that he obviously doesn't like the Bible; one wonders whether he still knows its texts quite as well as he did seventy years earlier in the novel.)

What looks like a game, a nonbinding poetic business, has in truth the character of a serious, life-shaping declaration about the writer's position: Ivan's metamorphosis points to the changes in the times and society. The variation of the pattern makes it clear how the author as copier and transformer (Böll in Dostoyevsky's shadow) understands himself. The discrepancy between the archetype and its image shows which spirit we are the children of.

This is a kind of self-insurance with the help of a newly worked-out ensemble of mythical figures. It is indirect characterization of one's own understanding of the world and oneself through the intellectual assimilation of Job and Antigone, Abraham and Don Juan, Hamlet and Faust. At a time like ours, lacking the definitive central symbols (literary archetypes, in other words), the poetic technique of seeking out symbolic figures that cast shadows, of presenting oneself in a guise appropriate to the times, acquires new meaning. Here we see, laid out in bold metamorphoses, biblical figures joining with the heroes and heroines of Greek myth. Judas and Clytemnestra meet, Isaac and Odysseus, Achilles and Solomon, and then, at once, the imaginary theater, dissolving time and space, swarms with Kirilov and Myshkin, Stavrogin and Raskolnikov, with the four sons of Fyodor Pavlovich Karamazov (Smerdyakov is on hand), with Grushenka and Father Ferapont, with murderers, whores, child molesters, saints, and devil worshippers.

If anyone—Shakespeare, as usual, excepted—can compete with Old Testament prophets and Greek singers of tales, *if* anyone has invented figures that provoke every new generation to rethinking, sketching out, and doing variations on the previously given material, then it is Dostoyevsky. Balzac's Rastignac, Dickens's Oliver Twist, Fontane's Effi Briest, even Tolstoy's Anna Karenina are closed characters (splendid, convincing, inviting identification, but fixed). By contrast, Dostoyevsky's figures offer themselves, open, unfinished, hungry for variation. Despite their accuracy as psychographs, they ask to be viewed as characters whose mystery lies in their power to surprise, that is, in their continual capacity for striking the reader as different, for bringing never-imagined sides into view, for growing beyond themselves, remaining behind themselves, slipping into other roles, God today, the devil tomorrow, here the cynic and there the Good Samaritan.

Dostoyevsky's characters are—in the terminology of the English novelist E. M. Forster (*Aspects of the Novel*), not flat but round. ("The mark of a round character is that he can surprise us in a convincing way.")

No wonder, from this perspective, that to this day Dostoyevsky is a favorite author among writers. With Dostoyevsky, the story can be continued, the thread can be picked up, the personnel can be supported in their actions through new techniques, hints, and psychological suggestions. (Franz Kafka, playing an interpreter of the examining magistrate from the novel *Crime and Punishment*, gave a preliminary demonstration of what productive and inspired thinking in the footsteps of Dostoyevsky might look like.)

The reaction "This character is wonderful, and so he wasn't changed by a hair" is something the author of *The Idiot* and *The Brothers Karamazov* would have taken as a misunderstanding of his actual—and most secret—intentions. Like his novels, his characters are built on surprising turnabouts, lightning-fast, stupendous variations. The most peaceable, the lovable figure of Prince Myshkin, could have been credited with a murder. On the other hand, the murderer Raskolnikov could transform himself in Siberia, accompanied by the prostitute Sonya, into a pious dweller in the unworldly house of the dead. This streetwalker and a double murderer stand closer to the world of the *startsi*, the cloistered monks, than to Russian society, where priests and great lords tolerate the poor Jesus as a good man.

And then Alyosha. He is the angel and rescuer, a cherub among the children of darkness—and a potential revolutionary. The erstwhile mystic could be imagined today a political rebel who will end on the block. Ivan, on the other side, the devil's interlocutor, could be saved—cured of madness and resurrected *in saecula saeculorum*.

"A new story begins, the story of the gradual renewal of a man, the story of his gradual transformation, the gradual transition from one world into another, the acquaintance with a new, hitherto fully unsuspected reality": The finale of *Crime and Pun-ishment* has an exemplary meaning and holds true for *all* Dos-toyevsky's characters. None can consider himself safe for all time, none has an undisputed faith, none, even the most depraved (the *apparently* most depraved), is lost once and for all against the horizon of an understanding of the world that orients all events toward God and interprets them from his perspective. No, under the aegis of a Christian anthropology, marked by the concepts of *humility* and *service*, Dostoyevsky doesn't acknowledge the words *lost forever*. Didn't even the haughtiest woman once give the poor an *onion*, even if only on a whim? And isn't the accomplice in a murder, the paid henchman, who only carries out what another thinks up, capable at any time of exchanging the ascent to heaven for the plunge into hell?

What damning judgments, true orgies of cursing, one hears in Dostoyevsky research, against the child of darkness, the cook Smerdyakov. He was born of a roaming idiot girl and begotten, most likely, in a drunken fit by the joker Karamazov, senior in the open air, between nettles and sage. (The top hat with the crepe in the mud, the boon companions from the club as spec-tators at the copulation, which they look upon as the pairing of man and beast: "The band broke out in laughter.")

But even this son of a drunkard and an antisocial retardate is described by Dostoyevsky, however uncompassionately he paints him, with cold precision. Smerdyakov is not betrayed, so to speak, but presented in the full force of his possibilities, and in a way that preserves him from rash judgments: "He may suddenly . . . abandon everything and go off to Jerusalem on a pilgrimage. Or he may suddenly set fire to his native village. Or he may do both" (123).

Judge not that you may not be judged. It is moving to see how consistently Dostoyevsky as a poet protects from a guilty verdict even those characters whom he condemns as a theoretician in an abundance of ideologically fixed positions. In letters and treatises, here and there, he may present himself as a Russian chauvinist, as a supporter of Slavic imperialism, an advocate of tsarist poli-tics—see his letter to the tsarevich in 1863!—as a xenophobe, indeed as a crude anti-Semite ("The Jew and the bank now rule all," he says [1873] in the *Diary of a Writer*, ". . . especially socialism [and] through it he will rip up Christianity by the roots

and destroy Christian culture. And when nothing is left but anarchy, the Jew will stand at the top of the whole pile . . . and
when all the wealth of Europe is wasted, the Jew's bank remains.
Then the Antichrist will come and anarchy will rule"). Dostoyevsky may occasionally (by no means always or without contradiction) hold forth on Europeans, Germans above all, on Semites
and Catholics, on the glory of a Russian politics of conquest and
the perfidy of his colleagues in a way that makes the reader begin
to doubt whether Dostoyevsky the novelist and Dostoyevsky the
pamphletist are actually one and the same person. Yet, as soon
as he begins to get serious, in novels and stories, he forgets all
his narrow-mindedness.

Then, just like Balzac, he acts contrary to the interests of the
class he so deferentially celebrates. He describes people the way
they *are*, in their Janus-facedness and ambivalence—and not, as
they *should be*, according to his ideological models.

What a powerful figure this monster Smerdyakov is. How grand
he is with his Luciferian wit. It's the one thing still left to him,
Smerdyakov the stepped on, the despised, the tormented, as his
ultima ratio. ("God created light on the first day, and the sun,
moon, and stars on the fourth day. Where did the light come
from on the first day?" [p. 121]: This is logic chopping as the
weapon of a creature who has been humiliated, and not entirely
by his own fault).

And what a character, furthermore, is Sonya Marmeladov from
Crime and Punishment: a whore and child of God, a figure of
misery who enters her father's death chamber as a flesh-and-blood
saint—but decked out, down to the red feather on her hat, with
the baubles of the devil:

> Sonya stared as though lost in front of her, seemed to have
> forgotten that she was wearing a colorful silk dress, bought
> fourth-hand and out of place here, with a long and ridiculous
> train and an enormous crinoline that filled the entire door-
> way. She also wore bright boots and carried a parasol, of
> which she had no need in the night, and a ridiculous round
> straw hat with a garish red feather. Beneath this jauntily
> boyish little hat, set at an angle on her head, a thin, pale and
> terrified little face looked out, with an open mouth and eyes
> immobilized by fright.

The ridiculous, the miserable, the out of place, what falls out of the world is seen as the actual, the here and now transcendent. Like Kierkegaard before him and Kafka after him, Dostoyevsky always denounced complacent this-worldliness not through glory (*exalted* this-worldliness), but through the twilight glow of the lowly, of what has been discredited by power, what is worthy of compassion, what has been dismissed. Not the (Russian) "pope" at the altar, but the priest under the sign of death, not the *ex officio* dispenser of the Sacraments, but the drunkard in the dive shows the outlines of the judging and forgiving Jesus: "And he will speak to us"—this is Semyon Marmeladov with an empty bottle by his side, a drunken official gone to the devil, in a state of extreme humiliation, mocked by his tippling partners around him: " 'You too come!' he'll say: 'Come, you drunkards, come you weaklings, come, you rotters!' And we'll all come forward, without being ashamed, and we'll stand before him . . . and he'll stretch his hands out to us, and we'll sink down . . . and cry . . . and understand everything."

It is a moving spectacle. The same Dostoyevsky who as a theoretician was obsessed with painting things in black and white, empowers precisely those figures of fantasy that, had he been ideologically consistent, he would have had to detest. He empowers them to articulate the central statements of the Christian message that were dearest to him, and he does so with the inevitability and persuasive force that befit figures of light. The whore expounds the story of the raising of Lazarus no less piously (because existentially) than the gentle monk Alexei does with the parable of the marriage of Cana. The atheist Kirilov looks upon the dead Jesus on the cross with the same earnestness as the fool in Christ, Prince Myshkin. And Myshkin, like Dostoyevsky (probably), has been marked by the sacred disease, epilepsy, and thereby proves himself a brother and fellow sufferer of the murderer Smerdyakov.

Here an author gives *his* disease first to the Jesuslike Don Quixote and a second time to the "Antichrist" who has killed and therefore hangs himself. And yet Smerdyakov is no more a thief than Dmitri Karamazov, but a person who, deep down in the dust, comes right out and stakes his life on his honor.

There are contradictions wherever we look: Dostoyevsky is an anti-European, an enemy of the Enlightenment, of rationality and the Euclidian explanation of the world. But in the enthusiastic vision of the old Russian nobleman Andrei Petrovich Versilov, he celebrates the Europe stamped by art, science, and wisdom. The writer who admitted that Jesus had a higher standing with him than the truth (insofar as he had to choose between them) has this principle articulated in *The Possessed* by the most depraved individual, Stavrogin. Stavrogin has raped a poor young girl, whose suicide he watches like a cynical psychological experimenter. Yet, in Dostoyevsky's secret language, which foreshadows Joycean nomenclature, Stavrogin means "the man on the cross."

What a muddled business, everywhere. We hear lines from the apocalypse used as a leitmotiv for the dispute between a sinner and a bishop (Stavrogin and Tichon) *and*—the same sentences!— in the touching meditation by Stepan Trofimovich: "I know your works: you are neither cold nor hot. Would that you were cold or hot! So, because you are lukewarm, and neither cold nor hot, I will spew you out of my mouth."

Demophilia, anti-Semitism, rejection of the Enlightenment spirit, all that is swept away, canceled, preserved, and heightened, as soon as Dostoyevsky inaugurates his giant debates about life in sin and salvation, the life of the great wrongdoers and the pious little people, of the simple in the spirit of the Lord. These debates are carried on by idiots and mutilated people, murderers and suicides, epileptics and eccentrics. And the one who is the starting point and end point of all conversations, Jesus in his lowliness— in various forms, evoked in a flash through quotations and references—is always in their midst.

Jesus is sitting at the table when Sonya and Raskolnikov expound verses from John (the story of Lazarus, a parable that is mentioned three times at a decisive moment in the story and so structures the novel). Jesus is a partner in dialogue when Alyosha in a moment of ecstatic rapture grasps the legend of the marriage at Cana as a parable of resurrection. Jesus is at the center of events when the deist Versilov suddenly brings Christ to the lost and lonely band at the end of the day (here too in an ecstatic vision); he is there—among the orphaned men and women. "How he comes to them, stretches his hands out to them" (think of the dream of the drunkard Marmeladov—always the same vision) and says: 'How could you forget Him?' And there falls as it were a blindfold from all their eyes, and there resounds the great, stirring hymn of the new and final resurrection."

One cannot repeat it often enough, Dostoyevsky's figures are first of all debaters and dreamers. They work little and talk a lot—and when they talk, they move right to the ultimate and loftiest topics. They don't talk about the weather, as people usually do in the nineteenth-century novel, but about immortality and sin, not about gossip, but about morality and terror, rebellion and guilt, the nation and the devil. And all the time they go for the limit, in speech and in action. When Dostoyevsky falls into a rage—and actually he's always doing that—the corpses get piled high, enormous crimes accumulate, there is whipping, and roaring, and whimpering. Scandals, outbursts, and wild public confrontations take place; women act like Furies and men, in their violent confessions, like exhibitionists.

It's always heaven and hell, Inferno and Paradiso. And all this occurs in a tiny space—in garrets and on staircases, in shanties and courtyards and above all, of course, in the theater of the soul. In Dostoyevsky, there are no long journeys from station to station. There are no wide-open Tolstoyan spaces, no powerful natural spectacles or dramatic changes of season. A scene like Levin's mowing in the open field among the peasants in the spring, as Tolstoy describes it in *Anna Karenina*, is unthinkable. Dostoyevsky's arena—a soul arena, a pan-demonium—is narrow. In his books, time limits, the action compresses, but the dialogues wander off, and the commentaries on events and the commentaries on the commentaries, the exegeses of the explanations needing to be explained, they stretch on—like the speeches of the lawyers in *The Brothers Karamazov*—over a hundred pages and more.

Dostoyevsky has his characters debate *murder and metaphysics*, the defendants as well as the district attorneys, defense counsels, judges. There are Shakespearean scenes in back rooms and entrance ways, *dramas sub specie aeternitatis* carried on by obsessed idea mongers of all classes and varieties in so passionate a manner, because for Dostoyevsky there is no topic that can be disposed of unequivocally, that is, quickly and briskly. Where the facts count for little, the motives behind the facts, by contrast, count for everything. Where the "what" is of no consequence the "how" is the question of all questions. Here there *has to be*, first of all, talk, debate and contradiction, confession and absolution, dreams and reflection on their content, by a public settling of accounts.

How many faces—and how many guilty parties—does the *one* death have in *The Brothers Karamazov*. How Janus-faced are the characters: constantly hovering on a thin thread (as the devil says) between heaven and hell—and never tied down, never safe on solid ground. As Lucifer, dressed as a bourgeois, a rather petty bourgeois ancestor of Thomas Mann's Mephisto, puts it, "Such abysses of faith can they grasp in one and the same moment that really one sometimes thinks, the whole thing is just hanging by a hair, and the person flies off." And this in-between kingdom, where everything—for salvation or perdition—can be done by the individual left to his freedom, was Dostoyevsky's turf. Here he took up positions and, prosecuting attorney and defender in one person, he delivered his pleas. This detective of the soul transformed his characters over and over and over in ever new conversations, frequently interconnected by parallels and contrasts, without ever closing the case and, like the Grand Inquisitor, saying his "dixi."

Ambivalence was Dostoyevsky's basic principle: ambivalence in sketching the psychographs, ambivalence in style. Narratives and visionary passages complete one another. Description is followed by speaking in tongues, shaped by intoxication and illumination, which Dostoyevsky traces back to the condition immediately preceding the onset of an epileptic fit. Like Nietzsche after him in *Ecce Homo*, he uses epilepsy to illustrate the meaning of inspiration: inspiration of the author, inspiration of Kirilov and Myshkin, the preachers—marked by *his* disease—of the dead and living God.

Dostoyevsky was a psychologist and theologian in one, a soul inspector and director of a *theatrum mundi*, as described by Andreas Gryphius. He was at once a detective and expounder of the law. Friedrich Dürrenmatt, a pastor's son and a poet, learned from the author of *The Brothers Karamazov* just as Dostoyevsky did when he went to school with that German-speaking writer Friedrich Schiller, who remained his great example for a lifetime, and with good reason.

Schiller was a criminologist and moralist, the author of *The Robbers*, a play in which, as we know, a father is murdered, as in *The Brothers Karamazov*. Schiller was also an expert on the

Spanish Inquisition and, in *Don Carlos*, the creator of the Cardinal Grand Inquisitor. He was the writer whose work Dostoyevsky wanted to see his brother Mikhail translate into Russian. Dostoyevsky confessed that he had "ground his way through" Schiller (and he liked to have his characters quote Schiller). The author of *The Robbers* was always concerned with "monsters" and the "minds" who "are tempted by the most repulsive vice for the sake of the power that adheres to it, for the sake of the power that accompanies it." Friedrich Schiller, it seems certain to me, was, along with Voltaire, the real godfather of the parable of the Grand Inquisitor, the "poem" that Dostoyevsky himself thought of, together with his representations of children, as the best thing he ever wrote.

The best? Perhaps. The most profound? Assuredly. And at all events the most controversial. It's controversial above all because it shows an atheist, Ivan Karamazov, with his eye on Christ holding up a mirror to the authoritarian and strictly hierarchical Roman Catholic church (and to the socialist avant garde, which in his view had a similar elitist structure). Dostoyevsky reproaches the church for despising the Lord on the cross in the same way that it despised man. The church knew the incapacity of the human race to endure the freedom Jesus had granted it, and so had made the devil's cause it's own. In the duel with the devil in the wilderness, the church had accepted the vile trinity of *miracle-mystery-authority*. It had satisfied the people and taught them to adore secular mystery just as they adored the power based on the identity of church and state.

Following in Schiller's footsteps, Dostoyevsky maintains that a small band of illuminati sacrifices itself for the masses and hence doesn't want to be disturbed by Christ when he appears in Seville around the time of the Grand Inquisition. Their work is completed, done forever; from now on, the pope and the church have their say. But unless Jesus wants to be condemned a second time and be executed amid popular jubilation, he has to keep quiet. (And Jesus really does keep quiet in Ivan's poem. Indeed, he not only says nothing, but he kisses the Grand Inquisitor on the lips. In other words, he returns, in the prison of Seville, the kiss he received from Judas in Gethsemane. This is a sign that the devil is to be conquered only through love, and—a unique case for Dostoyevsky—that logic chopping can be beaten only by silence.)

So the "Grand Inquisitor" is a song of praise to Jesus and a challenge to the devil's party, which has replaced service with domination and freedom with official authority (*potestas*, not *auctoritas*). A more dramatic way of presenting both the song of praise and the invective cannot be imagined. Ivan Karamazov makes his Cardinal Grand Inquisitor argue in a manner—grand, Luciferian, and eloquent—that only Schiller knew how to handle: " 'What I say to Thee will come to pass, and our dominion will be built up. I repeat, tomorrow Thou shalt see that obedient flock who at a sign from me will hasten to heap up the hot cinders about the pile on which I shall burn Thee for coming to hinder us. For if anyone has ever deserved our fires, it is Thou. Tomorrow I shall burn Thee. . . . I have spoken.' "

No doubt, Dostoyevsky is *arguing* here, Friedrich Schiller is *speaking* here. Here we see thought out to the end the idea originating in a meditation from Luke ("When the Son of man comes, will he find faith on earth?") This has been continually discussed by writers down through the centuries, all the way to Goethe who, as his notes from Italy prove, thought up a pope, Pius VI—a *living* pope, a *ruling* pontiff—who when Jesus returns can think of nothing better than having the Savior arrested and placed under the supervision of the Jesuits. Christ becomes the state prisoner of a Holy Father who is intent on theatrical representation ("I am completely spoiled for this hocus-pocus," wrote Goethe the Protestant from Rome).

Here we have the pope as comedian *playing* the Lord, while the *true* Lord is led away by the retinue of Jesuits. We see that Dostoyevsky's poem was not as daring as it seems at first blush—and certainly not implausible, given its author. Whatever anti-Roman heresies Ivan may advance in the parable of the Grand Inquisitor, Myshkin, Dostoyevsky's favorite figure, formulates the challenge to the Western, secularized church in even harsher terms. And as for Ivan, the "atheist" and the devil's partner, it is too often forgotten that of all the characters in the novel he, the disturbed and doubt-haunted one—the one who can "go under in hatred, but also rise again in the light of the truth"—is secretly the figure closest to Dostoyevsky.

He is close because of Ivan's love for children, which puts him alongside the secret preachers, with Myshkin and Alyosha leading the way, in Jesus' Church of the Children. He is close because of his rebellion against a world apparently penetrated by God, in which children are tortured. ("I will refuse until death," Camus says in *The Plague*, "to love the creation in which children are tormented." Ivan's humanity, stored up for the Auschwitz era, is a countersign to the Holocaust, which did not exclude children.)

Ivan Karamazov was close to his author, who read Pestalozzi and Fröbel. Dostoyevsky was a champion of children who, along with Dickens and Turgenev, was the first novelist in world literature to present girls and boys who were more than "little grown-ups." Ivan was close to him as a rebel on behalf of those children with whose emancipation Dostoyevsky—like Novalis—identified the beginning of the Golden Age. This creature was close to his creator as his secret brother under the sign of suffering: "Such notions as giving back the entrance ticket and the Grand Inquisitor," Dostoyevsky wrote in an annotation to *The Brothers Karamazov*, "smell of epilepsy, of excruciating nights."

Finally, Ivan was also close to his inventor because his doppelgänger, the devil, expresses literally what Dostoyevsky himself thought: "Not like a child (who knows no doubt), I confess to faith in Christ. But my hosanna has gone through the great purgatorial fires of doubt, as the devil says of himself in my last novel."

The diary entry for the year 1890 speaks for itself. Berdayev was right when he defended the thesis that Dostoyevsky's own voice echoes in the words of Ivan Karamazov. He himself, not only his character, felt that the divine harmony of the world was bought too dearly with the suffering of a single child: "And so I renounce the higher harmony altogether. It's not worth the tears of that one tortured child who beats itself on the breast with its little fist and prayed in its stinking outhouse, with its tears to 'dear, kind God' " (pp. 225–26).

I consider this one of the grandest passages in Dostoyevsky's *oeuvre*, steeped in pain and compassion. It made André Malraux exclaim, in answer to the question whether Dostoyevsky was a reactionary, given his religious mode of thought, which here and there obstructed his view of existing social abuses: "A person who has reached Dostoyevsky's depths, as expressed in Ivan Karamazov's rebellion against unhappiness, cannot be a reactionary. 'At the moment when an innocent child is tormented by cruel men, I give back my entrance ticket to paradise': Anyone who talks that way is close to the forces of revolution. There is no reactionary who didn't accept the world as it is."

Keeping all this in mind, there is not the slightest doubt that Dostoyevsky himself supported point for point the correctness of the condemnation pronounced by the spirit of Jesus' rebellion: He was opposed to a church that for the sake of maintaining the power of a few kills souls, lets children die, removes freedom from sight, and gambles away peace among men. "I want to see with my own eyes the lamb lie down with the lion and the victim rise up to embrace his murderer. I want to be there when everyone suddenly understands what it has all been about. All the religions of the world are built on this longing, and I am a believer. But then there are the children, and what am I to do about them?" (225).

Is that really the speech of a cynical free spirit, who holds that whatever is possible can also be justified? Is Ivan's dictum "I am a believer" a mere flourish? And even if it were, in his opposition to a world where the horrible scenery of future concentration camps is anticipated, and Russian or Turkish sadists, in bold poetic adumbration, appear as Mengeles or Eichmanns, how near he stands to the prisoner who walks silently out into the streets of Seville. And how near he stands to Alyosha, as he was originally planned—Alyosha who with his children discusses the temptation of Christ in the wilderness.

And is this Ivan nevertheless an atheist? As I see it, he is, since it says so in the text. After all, why not, if we reflect that Dostoyevsky had the peculiarity of always giving the best and most telling arguments precisely to the character whose position struck him as ambiguous (like his own, like his hosanna on the edge of Purgatory).

No, he let none of his characters fall, not a single one: least of all the sufferers, the ones marked by sickness and confusion. No wonder, then, that his confession to Christ—"without Christ there will be nothing, that is what we must believe in"—was a confession with its eye on the Man of Sorrows. Dostoyevsky stressed not the Risen Christ—despite his Johannine faith, he scarcely speaks of him in the novel—but the tortured Christ: the one addressed by Pascal as the man who "will suffer till the end of time."

When the author of *The Idiot* and *The Brothers Karamazov* writes about the one murdered on the cross, he argues from the position of a candidate for death, who knows quite precisely what he is speaking about. Why else the continual descriptions of the last seconds before the guillotine falls? Why, time after time—in *The Idiot*, too—the copying of the dead Christ as painted by Hölbein (if Jesus "could have seen his picture as a corpse on the day before his execution, would he have still let himself be crucified, and would he have died as he did afterward")?

"No, one may not do that to a man": The cry of Myshkin at the execution of a murderer in Lyon is identical to the rebellion of Ivan Karamazov against the torturing of innocent children everywhere in the world. And the pathos, here explicit and there alluded to, through the connection of the appeal to Christ's death on the cross *and* through the countervision of "Jesus among the children," produces a revocation of Hölbein's picture, as planned in *The Idiot* by Nastasia Filipovna, the "great sinner." This testifies to a secret dialogue that Dostoyevsky's figures carry on with Jesus of Nazareth. They would like to avenge Jesus' disgrace by occupying in his stead, like Kirilov in *The Possessed*, the freedom he promised in the act of suicide ("redeemed," as the Crucified never was redeemed). This is the Jesus whom the dying remember in their last hour, the Jesus whose life Dostoyevsky—like Pascal and Kiekegaard—wanted to write. And this is the Jesus whom he, knowing very well the border between poetry and preaching, nevertheless had good reasons for approaching only indirectly and approximately. Dostoyevsky would approach this Jesus only with the help of dreams, visions, legends, and pictures—only by referring in chronicle fashion and imagistically to the pious practices of the monks, particularly the starets Zossima. He would approach this Jesus only—and above all—by discovering a person, Myshkin, the idiot, who from the perspective of a fool, the standpoint of the pure simpleton and innocent fool, illustrates how badly the world needs salvation.

Myshkin is no saint, but a clown; no representative of power, but a man struck by epilepsy, impotence, and, in the end, madness. And he is the "most Jesuslike figure" in Dostoyevsky, not the mirror image of Jesus (that would be too direct for Dostoyevsky), but a follower in an unholy time, humble and gentle, full of patience and grief. He is a sacrificial victim, not a doer, a brother eccentric rather than a man who knows what he wants. Nevertheless, he is the only novelistic character in world litera-

ture—the first and the last—who gives a profile to Jesus of Nazareth as a possibility person (in Musil's sense). He does so through
the figure of the "other," who in his foolish humanity, his charm,
vulnerability, and childish innocence becomes a judgment on the
world as it is—the man in the drawing as a *skandalon*.

Myshkin, Alyosha's older, deeply wounded brother in the
Lord, the pure fool ("only help from a fool is real help," said
Walter Benjamin) is an incarnation of those Dostoyevskyan fig-
ures, about whom one of their most skillful interpreters, E. M.
Forster, has said:

> In Dostoyevsky the characters and situations always stand for
> more than themselves; infinity attends them; though yet they
> remain individuals they expand to embrace and summon it to
> embrace them; one can apply to them the saying of St. Cath-
> erine of Siena that God is in the soul and the soul is in God
> as the sea is in the fish and the fish is in the sea. Every sen-
> tence he writes implies this extension, and the implication is
> the dominant aspect of his work. He is a great novelist . . .
> (but) he has also the greatness of a prophet, to which our
> ordinary standards are inapplicable. (*Aspects of the Novel*,
> 192–93)

A prophet and a marked man, *Hosanna and Purgatory*. E. M.
Forster formulated his homage a half century after the remark,
explicitly recalled by André Malraux, that Dostoyevsky's first wife
is supposed to have said on her deathbed: "I have always despised
you, because you were once a convict."

The author of *The Brothers Karamazov* knew why he, along
with Ivan, moved into the twilight a world in which, in his day
as in Jesus' time, humility does provoke humiliation; but humiliation, in turn, goes to ruin at the hands of humility.

This can be gleaned from the parable of the Grand Inquisitor,
the poem by Ivan, one of whose important functions in *The Brothers Karamazov* is to recall past and ongoing suffering—the suffering of the poor, the unredeemed, and the disturbed beneath
the cross.

"Behind Dostoyevsky's coffin," Kafka noted in his diary on 15
March 1914, "the students wanted to carry his funeral wreaths.
He died in the workers' quarter, on the fifth floor of an apartment
house."

FRANZ KAFKA

◆

THE CASTLE

HANS KÜNG

◆

Religion
in the
Collapse of Modernity

The Castle by Franz Kafka is a work of world literature. On this point, at least since the post–World War II Kafka boom in Europe and America, there can be no question. But is *The Castle* a *religious* work? Despite the important critics who have championed a religious interpretation of Kafka—the editor of his posthumous works, Max Brod, and his English translator, Edwin Muir—one may be allowed to have one's doubts about this.

What is supposed to be religious about this bafflingly real-unreal story, with its long conversations, its often dreamlike, grotesque situations, its continual fresh complications, but its ultimately static account of the man with the initial K. (originally "I")? K. has been called from far away, but when he arrives he cannot practice his métier as a land surveyor either up in the count's castle or in the village that belongs to it. In the course of the novel, he doesn't even find the entrance to the castle or manage to settle down in the village community.

Indeed, what is supposed to be religious about this story? In his inexplicably tireless striving for access to the so-close-but-oh-so-far Castle, K. falls in with two women who are connected to it. First he loves Frieda, the mistress of the high-ranking Castle official, Klamm, and then Olga, the sister of Amalia. (Amalia is persecuted but resists and is therefore ostracized with her entire family.) But he loses both, and so fails to reach his goal either in his occupation or in his love life.

Finally, what should be religious about K.'s story? He runs around in the immense, labyrinthine bureaucracy. At first he is mysteriously appointed an assistant in the school and humiliated; then he is called to a hearing. Completely exhausted, he can no longer perceive the one chance of access he is—perhaps—given. And the more he tries to decipher the mystery of the Castle, the more it escapes him. The once proud land surveyor is thus lowered to living in hiding as the servant of the maids at the inn—and at this point the novel breaks off. One last time, what is religious about all this?

To be sure, it would be seductive for the theologian to unlock this novel, darkly mysterious as it is for rational understanding, the way the old church fathers did with the incomprehensible passages of the Bible. We could simply understand it as an allegory, as an imagistic expression for certain religious ideas. In this manner, one can discover—or, if necessary, read everywhere into the text—the secret of divine, even Christian, reality. Why not? After all, the text itself leaves many questions open: Is K. actually a land surveyor or not? Was he really called or told a lie? Did he come by accident? What was his intention in coming? And so forth. There are many methods of explicating Kafka, and there is almost total chaos among the interpretations by Kafka experts all over the world; in Hartmut Binder's helpful two-volume Kafka handbook, Richard Sheppard cites well over 150 articles on *The Castle* alone. In the face of all this, the theologian could not be blamed for deciding, without further ado, for the *religious-allegorical* interpretation by the prominent Jewish writer Max Brod. This is the oldest and long the most popular reading. (We owe to Brod the publication of the novel in 1926—against the will of his friend Kafka?—two years after Kafka's death.)

Behind *The Castle*, Brod says, lies hidden Kafka's struggle and striving for divine grace. With the authority of Kafka's friend and editor, Brod comes to the following conclusion in comparing *The Castle* with Kafka's earlier, likewise highly cryptic and unfinished novel *The Trial* (see his famous "Afterword by the Editor" in the first edition of *The Castle*, for which Brod himself provided the title): "It is essential that the hero in *The Trial* is persecuted by an invisible, mysterious authority, summonded before the court, while in *The Castle* he is shunned by just such an authority. 'Joseph K.' (in *The Trial*) hides and flees. 'K.' in *The Castle* asserts himself, attacks. Despite the opposed directions, however, the basic feeling is identical. For what is the meaning of *The Castle*, with its strange archives, its inscrutable hierarchy of functionaries, its whims and deceits, its (thoroughly justified) claim to unconditional respect and obedience? We need not exclude more particular interpretations, which may be completely valid, but are enclosed by this most comprehensive reading the way the inner shells of a Chinese wood carving are by the outermost shell. But, that said, the Castle, to which K. gains no access, which he cannot, for some incomprehensible reason, even properly approach, is precisely what the theologians call 'grace.' By that I mean the divine guidance of human destiny (the village), the efficacy of accidents, mysterious resolutions, gifts, and damages, the unearned and unobtainable, the judgment of 'non liquet' passed on the life of everyone. Thus, in *The Trial* and *The Castle*, we find presented both of the deity's modes of appearance (in the sense of the cabala)—judgment and grace" (Fischer Paperback Edition in 7 Volumes, p. 349). Given this sort of obliging interpretation, why shouldn't the theologian seize the opportunity decisively? Why not, in fact, understand *The Castle* as an allegory, as a parable of divine grace?

But here I can't avoid making a confession. After studying the novel again and again, with the best will in the world, I still find nothing religious in it. And this is not just because its general atmosphere is depressing, cheerless, with no promise of salvation. *The Castle* nowhere lets us glimpse a redemptive way out. There is practically no mention of God, the divine, the religious. But above all the Castle itself, this dismal giant bureaucracy, is a much too ambivalent and threatening quantity to be identified with the Absolute or "heaven," much less grace. Nor can the village be equated with the "world of human beings."

Try the countertest: Couldn't one rightly use the same allegorical system to decipher the Castle as hell? In this novel's contradictory history of interpretation, this has in fact been done—by Siegfried Kracauer against Max Brod. Because of such positive or negative mystagogy, one is inclined to prefer the sober interpretation of Hannah Arendt that in the first instance the novel describes the stubborn struggle of a person of good will against the overpoweringly complicated old Austrian bureaucracy, which set itself up as God's deputy and which Kafka had to deal with every day in his years as a lawyer and employee of the Prague "Workers Accident Insurance Institute."

As always, I see no possibility of directly translating Kafka's world of images into the language of theology, nor, of course, into the language of psychology, philosophy, or sociology. Kafka's last great work may not be made over into grist for the mill of mystifying speculative thinkers, whatever their discipline. The upshot of all this is that I as a theologian cannot subscribe to such a directly religious interpretation, although it may be shared by most theological experts on Kafka (whether Jewish, Protestant, or Catholic). And for analogous hermeneutical reasons neither can I endorse any *direct psychoanalytical, philosophical, or sociological interpretation* that encumbers the novel, not with a religious conceptual system, but with a psychoanalytical, philosophical, or sociological one. No, in *all* these instances, Kafka's work becomes "program music" (Heinz Politzer writing against Max Brod). The work of art is only the occasion for preaching already given theorems and unverified dogmas, which exist, as we know, not just in theology but in philosophy, psychology, and sociology, too.

———————◆———————

Thus, given such infiltration by nonliterary considerations, would it not be better to cut through the Gordian knot of interpretation and take the novel simply as a brilliant *literary document*, to work on it strictly as a text, and analyze its specific narrative structure? The Tübingen philologist Friedrich Beissner, an experienced critic of Hölderlin, noted in his 1952 lecture on Kafka (p. 9) that, "Hardly anyone raises questions about Kafka's *art*." In making this point, Beissner gave the decisive impetus to an internal literary critique. Formal and structural analysis are in the foreground here. Kafka is evaluated as a "teller of tales" (1952), as a "poet" (1958), as a painter of "dreamlike inner life" (1972)—all these titles from Beissner. And this essay has been supported and modified by Beissner's students—especially by his doctoral student Martin Walser, who wrote his dissertation "Description of a Form" in 1951 (published in 1961).

Shouldn't all other disciplines concede this point, along with the theologians? On a novel like *The Castle*, a work of literature, the literary scholars have to be consulted first. Kafka himself said that *The Castle* was shaped with the greatest "expenditure of art." And so readers should explore and judge it in accordance with internal, aesthetic criteria and not some sort of grand philosophical views. As a matter of fact, in the last few decades an enormous amount of objective analysis of Kafka has been done, investigating in precise detail his peculiar narrative methods, his structural forms and elements, his use of language and metaphor in both individual pieces and his work as a whole. But on these issues Walter Jens will have to report.

As a theologian, I am interested in something that has also struck some literary scholars—the fact that while the exploration of the work as a text remains fundamental, we cannot overlook the question of the reality content. How is reality mirrored within the subject? What is the relation between the work of art, the inner world of the artistic subject, and the historical situation and social pattern? Indeed, these questions are now posed in earnest. We can thus completely agree with Hermann Hesse when as early as 1956 in his *Writings on Literature 2* (p. 491) he points out: "Kafka's stories are not dissertations on religious, metaphysical, or moral problems, but poetical works." Still I do not share Hesse's exclusivity when he concludes that "Kafka doesn't have anything to say to us, either as a theologian or a philosopher, but only as a poet. It's not his fault that his tremendous fictions have become fashionable today, that they are read by people who have neither the gifts nor the will to comprehend poetry."

What Hesse misses here is Kafka the *human being*. For the "purely literary Kafka" does not exist, any more than Kafka the philosopher or Kafka the theologian. Kafka's work is only seemingly ahistorical. And any idealogically unbiased and comprehensive interpretation of the work can in no way be allowed to exclude the writer's biography, literary tradition, and the historical background in general.

Literary scholarship has shown no lack of meticulous detective work *in tracking down the biographical material* in Kafka. Klaus Wagenbach and Hartmut Binder, adopting a comprehensive rather than a selective approach, have researched the exact circumstances of Kafka's life and made an immense contribution to faithful interpretation of *The Castle*. Here some interpreters try, all too complacently, to pat on the back the man whose shoulders they are standing on: Max Brod. Kafka's most intimate friend and editor of his literary remains has already provided the crucial biographical background data for *The Castle*: Behind the figure of Amalia is concealed Kafka's earlier fiancée, Julie Wohryzek. Behind the figure of Frieda is primarily the Czech journalist Milena Jésenká, with whom Kafka was linked in a passionate but brief friendship, but who refused to leave her husband (K.'s great antagonist Klamm). The crucial finding of positivistic-biographical Kafka research is that "*The Castle* is an autobiographical work in the extreme sense" (Binder, *Commentary*, II, 269). Thus, owing to this "new view" there is no longer any question of religion. But this is by no means a clear case.

Granted, *The Castle* is an autobiographical work. But that's not the whole story. With an author like Kafka, problems of his life and his era, the history of his life and mind, cannot be so simply separated. To do so would be to succumb to an overly narrow biographical approach. But if we join Binder (*Commentary*, I, 9) in (rightly) presenting Kafka not as "purely traditionless and withdrawn from all empirical connections," could it not be— *pace* Binder—that Kafka ultimately does stand as something like "a main representative of literary modernity, as a certain endpoint of European intellectual history"?

For this reason, we should try to escape "the hermeneutic narrowness of purely internal interpretation, without slipping back into the old mistakes of the allegorical, symbol-translating, philosophical, and sociological school." Unlike narrow positivistic analysts, we should not tear "literature and the individual work of art . . . out of its overlapping intellectual contexts" (quoted from the informative research report by Peter U. Beicken, pp. 161, 175). In order to arrive, as a theologian, at a responsible reading of Kafka, I would like to propose something like a *structured-integrative method of interpretation* that neither monistically rejects other methods nor indulges in a promiscuous methodological pluralism. My approach would rather build on the philological, literary-historical, and biographical method and still—since the work of art is a unit—remain open to the study of larger psychological, social, and philosophical connections.

Positivistic research has correctly pointed out the great importance of the *family situation* for Franz Kafka, who was born in

Prague's Old City in 1883, two years after Dostoyevsky's death. Kafka had a strong, successful but thick-headed father, and a retiring, empathetic mother. He was the firstborn, a child who in growing up was very often alone, continually handed over to the care of domestics, and "evidently could not build up the necessary primal confidence in the people he was permanently connected to for a healthy personality structure" (Binder, *Commentary*, I, 22). The upshot of this was a disturbed relationship with other people as well. Kafka's problem was based on a lack of feelings of self-worth, and on a neurotic attitude toward sex, owing to passivity, distance from the community, low vital energy, and a bachelor existence. In Kafka's late works, the failure of human relations is taken for granted. He comes to grief in love, marriage, work, community life, in everything; and this is given literary expression in *The Castle*—alienated and distorted in Kafka's "dreamlike inner world" (H. Politzer).

Building on Brod's testimony, all students of Kafka agree in stressing that along with his family Kafka's *Jewish origins* played a powerful role in his life. We can easily imagine what a shocking effect the somewhat innocuous film version of the novel would have had if—and scarcely a single detail would have had to be altered—instead of Maximilian Schell, a recognizably Jewish actor had played K.: Then we would have had the Jew as a prototype of the stranger in society, of the unwelcome one, the person watched with mistrust, the melancholic type who would like to adapt to society and yet keeps meeting hostility.

Despite everything, is it true that Kafka as an extreme exponent of a deracinated, alienated Western Judaism "was remote from the consciousness of a European stamped by Christian tradition and its decay" (H. Binder, 10)? And does this mean that the alienation of Kafka the Jew and of the land surveyor K. has nothing at all to do with the alienation of the modern person?

On the contrary, Kafka the Prague Jew, who wrote his works in the two decades that changed the world, between 1904 and 1924, participated in the mainstream of European culture. He had Jewish friends with a thoroughly European education, such as Max Brod, Franz Werfel, and others. He had come to grips with Kleist, Grillparzer, Hauptmann, and Hamsun. As early as his gymnasium years, he had been a convinced Darwinist and follower of Nietzsche. He had turned to socialism and rejected the Jewish faith. He had studied and graduated from a German university, taken part in lectures and poetry readings set up by the "German Students Reading Room." But later he underwent a transformation, studied Augustine's *Confessions* and Tolstoy's philosophical writings, and finally turned to the study of Hebrew and Zionism. No one like this could be a provincial Prague ghetto Jew. Kafka was in fact a "typical Jewish" *representative of late modernity, of the generation after the First World War.*

In all this, Kafka had an enormous—and symptomatic—interest in Kierkegaard and Dostoyevsky, the two great figures who as early as the nineteenth century diagnosed the looming crisis of modernity. What interested Kafka the Jew in Kierkegaard the Christian? Surely it was not only the quite analogous difficulties Kierkegaard had with sexuality and marriage, but also Kierkegaard's work. He studied it and concentrated, though by no means exclusively, on the passages emphasizing man's anxiety, impotence, and forlornness. But Kafka also read Kierkegaard on the possibilities for action: "And the following passage is not from the Talmud," but actually from Kierkegaard: "As soon as a person comes bringing something primitive with him, so that he doesn't say: One must take the world as it is . . . but says: However the world may be, I stick to an original notion that I do not intend to change as the world sees fit: At the very moment that this word is heard, a transformation takes place in the whole of one's existence. As in the fairy tale, when the word is spoken, the castle that has been enchanted for a hundred years opens up, and everything springs to life: Thus existence becomes pure attentiveness" (quoted in Brod, pp. 150–51).

Of course, belief in Jesus Christ was not possible for Kafka, and, unlike Kierkegaard, he did not look at individualism, solitariness, and bachelorhood as an ideal. In no way did he wish on principle to live alone. In the last half year of his life, at least, he experienced the happiness of living together with Dora Diamant from Berlin, who accompanied the mortally ill Kafka to a sanatorium in Vienna and cared for him till his death.

Early on, Kafka read a biography of Dostoyevsky and all his life he rated him highly. He read Dostoyevsky to his favorite sister Ottla, along with Schopenhauer and Kleist. And in one of his first letters he compares his "discovery" of the love of Milena with his "discovery" of Dostoyevsky: He tells how after they read the manuscript of *Poor Folk* around three o'clock in the morning Dmitri Grigorovich and Nikolai Nekrasov rang Dostoyevsky's bell, hailed him as the greatest Russian writer, and how, after they left, Dostoyevsky stood weeping at the window, with the feeling: "These splendid people! How good and noble they are! And how common *I* am . . . if I just tell them, they won't believe it."

Kafka was a man of the modern world through and through. On the strength of his Jewish alienation, he felt the *crisis of the modern paradigm* sooner and more strongly than others did. Science, technology, industrialization, and democracy—the forces of modernity—lost their fascination for Kafka, and presented themselves to him above all in the form of an enormous, inaccessible, impenetrable bureaucracy, the world of the Castle in fact. It is true that Kafka, who was very interested in political and social issues, in his literary alienation scarcely allows a glimmer of the modern problem of production to appear in *The Castle*. But he understands capitalism as a system of dependencies, and in the novel he shows quite clearly the subordination to a bureaucratic power structure of the individual person, of the family and the group. He shows too their external and internal dependency, which will not allow life to develop freely.

Thus, in *The Castle*, Kafka is *also* concerned with a critical analysis of the age, translated into images and puzzles, although he presents it from a higher standpoint. And Adorno was not wrong when he called the repellent, shabby, and irrational features of Kafka's world of compulsion, which proceeds with the uncanny precision of a nightmare, "the cryptogram of the brilliantly polished late phase of capitalism" (*Prisms*, p. 319). Thus a *social-critical* reading of *The Castle* is justified, so long as it does not pervert the philological, literary-historical, and biographical interpretation into its exact opposite and confine the whole of the novel to this narrow perspective.

The same holds for existentialist interpretations. There is no denying that the central figure of the land surveyor, who appears as the challenger of the existing order, includes much of what Sartre and Camus have found in Kafka; K. contains not only the impenetrable, absurd, labyrinthine qualities of this world, but also the contradictions of human existence, anxiety, care, suffering, death, the necessity of the free, yet continually threatened and ultimately doomed project of life.

We are now prepared, as far as method and content are concerned, to discuss the central idea of the novel—*the Castle* itself. For according to the novel the goal of K. the man is evidently not merely man nor being human. The point K. is entirely oriented toward, which he strives for, albeit in vain, with all his powers, the point he strives to reach by all the roundabout ways possible (women are important here) is the Castle. The Castle is the goal of his longing, the focus of his thinking, the motor driving his will. What does it mean?

There can no dispute here. This Castle, from which everything depends, not only for Kafka, but also for the village, remains confusingly vague, remains essentially undefined, always mysterious. In the whole novel, there is not the least indication of what the Castle means. We have already seen that it cannot mean God or the divine. Only one thing, I believe, is certain from the text; the Castle always towers over humanity, always outdoes and transcends it. Man may always try to come closer, but cannot reach it on his own, if he is not called. The Castle is the goal to which K. finds no way. It is thus an expression of *transcendence* that remains *mysterious*.

Here one has to go along with those interpreters, such as Erich Heller, who early on spoke of *"symbols . . . of a negative transcendence"* (p. 103). In so doing, we are *not* falling back on the *allegorical* exploration that we rejected at the outset, where the interpreter simply "says something different" ("álla agoreúei") from the immediate, literal sense, where he arbitrarily substitutes another meaning and injects his own thoughts into the text ("grace" instead of "Castle"). No, a *symbolic* explanation is given where the interpreter discovers in the text itself the essential relatedness of an image to a content lying behind it. This occurs when a text proves itself to be what the Germans call a *Sinn-Bild* ("meaning-picture," or "symbol"), namely a symbol for a reality that the author obviously has in mind (taking the Castle to mean "transcendence").

Kafka was quite conscious of the symbolic meaning of his work.

He once did a tremendous little meditation on the "Parables." And on this symbolic level a careful *religious or theological interpretation* is possible. I will leave the reader to decide whether we can go as far as Claude David, who in what is also a quite restrained interpretation calls *The Castle* a "theological fable." This much, at least, is certain: The Castle, the world of transcendence, exists.

A communion, even though a puzzling, impenetrable one, exists between the world of the village and the world of the Castle.

A way leads into the interior of the Castle. It may be long, infinitely long, and it may be obstructed by ever new rooms and ever new barriers, but it does exist. And Barnabas the messenger took it, at least as far as the chancelleries or front building of the Castle.

Once one arrives in the Castle, "something is there." This something is offered to Barnabas, and it is only "Barnabas' fault if he gets nothing out of it except doubt, anxiety, and hopelessness."

For all his consciousness of the loss of transcendence (symbolized by the church tower in his home town), even the land surveyor never gives up the hope of winning, through the Castle, the right to reside in the human community of the village, to get into the Castle, and to be received in it, which means to win back transcendence.

All these are points that a theological-symbolic interpretation can answer for. Thus, the Castle is not an expression for grace, but for a *coded, enigmatic experience of transcendence*. In such an experience, transcendence remains mysterious, impenetrable, alarming, but a way is left open to humans, and hope is not rendered impossible. So is *The Castle* a religious work? Well, not *directly religious*, but of the *greatest religious relevance*.

Kierkegaard as a radical believer speaks of the absolute paradox or the paradox of the Absolute. Dostoyevsky, the skeptical believer, has at least some of his characters give positive expression to faith. But in his fictions Kafka draws back, sibylline, undefined, unfathomable. No more than Dostoyevsky is he a naturalist à la Zola, who tried "scientifically" to dissect the person simply as a product of heredity and environment. In this positivistic, scientific, bureaucratic world, where what is visible, graspable, and calculable is considered the actual and ultimate reality, Kafka holds on tight to transcendence. Unlike Nietzsche, from whom he learned in his early years, he was no atheist denying the supreme value and declaring that God is dead. And he was certainly not a nihilist denying any value not just to the highest value but to all of them, a man without a goal. But he is, as far as we can determine in this novel, a person continually tormented between the Castle up above and the powers below, a person torn between doubt and hope. And all this takes place in a depressingly gray world, which for good reason has become proverbial in all languages in the decades after his death: the "Kafkaesque world."

"Kafkaesque" suggests the labyrinthine world in its late phase. It conjures up the world of our century with its absurd world wars, its concentration camps and gulags, which so far surpassed all Kafka's visions of terror. But it also evokes our world's anonymous forces, its unconquerable compulsions and hidden seducers, its countless assurances, and, nevertheless, continually increasing uncertainties. Kafka, we recall, worked for an insurance company, Assicurazioni Generali!

Here the *paradigm of modernity*, which began so hopefully, has come to an end, in a way completely different from *all* earlier paradigms: It is overshadowed not only by anxiety and helplessness, but—and who could overlook this?—by an unprecedented distance of God, indeed the "eclipse of God." Martin Buber, Kafka's Jewish interlocutor, made that the key word for the epoch: "The darkening of the light of heaven, the eclipse of God is in fact the character of the hour of world history in which we live" (*Works*, I, 520).

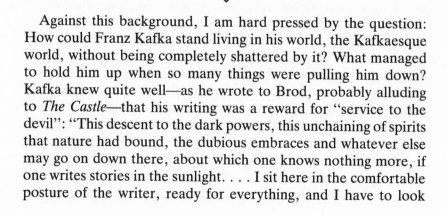

Against this background, I am hard pressed by the question: How could Franz Kafka stand living in his world, the Kafkaesque world, without being completely shattered by it? What managed to hold him up when so many things were pulling him down? Kafka knew quite well—as he wrote to Brod, probably alluding to *The Castle*—that his writing was a reward for "service to the devil": "This descent to the dark powers, this unchaining of spirits that nature had bound, the dubious embraces and whatever else may go on down there, about which one knows nothing more, if one writes stories in the sunlight. . . . I sit here in the comfortable posture of the writer, ready for everything, and I have to look idly on—for what else can I do but write—as my real self, this poor, defenseless thing . . . is at the drop of a hat . . . pinched, thrashed, and almost pulverized by the devil" (*Letters*, pp. 384, 386).

But testimony like this does make it clear that Franz Kafka himself, the writer, the man, by no means lived exclusively in his Kafkaesque novelistic world. There was for him not only the "below," but the "above," not only the "dark powers," but also the "sunlight." Despite all the "dubious embraces," he remained "ready for everything beautiful." Kafka considered suicide, but rejected it.

Kafka's *works* don't tell us everything about Kafka the *man*, about the source of his energy, his staying power, and even his writing. They don't tell us everything about his faith, his attitude toward religion. Excitingly, there is the mysterious *other side* of Kafka that could not enter into his work, but was reflected in aphorisms and reports about his life by himself and others. From his youthful days, Kafka was anxiety ridden and then became deathly sick. Like Pascal, he had to stop writing at an age when Dostoyevsky had really just gotten started. But it's idle to speculate whether he would have finally worked this other, more positive, side of life, of religion, into his writing. Even *The Castle* remained a fragment. It is only thanks to Brod that we know about how it might have turned out: K. would struggle on, would finally die of exhaustion, but on his deathbed he would get word that he was "allowed to live and to work here" (*The Castle*, p. 347). A more than ambiguous end. We have to come to terms with the fact that what positive value Kafka found in religion never took shape in his work.

But it is certain that Kafka was personally more religious, more believing, more hopeful, than his works reveal. Brod continually points to the "positive feature" (p. 156) in Kafka, his humor (when he read the first chapter of *The Trial* to his friends, there was "uncontrollable laughter"), his "serenity and cheerfulness," "the gentle, levelheaded, never hasty quality of his nature," in short, "the joy in life and the world." This joy shines through with elemental force even in the Vienna days with Milena and, more weakly, with Dora, his companion for the last half year, in the face of all his anxiety.

Still, first of all, there is something more important that finds expression in Kafka's own *diaries*, for instance in prayerlike passages of touching urgency, in a way that would be unthinkable in his work. These are reflections, meditations, examinations of conscience before the hidden God, as it were. In February 1916, for instance, after a depressing confrontation with his first fiancée, Felice Bauer: "Have mercy on me, I am sinful down to the last corner of my being. But I had gifts that were not entirely despicable, some modest capabilities. I played havoc with them, thoughtless creature that I am. I am now close to the end, just at a time when externally everything might be turning out well for me. Don't thrust me among the lost. . . . If I am condemned, then I am condemned not only at the end, but condemned as well to protest till the end" (p. 370).

In the second place, important material can be found in the *aphorisms*, what Brod called "considerations of sin, suffering, pain, hope, and the true path." These were composed at around the same time as *The Castle*; they offer uncommonly rich theological reflections on evil and the devil, the Fall and guilt, Paradise and expulsion from Eden, the appearance of the Messiah and definitive salvation, about truth and the "indestructible" element in humanity.

In the third place, there is important material in Kafka's *conversations* with *Gustav Janoch* (although it is hard to scrutinize critically the sources of the individual statements). Here Kafka reflects on "the longing for the divine" (p. 66); he rejects literature in which "religion is completely distilled into the aesthetic" ("the religion of this kind of literature is snobism," p. 70); he meditates on original sin and freedom, on Judaism and Christianity, on Christ and God: "What we really can grasp is mystery, darkness. God dwells in this. And that is good, for without this protective darkness we would overcome God. That would correspond to the nature of men. The son dethrones the father. This is why God must remain hidden in the dark. And since man cannot press forward to him, he at least attacks the darkness surrounding God" (pp. 79–80).

———————◆———————

Time does not permit me to say more about Kafka, as with all our other authors. We are at the end not only of this chapter, but of the whole series of presentations. So may I be allowed to draw up a little résumé from my point of view.

What happened to religion in the modern era, and what happened to modernity as a result of religion? That question was our point of departure. We have described a mighty arc from the beginning of the modern period to the beginnings of the twentieth century. There is no missing the fact that the modern era looks different, depending on whether we look from Descartes, Pascal, and Galileo, and the whole age of the Enlightenment forward into a hopeful future, or backward from Kafka and the gloominess of his world toward the centuries before, at once sobered and terrified. To be sure, for theologians and Christians in general looking back in anger, in accusation and complacent superiority, is out of place. But we may glance back in mourning for the losses, for the fact that we were unable to master the destructive, suicidal forces of modernity. Realizing that the theologian is involved in the guilty history that the church, theology, and religion all helped to bring about, we need to do *grief work* over modernity. This means more than complaining about the losses. It means laying claim to what has not yet been redeemed and what may be won for the future.

Really, how different would it have been if, at the beginning of the new science, technology, and industry, the leading minds of the modern age had taken seriously *Pascal's* appeal to the reason of the heart, the *esprit de finesse*, reason sublated in faith?

Suppose that in the spirit of the Reformers the Church had clung to the justification of man not through deeds and achievements but through the humanizing power of faith, which *Gryphius* had embodied through all the crises of the age.

Suppose that in the course of the Enlightenment the unbelief and frivolity of Voltaire had been less successful in imposing itself than the ethics and critical piety of a *Lessing*.

Suppose that the new understanding of God, God in the world and the world in God, announced by Schelling, Hegel, and *Hölderlin*, had held up even through the critiques of religion launched from Feuerbach to Nietzsche.

Suppose that the romantics', especially *Novalis'*, vision of peace, of the reconciliation of religion and society, and thus of a higher epoch of culture, had taken concrete form.

Suppose that *Kierkegaard*'s demand for the reintroduction of Christianity into Christendom, and *Dostoyevsky*'s protest against the Inquisition and totalitarianism in church and state, like his appeal to Christ even in the utmost pain and distress, had been heard.

What was all this except a cry backward, or rather forward to the true God, and an appeal to humanity, to the love of man?

But the voices of Europe's good spirits died away, and often enough the warnings of the prophets were covered with ridicule. At the end of this modern era stands—how can we conceal it?—*Auschwitz*, along with the Gulag, the permanent code word for an unprecedented crime. What in Dostoyevsky was still an individual parricide, has, in the Kafkaesque world of our century, turned into genocide. "If God does not exist, all things are permissible." The Dostoyevskian vision of the suffering of innocent children now receives a previously unimaginable collective dimension: millions of people gassed and annihilated, among them *Kafka*'s sisters, Elli, Valli, and Ottla, as well as his great love Milena. And no doubt he, too, would have perished, had he not already died *tempore opportuno* in 1924, after suffering for seven years from tuberculosis.

In view of the Holocaust, Dostoyevsky's theodicy question lies on our century with a weight that is still unlike any other. Deep darkness, eternal aporia, indecipherable mystery, which dooms to failure any theology given to ingenious speculation about God. No, even in the face of Auschwitz I can as a Christian give no other answer than that of Job the Jew, of which starets Zossima spoke. In the final analysis, I can only point to the Crucified, of whom Alyosha reminds his brother. And I can appeal to nothing except the attitude of faith that offers ever fresh resistance to evil. I can appeal to the deeds of love, practiced even in the concentration camp, to the hope against hope that was lived even in extremis and de profundis.

————————◆————————

For me as a believing Christian, however, Auschwitz is for precisely this reason not the last word in world history. On the contrary. Forty years afterward, Auschwitz demands the *alternative vision of a renewed religion in a renewed society*. The eclipse of God, the subsequent twilight of the gods, the downfall of the modern pseudogods *can* be followed by a new morning in a paradigm of *postmodernity* (a name for what is as yet unknown). Of this dawn, even in the dark life of Franz Kafka, writer and moralist, a mysterious, narrow streak of light has already become visible. "Thus I would entrust myself to death," he wrote as early as September 1917, after the doctors confirmed that he had tuberculosis, and he decided to break his second engagement. He went on to say: "Remnant of faith. Return to the Father. Great day of reconciliation" (*Diary*, p. 390). At this point, doesn't Franz Kafka find himself, after all, with Dostoyevsky and Kierkegaard, Novalis, Hölderlin, and Lessing, and Pascal and Gryphius, too?

Yes, let us look forward. If I read the signs of the times rightly, toward the end of our century *rebellion against the Kafkaesque world* is everywhere afoot: among all the scientists, technicians, and doctors, who are intent upon ethics and even on religion; among men and women of all professions who are dissatisfied with a spiritless one-dimensional life and long for something definitively valid; among the younger generation, with their minds open to alternative approaches, who yearn for a new scale of values, a less materialistic orientation, a new horizon of meaning; but also among many poets, writers, and journalists, some of whom have joined with us here in Tübingen in carrying on this theological-literary symposium.

For all critical observers of the age, there is no overlooking the fact that nowadays, in our atomized modern society, religion can provide an urgently needed existential security and an intellectual home. But it can also develop an incomparable power of resistance against the destructive forces, against the modern process of alienation, against totalitarian systems of every shade, even black. Religion thus can have an eminently humanizing, liberating function, and de facto it has again and again had this function—religion, not as the opium, but the remedium, of the people.

All this, however, is true not only of Christianity, but also of Judaism, of Islam, and the great Asiatic religions as well. That immanence is everywhere bound up in a humanly liberating way with transcendence, the horizontal with the vertical, life down in the village with the mystery up in the Castle.

No, the great visions of Gryphius, Lessing, Hölderlin and Novalis, visions of peace, freedom, and humanity, have not been refuted. They were simply not realized in the modern era and they point to a different future. And the lofty intellectuality and morality of Pascal the Catholic as well as the radical Christianness of Kierkegaard the Protestant have to be taken in here just as much as the mystical depth of Dostoyevsky the Russian and the enigmatic darkness of Kafka the Jew.

To sum up, we have surveyed literature and religion in one: This is a theme covering a grand past that stretches back for thousands of years. Literature and religion in one: a theme of hope for a new future—an era that can bring forth literature in which great theology and great aesthetics enter once again into an exemplary intimacy.

WALTER JENS

◆

Don't Let Man
Go to the Dogs

"Inability to bear living alone, but not inability to live, quite the contrary. It is even likely that I understand how to live with someone. But I am incapable of bearing the onslaught on my own life, the demands on my own person, the assault of time and of old age, the vague rush of the desire to write, insomnia, the nearness of insanity—all this I am incapable of bearing alone." This is a diary entry from the summer of 1913. Franz Kafka, a bachelor three times engaged, sets down the arguments for and against marriage, in actuarial fashion, precisely, one point after the other.

The result is a very weak case for marriage, and a very strong case against it. There is hope from the engagement with Felice Bauer (who shows up in his work as Frieda Brandenstein or Fräulein Büstner: F. B. in many variations), but this hope sounds more like a formulaic wish than a secure conviction.

The result of Kafka's soul-searching sounds like a whispered, half-bewildered "yes" uttered in the form of a question, and then confronted with a stunning "no." The picture of two parental nightshirts on the turned-down beds is not encouraging. As for his literary partners in dialogue—Kierkegaard, Grillparzer, Kleist, Flaubert, Dostoyevsky—Kafka notes with satisfaction that of all his masters (Pascal is also on the fringe of this group), with the exception of Dostoyevsky, not one was married.

"I must . . . be alone. All that I have accomplished is the result

of being alone. Everything that is not related to literature, I hate."
This is the confession of a man who, like many others of the house
and lineage of Tonio Kröger, was not just alone, but completely
isolated, locked out, and exiled. He was a German (of Czech
descent) who belonged to the eight percent of the inhabitants of
Prague who spoke German, a writer who pushed for Czech self-
determination in the midst of a nationalistic German upper class
that swore allegiance to Vienna, not to Prague. He was a Jew
among Christians, a man who knew Luther, but also Schwejk, a
bachelor among fathers, children, wives, and husbands—all those,
that is, of whom Kafka's beloved Flaubert once said (without
drawing any conclusions, of course) "Ils sont dans le vrai."

Kafka was *aphorismenos*, separated from the world like the
later Kierkegaard; a *Claudio* figure like one of the heroes from
Hofmannsthal's *Death and the Fool*. He was a *Claudio* (that is,
isolated), only much more lost. He was lost in the language itself,
which he did not have, but rather first had to *produce*, surrounded
as he was by pastry shop Bohemian, jabbering Yiddish, operetta
and bureaucratic German. And so he created the severe but poetic
lawbook German of a man who was in the right company only
when he dealt with himself. "It bores me to carry on conversations
(even if they relate to literature), it bores me to visit people, the
sufferings and joys of relatives bore me to my very soul. Conversations take the importance, the seriousness, the truth out of
everything I think."

Franz Kafka was a bachelor whose protagonists were all bachelors: Rossmann, Bendemann, Samsa, Joseph K. (The surveyor
belongs to this group as well, even if at some point in the distant
past, he had once been married.)

There are no women here (with the exception of the singer
Josephine). Not so much as a mother-and-son in the midst of all
of these young or at least seemingly young men who, in the
shadow of their *fathers*, try in vain to emancipate themselves.

Kierkegaard's fate seems to be repeated in Prague: Incapable
of social bonding, unwilling (and in no condition) to relate to
anyone but himself (and his father!), Kafka warns his fiancée
Felice Bauer (and with her, all other women as well), implores
her not to let herself get involved with him. And he is being
totally honest. More honest, in any case, than Kierkegaard, who
was allegedly sparing Regine Olsen his religious melancholy. In

reality, he was thinking only of his existence as a writer, which demanded isolation. He tried to circumscribe that existence with the help of a great deal of metaphysics and biblical psychology, whereas Kafka laid his cards on the table.

I'm warning you about me, I am different, you will become infected with my nonexistence in the world. Again and again Kafka varied this appeal, vilified himself, played the nonperson (like Kierkegaard in "Diary of a Seducer," but also like Sortini, with his obscene repulsion of Amalia in *The Castle*). And again, very much like Kierkegaard, Kafka wrote "confusing letters behind the clouds," clandestine messages passed between prisoners. According to Kafka, writing to Max Brod in 1918, concerning his Danish brother in the spirit—the purpose of these letters was to warn his fiancée about the *torture* of monomaniacal writing.

Abominable things, written with the sharpest of pens. Kafka wanted to spare those who loved him what Kierkegaard exacted from Regine Olsen. He wished to spare them not least of all for a very concrete reason: "Could you stand it?"—from a letter to Felice in June 1913—"To know nothing of a man, except that he sits writing in his room? And to spend fall and winter in this way? And then toward springtime, to welcome the half-corpse at the door of his study? . . . Is that kind of life possible?"

Anyone who, like Kafka, conceived of writing as a *form of prayer*, as an endless monologue in the midst of a world in which God—maybe—once was and into which he—but who could know?—might sometime return; anyone who tried to write according to the maxim "There is no having, only a being that longs for the last breath, for suffocation," would, as a poet, *have* to be literally asocial. Any writer like that would, as Kafka did, *have* to understand loneliness and isolation as a sine qua non condition of his work. "This writing," he says, in a letter to his friend, the physician Robert Klopstock, "is, in the most awful way (outrageously awful, I won't even talk about it) for everyone around me, the most important thing on earth. It's something like the way insanity is important to the madman (if he lost it, he would go 'mad') or as pregnancy is important to a woman. . . . And that is why in my trembling fear I hold my writing in a tight embrace to protect it from every disturbance. I protect not only my writing, but also the solitariness that goes with it."

Much as Kafka suffered from loneliness, he thought he knew

that the total isolation in which the writer is confronted by a humanity that is at odds with itself and does not reach him was still better than that most abysmal of all lonelinesses, being lost as a couple (*Ils sont dans le vrai?* Not for the author of *The Castle!*).

And yet all his life he yearned to be incorporated into a community, longed for a reliable social connection—and not only in the private sphere. Still he nurtured the desperate hope of being reconciled with his people, of becoming a Jew among Jews—rising, as he says at the end of his "most Jewish" story, "Josephine the Singer," to the "heights of redemption" of the people.

Still, at the end of his life, he dreamt of a modest existence in Palestine, the life of a waiter, for example, or of a craftsman in a workshop ("I mean, I wouldn't want it *that* much") in some southern country good for curing him of tuberculosis.

Still—again and again—there is the pride in his country, the enthusiasm at watching a Jewish theater group, the emotion over seeing Jewish children. Kafka was swayed by the motto: "Come back to your people." And there are the stirrings that Kafka feels when a perfectly common troupe begins to sing and dance in a perfectly common, even shabby cafe: "At some songs, at the speech about the 'laughter of Jewish children,' at some glances toward this woman on the podium, who, because she is Jewish, draws us listeners (because we are Jewish) to her, without the desire or curiosity for Christ, my cheeks began to tremble."

In a matter of seconds—flashing and then quickly extinguished again—the vision of the *great community* keeps turning up. Within its circuit, the antithesis between *solitaire* and *solidaire*, *einsam* (lonely) and *gemeinsam* (communal), is resolved. It is resolved in a community that stands for something paradoxical like the "Jewish" (read: Kafkaesque) cross, under whose aegis the vertical and horizontal meanings complete each other.

How can the individual, with his eyes raised to the Law, do justice simultaneously to himself *and* to others? How does one succeed in not forgetting the "village" because of the "Castle" and the "Castle" because of the "village"? How can the writer practice the asceticism demanded of him and yet not fall out of the world? How is it possible—this is Amalia's problem in *The Castle*—"to stand eye to eye with the truth" (even if only for a fraction of a moment), without for that reason being pointed out, that is, socially stigmatized and, like too many of those in the know, being expelled from society?

What Amalia in *The Castle* was only able to think or suffer through, on the border of inhumanity and madness, Kafka tried to conceive in allegories, parables, and paradoxical images. How can one live on the "Jewish cross," with its beams pointing vertically to the Castle (the Law, the Indestructible) and horizontally to the village (the community, marriage, social behavior, communication with one another)?

The question is: How can Amalia—Kafka's greatest and most human figure—live before the face of God and at the same time be respected? Where does the Torah reader, sunken in monologue, find his congregation?

There is no doubt that Kafka, who thought this question through more consistently than any other writer in our century, had no answer to give—no solution, no end result. The novels end as they began: open. The surveyor is as close to the Castle in the first line as in the last.

Instead of results, there are more and more exact questions. Instead of analysis of the goal, there are descriptions of the path. Instead of defining salvation and deliverance, Kafka presents possibilities with regard to salvation (Is it back in the past? Is it to come?). ("There are innumerable hiding places," he says in 'Reflections' n. 26, "only one deliverance, but as many possibilities of deliverance as there are hiding places.")

Solitaire-solidaire: For Kafka, the antithesis remained between what *wanted* to be sublated to dialectical completion, to the interplay that created meaning, and what, on the other hand, *could not* be sublated ("What do I have in common with the Jews?"—runs a diary entry from 1914—"I hardly have anything in common with myself, and should stand quite silently in a corner, content that I can breathe.")

And in spite of this, once again Kafka had the bold hope that in the darkness and forgetfulness of salvation that marked the here and now, the dim light pointed to a once-present glow that guaranteed meaning and order. He hoped that grief would stand for punishment, punishment for guilt, guilt for the existence of the "Other," demonstrated at a third remove. He hoped that, with the help of the category of "constructive destruction," the positive might—perhaps—come into view from out of the negative.

Perhaps, mind you. *Only* perhaps. For Kafka, there was no *certainty* as to whether the kings still lived under heaven or whether the couriers passed along the messages (which had long ago become meaningless) to each other. The screams, appearances, actions, and conversations might be reality, but might just as well be (as *The Castle*, above all, shows) only echoes, mirages, dreams, and hallucinations. The light on the grimace—does it emphasize the demonic element in a character or does it symbolize, if it can be interpreted as a mirroring, the reflection of the Law? No, Kafka gives no answer. He knew none, and so did not pretend to know one. In circumscribing possibilities, he took care not to define realities. "Seen with terrestrially sullied eyes," he writes in the third octavo notebook,

> we are in the situation of travelers in a train that has met with an accident in a long tunnel, and moreover at a place where one can no longer see the light at the beginning of the tunnel. And the light at the end is so tiny that our gaze must continually search for it and is always losing it again, so that beginning and end are never certain. Around us, however, in the confusion of our senses, or in the hypersensitivity of our senses, we have nothing but monstrosities and a kaleidoscopic play of things that is either enchanting or exhausting, depending on the mood and astonishment of each individual. What should I do? or Why should I do it? are not questions to be asked in such places.

I do not think that this is a parable stamped with nihilistic or even atheistic pathos. On the contrary, it's clear that the darkness of the day corresponds to the brightness of order (hardly recognizable, of course). We don't know, however, whether this order is in the past or is to come. But in any case it seems to be in existence and so, even if only by inference, an active presence.

Was Franz Kafka a *homo religiosus*? Certainly. Was he therefore also an author who rightly associated himself, as last in line, with Pascal, Kierkegaard, and Dostoyevsky—authors with whom scholars continually compare him? That, too, can't be doubted. He was a poet, then, who all his life acknowledged the famous maxim ("Reflections," #50) that man could not exist "without a lasting trust in something indestructible within himself." Yes, that, too, is true.

Kafka was not an author shaped by untroubled belief. Indeed, he was hardly shaped by troubled belief, but rather by the *wish to believe.* (He was deadly serious when, in a letter to Max Brod at the beginning of 1918, he mentioned the establishment of "a church, an asylum," as "something that will undoubtedly come about and is already rising around us at the same pace as our integration.")

But does that mean that Kafka, like Kierkegaard, or perhaps only like Dostoyevsky, was a theological author? Was the author of *The Castle* a prose writer in whose work certain ciphers are allegorical, so that the "village" would stand for the "world" (or fallen humanity) and the "Castle" for "heaven" (or nothing or authority or bureaucracy)? Not exactly.

Theological "interpretation," Hermann Hesse has said with great clarity, "is good for people who never found entrance to the inner depths of a work of art, because they stand at the gate, trying hundreds of keys at the lock, not even seeing that the gate is already open."

Well, that gate is unfortunately not quite so open. While it seems certain that readers who would like to discover allegories and simple equations in poetry cannot make use of Kafka, it must be stressed just as decisively on the other hand that the author of "Reflections" and "The Penal Colony," of "Josephine" and of the great novels, made very good use of religious images, biblical archetypes, and symbols borrowed from theological exegesis when it came to sketching in the utopia of his imaginary Jewish cross, or to do an exegesis on the rabbinical question of the light (Is it at our backs or before our eyes?).

Kafka knew Judaism, and he knew the Bible, especially the Law, the preachers, and the prophets: "Only the Old Testament sees—nothing more to say about it." He treated Jesus with respect, patience (as the result of careful listening and meditation that produced sympathy), and even with a certain friendly, foreign admiration (he called Christ "a light-filled chasm"). I am of course not sure if this quotation, from Gustav Janouch's *Conversations with Kafka,* may claim authenticity. In any case, Kafka praised Jesus not least of all for his interest in the world (the whole cosmos, Kafka says, becomes "open" on the birthday of the Nazarene). Nevertheless, in spite of all his affection, he never leaves his position as an observer. In the case of the Old Testament, by contrast, he sees himself challenged as an author. There he discovers a dreadfully foolish Abraham, a pompous fellow whom God didn't even have in mind. In this way Kafka can emulate Kierkegaard and raise to sheer absurdity the paradox of pious murder. Here he has the opportunity to transfer Moses and Sarah into the reality of his time, to locate Canaan on the Moldau and the wilderness in that realm of the soul where he, Kafka, has dialogues with Felice and Milena. Here he gets the chance to put to use Old Testament notions of God and the commandments of the Law so as to clarify his understanding of himself and the world. The dubiousness of paternal authority, the revolt against sexual taboos, the observance of ritual-like ascetical precepts—these are cardinal questions of Kafka's existence, illuminated against the background of Old Testament notions of belief.

In short, the author of *The Castle* was a writer who drew up his parables against the horizon of Jewish understanding of law and redemption, original sin, guilt and punishment, without, for all that, ever having been a believing Jew (or Christian): "I have not been brought into life by the certainly already sinking hand of Christianity, as Kierkegaard was, and have yet to catch the last corner of the prayer shawl, like the Zionists, as it flies away. I am end or beginning."

End or beginning, but he was never the middle. Kafka was never the center of a development created by faith and confirmed by history. Never the symbol of exodus, between prophecy and messianic redemption.

And yet, as far removed from orthodox Jewish piety as Kafka was, he did not shake free from the rabbis and miracle workers, the servants of the law and the actors around his friend Jizchak Löwy, to whose productions he devoted a sixth of his diaries. The Eastern Jewish world, above all, fascinated him—as it did Joseph Roth or Arnold Zweig, in a way that made it clear how important to Kafka was the obvious, not cumulative, but existence-determining translation of faith into reality. Such faith stood for something that was worlds apart from Hermann Kafka's dignitary's Judaism, as glossed in his *Letter to His Father*: "At bottom the belief that directed your life consisted in your believing in the absolute correctness of the opinions of a certain Jewish social class. . . . One cannot make it comprehensible to a child, who is watching too closely out of sheer anxiety, that the few futilities you carried out in the name of Judaism, with an indifference matching their futility, could have a higher meaning."

When Kafka polemicizes against the nonchalant liberalness of his father, he speaks like Joseph Roth after him, who in the essay "Jews in Their Travels" ridiculed the assimilated types who would have the temple changed into a Protestant church, a Sunday temple, where they let themselves be lulled into a devotional mood, while the organ music played.

And now Kafka the Jew took his stand against them. He was a writer whose responsibility toward the heritage that made him what he was showed itself at the very moment that he met a Christian, Milena Jésenká. To Milena, as if standing before a foreign authority he had declared binding on himself, he explained his Judaism, cursed his diaspora existence, bemoaned his distance from paradise, explained his peculiar status as a specifically Jewish one. ("Consider . . . Milena, the kind of person that comes to you, the thirty-eight-year journey that lies behind me, and, since I am a Jew, an even longer one.") It's striking to see how he has changed himself into a "rabbi" ("almost white-haired from the past nights"), how he tried to bring Milena close to the people closest to him, poor Jewish emigrants, and then how, in the middle of it all, self-hatred, an infernal rage of Jew against the Jews, suddenly threatened to triumph. "Sometimes I would like to stuff all of them (the Jews), myself included, into a drawer in the linen closet, then wait, then open up the drawer a little to see whether they had all suffocated already. If not, shove the drawer in again and keep on this way until the end."

This was an Auschwitz phantasmagoria written around the time that *The Castle* was coming into existence. It was the nightmare of a Jew to whom the liberal stance of the assimilated Jews meant nothing, to whom orthodox Zionism meant more (*something more*), and Eastern Jewish piety with its wealth of visions, enchantments, wild usurpations of the world, and ecstatic appropriations of God meant a great deal. In the Hasidic stories, not in the Torah or the Talmud, Kafka found what suited him: the understanding, based on paradoxes, of a mysterious, very quiet, encoded dialogue, a dialogue that needed explication, between man and man, in the direction of God: "These stories, I don't understand how," he writes in a letter to Max Brod, in September 1916—"are the only Jewish thing in which I always and immediately feel at home, regardless of my condition. In everything else I am only blown in, until another draft of wind carries me out again."

Kafka was attracted not by Zionism, to which he would only concede the label of a "prelude to something more important," but rather by the legends of the Ba'al Shem Tov and the parables of the Great Magid (both translated into German by Martin Buber). It was the arsenal of Hasidism that became for Kafka the parable writer a treasury of faith, that found in him a kindred soul, and that increasingly fascinated him. No wonder some legends of Hasidism read like Kafkaesque studies, and that in turn aphorisms by Kafka resemble wise sayings in twice-told tales from the cabala. In both cases, what we have is, to echo the writer of the diaries (note of January 16, 1922), "an assault on the last earthly frontier" ("an assault from below, from mankind" and an assault "aimed down at me from above").

Kafka describes a poetry that had for him the character of a relentless battue ("it can, this seems most compelling, lead to madness"). In this poetry, the interplay of lowliness and sovereignty, of the view from the dust and the view from the stars, acquires, in a suddenly illuminating formula, the vividness that marked Kafka's later work, especially his last novel.

The Castle is a book that describes how an individual, the surveyor K., would like to become a naturalized citizen where, to speak with Ernst Bloch, "no one was" before him—at home in a world where God becomes reconciled with humanity, and humans with each other.

So we have the description of a utopia, in other words, that Kafka ventures into by inventing a protagonist for whom this utopia drops out of sight but is never refuted. The quintessence of the novel is that there *might* be a home/homeland on the border of the village and the Castle, under the sign of the *skandalon*, of the religious paradox of a Jewish cross with its one beam pointing heavenward, into the infinite, and the other pointing toward the earth. There might be, but it *isn't there* yet, and it's questionable whether that Castle—though perhaps still useful as an allegory—

even exists. It might be identical with the phantasmagorias of the surveyor, those reactions produced by the blindness but also by the sudden clairvoyance, of a man seeking asylum.

But however the Castle may look from the standpoint of the author or the perspective of the hero, it is, in any case, a *twilight kingdom*. Its essence is ambivalent and Janus-faced. In this realm, God can play the devil and the devil can play God. It is a region where relationships arise only through the refusal of contact and meetings only with the help of dismissals.

The Castle, then, is an imaginary palace that the author sketches out with the help of his hero's conceptions, so that in the end it remains an open question whether the surveyor has rightly assessed the object-world that meets him, in other words has judged it for what it is, or whether the story that K. experienced could be presented altogether differently from the perspective of Amalia, Frieda, Olga, Barnabas, or even Klamm.

In fact, one must be cautious. Kafka makes it clear from the beginning that the view of the surveyor is not the only possible way of seeing things. The truth could easily be different. (This seems particularly obvious at the beginning, where the narrator, for the length of a phrase, emancipates himself from his hero.) The fact could rather be that K., the surveyor, is in the situation of the chained prisoners in Plato's allegory of the cave. Incapable of movement, they take for real people the shadows of puppets that are carried behind their backs on a small balcony, and mistake the images of carved figures, projected by a fire onto the wall the prisoners are facing, for living beings of flesh and blood.

It *might* be so, of course, but then it would also remain indisputable that amidst the truth attested to only in the form of images, and contradictorily at that, amidst all the ambiguity, a promise of a meaningful existence nevertheless begins to emerge. For Kafka, such an existence could be represented only *ex negatione*. There is luster in his work only where twilight reigns. To take shape, truth needs the comical. Connections can be made only where the incongruous, ludicrous, and even the grotesque come into play.

Naturally, this doesn't mean that the piled-up atrocities and obscenities would all have to be interpreted metaphysically. It doesn't mean that Sortini, the ascetic with the dirty mind, is a messenger of God and that the bureaucratic stepladder, on which characters resembling robots and marionettes do their stunts, would stand for the world order. That's not it at all.

Interpreters of Kafka should not speak of "is" or "represents" or "means." Analogies between incidents, things, characters, and their (apparently single-minded) meaning are forbidden, at least between "judgment" and "the Castle."

And, nevertheless, for Kafka *writing is a form of prayer*. Nevertheless, Kafka was caught up in *the hunt until madness sets in* and the *assault on the last inner frontier*. He was concerned with defining in poetic terms an understanding of himself and the world, and against the background of this definition there are no answers, only questions. Nothing is fixed; everything is open. The rule that holds for Dostoyevsky—limitless possibility even in the most insignificant case—applies only to his characters. With Kafka, however, this rule applies to every detail. Nothing, no gaze at a snowy landscape, no awakening in a gymnasium, no dance around a fire engine, is understood correctly unless the reader senses that for Kafka the grandeur and the pathos of Luciferian or messianic struggles belong precisely to the most everyday occurrences. As always, the rebels and harlequins, dullards, evil creatures, jokers, beggars, braggarts and whores, the ugly villagers and the absentminded bureaucrats, the negligent and the overzealous sinners, present themselves on stage. And with every gesture they all clearly say: We are not alone; people are watching us; we have scars; we are marked.

"Assault from above, down onto me." There is no chapter in *The Castle* whose actions would not have to be interpreted according to this principle formulated just before the beginning of the novel. It is not the Castle, nor the officials, nor the bureaucratic apparatus, but the way that the people deal and speak with one another, how the surveyor tries to find a place to stay, is rejected, remains in place, moves about in a circle—this alone guarantees the metaphysical significance of the novel.

An insignificant man is fighting here, a conformist, considerably in debt, an exploiter of women and a monomaniac, an infantile egocentric. He has a thing about the Castle. He engages in an inconsequential, occasionally involuntarily comical, struggle, behaving half as Don Quixote, half as a Jewish villager. He is an *am-ha-aretz*, who dares to defy the pure and fine spirits, the specialists and interpreters of the Law. He stumbles unflinchingly, goes astray, mistakes giants for dwarves and dwarves for giants, enters staunchly into coalitions that, however informed he may be, afterward prove to be calamitous. He falls down, gets up again, tries his hand as a surveyor, then as a school porter, constantly trying on different masks, while the world around him, fixed and unchangeable, stays what it is. And yet this ridiculous man, who can't even describe the façade of the Castle coherently, but constantly gets lost in inadequate comparisons, this nobody is like a Homeric *Outis* (nobody). In his unremitting struggle against the evil authority of the Castle, he is Odysseus among cyclopes, sorceresses and sirens (now called Klamm, the Brueckenhof landlady, Frieda, and Olga). Still more, in all of his wretchedness, K. has become a Job who will not let go of his dream Castle, which in the end will literally bury him beneath itself. It will give him, the dying man, a provisional homestead in the village. (And in getting this permission—here is the point of all the paradoxes that Kafka develops over hundreds of pages—K. is graciously presented with something he already had from the beginning.)

No, the conclusion of *The Castle* isn't consoling, but imbued with cynicism. It is a reversal of Goethe's *Faust*: the one man forever striving remains unredeemed. Any reader who expects anything else (Max Brod did, taken in by a highly idealistic error) only proves that he hasn't understood Kafka's intentions. No justice can be expected from authorities who criminalize a woman, Amalia, for seeing the truth for a second. Domination is in charge here, not authority (in the sense of humaneness and competence). Here the hideous Kierkegaardian, Dostoyevskian, Kafkaesque father—the destroyer, not the reconciler—is in charge. The counterdeity—Sortini with the phallus symbols, the shaft and the fire engine—celebrates its macabre triumphs and destroys in the same way both those that oppose it and those that sacrifice to it. Amalia, the only truly free person in the novel, is ruined in the same way as her sister Olga, who, in order to preserve the family's honor, gets involved with the officials.

And yet, in the same way, absurdity can always (at any time) change over into majesty. A surveyor tilting at windmills plunges into Job's shadow; a nobody whose character is secretly a composite of archetypes suddenly gains the greatness of a servant of

God. In the same way, what is dirty and depraved could also turn
into sudden brightness: Then there would be no more darkness—
as the case of Amalia shows—but inextinguishable light, light in
the darkness. Satan and seraphim, heaven and hell, the wilderness
and the land of Canaan, lie close to one another in Kafka. The
loneliness of exile is near the "farmland," from which the author
of *The Castle*—as a diary entry from January 28, 1922 proves—
believed himself to be exiled. Kafka was an emigrant in the wilderness, who nevertheless did not want to give up his homeland,
a solitary writer, but a Jew. "Perhaps I do remain in Canaan after
all, and in the meantime I have been so long in the wilderness,
and there are only visions of despair, especially at those times
when even there (in the wilderness) I am the most wretched of
creatures, and Canaan must present itself as the only land of hope,
for no third land exists for mankind."

For no third land exists for mankind. What constitutes Kafka's
greatness and gives him his place under the heading of "Theology
and Literature" is that he knows no "adiaphora" (indifferent
things), no states of indecision, no episodes and pauses for catch-
ing one's breath, when the reader can relax, no "neutral" genre
scenes, where one can just say to one's heart's content, "That's
too broad a field, Louisa."

One can't get at Kafka with the categories of the bourgeois
novels, where the people are completely at home. Here in the
haylofts, bars, schoolrooms and backhouses, there is fighting,
judging, rushing about, silence and lovemaking, heaven and hell
present as ever. The upshot is that—again the diary entry from
28 January—there is the possibility "even for the humblest to be
raised to the heights as if with lightning speed, though they can
also be crushed for millennia as if by the weight of the seas."

There is no word, in the fictional passages of Kafka's works,
about God and the devil, about the cross and redemption—and
yet the spirits of Pascal, Kierkegaard, or Dostoyevsky are all
present. We see this when the temple prostitute, Olga, swears to
the heroism of her sister, who keeps her eyes open where all
others, blinded by truth, close them. "But Amalia bore not only
the suffering, she also had the understanding to see through it.
We saw only the results, she saw the reason, we hoped for some
kind of small remedy, she knew that all had been decided, we

had to whisper, she had only to be silent, she stood eye to eye with the truth and bore this life then as today."

Man, as he could be, at the border between the land of Canaan and the wilderness, caught and shown meeting with the "other"— that is what Kafka tried to present between 1904 and 1924, the period when "Wedding Preparations in the Country" and the story "Josephine the Singer" were composed. He presented this vision of man with a consistency and urgency that enabled him, the nonbeliever and the man under attack, to hold his own with any self-assured believer. Or at least he could hold his own with respect to the inexorable demands of writing (which is for Kafka the appropriate mode of self-reflection in exile). For Kafka—as for Lessing—the Blochian principle holds: "The best thing about religion is that it makes heretics"—heretics for whom God is a *problem* and not a *fact*.

Franz Kafka is the "other." Kafka is an author who *ex negatione*, symbolically, and prophetically showed what it means when the spirit that blessed Canaan enthrones itself as counterspirit in the "Penal Colony": This is Kafka in Auschwitz, when Auschwitz did not yet exist.

Kafka, the Jew among the Christians, was the outsider who considered Judgment Day a court martial. He held belief in a personal God responsible for the fact that trust in the indestructible element in man remained hidden from him. Kafka was the doubter among the orthodox. And yet he was one of the very few writers who managed, line for line, to say, in indirect religious language, that an existence without God, an existence in which metaphysics was extinguished, would no longer be human, that beyond the wilderness and Canaan one could only vegetate, but not live; that the autonomous person, incapable of casting and bearing shadows, is shapeless.

And all of this is never expressed in treatise form or postulated in a sermonizing way, but rather made present through parable, image, and allegory. This means that the Absolute appears at the end as the most perfectly obvious thing and the second world beyond, which breaks into the first empirical one, appears as the normality of all normalities. ("The world of Franz Kafka," Kurt Tucholsky, one of his greatest admirers, has said in reference to *The Trial*, "is in his thought . . . rational . . . logical, mathematical in its order; it even lacks that faint dose of the irrational that first gives the rational man pause. There is nothing more terrible than a pure mathematician of the understanding.")

Rationality of the irrational; the obviousness of paradox; the everydayness of the metaphysical: However one defines Kafka's ability to elucidate the reality-determining omnipresence of the transcendent by means of an extreme realism, of a truly obsessive joy in detail, a grotesque, blood-curdling comicality, one thing is certain: Hardly anyone has pressed the question of whether man could live without God so close to the brink of an answer as Kafka did.

No wonder, then, that he—like Dostoyevsky—became a favorite author of a group of notable writers, from Hesse to Martin Walser and Peter Weiss (see the Kafka hymn in the first volume of *The Aesthetics of Resistance*, with its analysis of *The Castle*: "This being surprised in a supposed shelter, this sudden invasion of the inconceivable!"). Such writers can judge what it means to talk, in thousands of pages—in books that, as Kafka said, "must be an axe for the frozen sea in us"—about the relationship between individuals against the horizon of the Absolute. The literary heirs of Kafka know what it is to spend one's whole time speaking, supposedly, about nothing but staircases and back rooms, letters and telephone calls, sexual intercourse or madness, and thus to make visible what it means to have God at one's back and paradise behind one. They know what it is to have to live in the desperate hope of redemption at the end of the day, in the darkness of the here and now—very lonely and yet hoping for the new community under the sign of an inner meaning realized both in the vertical and the horizontal axis meeting as one. This is a meaning that takes shape under the aegis of humility in favor of the Insulted and the Injured.

"Humility," says Kafka in the manner of Pascal or Dostoyevsky, "gives everyone, even the lonely person in despair, the strongest relationship with his fellows, and does so immediately, although of course only with complete and lasting humility. It can do this because it is the true language of prayer, at once worship and the strongest bond. The link with others is the link of prayer, the link with oneself is the link of striving; from prayer we get the power to strive." Here for the duration of a single sentence a Jew points to the ideal image of the cross, under which sign praying to God means at the same time, to vary slightly a line from the *Castle* fragments: "Don't let man, whoever he is, go to the dogs."

The text literally says, "You shouldn't let this man"—in the sense of person—"go to the dogs." This is the quintessence, in the double sense, of what Hans Küng and I have tried to do with a literature written under the sign of Jesus of Nazareth and under the sign of man.

Is this conclusion slightly pathetic? Is it too theological? Very well, then let us conclude less solemnly by giving both poetry and theology their due, with a characterization of Kafka provided by the physician Dr. Robert Klopstock in 1921: "His guides are Jesus—and Dostoyevsky."

Jesus and Dostoyevsky. Here we have theology and literature united in a *concordia discors*, whose breadth and polyvalence these eight portrait sketches have aimed at clarifying. Our sketches have portrayed Janus-faced authors, rich in radical contrasts; they have sought to show how multifarious and contradictory the possibilities of literature are, when the point is to bring into focus the "Other," "the ground of being," and the "unconditional" that holds man in the world, but leaves him unclear about it. And in this ambivalence, this meaning-making darkness and existence-shaping riddle, that "Other" can be represented only by poetry.

These eight biographies were designed to show by example that man, in his confrontation with the Absolute, can be brought into our field of vision only by the literature that—undogmatically, but led by *docta spes*, the anxious utopia—risks the "great leap," and, in the sense of Pascal's metaphysical wager, plays *va banque*. All or nothing.

"Beyond a certain point," Kafka wrote, "there is no more turning back. This is the point we must reach."

BIBLIOGRAPHY

BLAISE PASCAL

Béguin, Albert. *Blaise Pascal*. Hamburg, 1959.

Davidson, Hugh McCullough. *The Origins of Certainty: Means and Meaning in Pascal's Pensées*. Chicago, 1979.

Friedenthal, Richard. *Entdecker des Ich: Montaigne, Pascal, Diderot*. Munich, 1969.

Friedrich, Hugo. "Pascals Paradox. Das Sprachbild einer Denkform," in *Zeitschrift für romanische Philologie 1936*, vol. 56, 323–70.

———. 2nd ed. Bern/Munich, 1967.

Goldman, Lucien. *Der verborgene Gott. Studie über die tragische Weltanschauung in den Penseés Pascals und im Theater Racines*. Neuwied/Darmstadt, 1973.

Gouhier, Henri. *Pascal et les humanistes chrétiens: L'affaire Saint-Ange*. Paris, 1974.

Guardini, Romano. *Christliches Bewusstsein: Versuche über Pascal*. Munich, 1950.

Harrington, Thomas More. *Vérité et méthode dans les "Pensées" de Pascal*. Paris, 1972.

Kummer, Irène Elisabeth. *Blaise Pascal*. Berlin/New York, 1978.

Kruse, Margot. *Das Pascal-Bild in der französischen Literatur*. Hamburg, 1955.

Lacombe, Roger-E. *L'apologétique de Pascal: Étude critique*. Paris, 1958.

Léveillé-Mourin, Geneviève. *Le Langage chrétien, antichrétien, de la transcendance: Pascal–Nietzsche*. Paris, 1978.

Lønning, Per. *Cet effrayant pari: Une "pensée" pascalienne et ses critiques*. Paris, 1980.

———. *The Dilemma of Contemporary Theology: Prefigured in Luther, Pascal, Kierkegaard, Nietzsche*. New York, 1962.

Mesnard, Jean. *Les pensées de Pascal*. Paris, 1976.

Patrick, Denzil G. M. *Pascal and Kierkegaard: A Study in the Strategy of Evangelism*. London/Redhill, 1947.

Rehm, Walther. *Experimentum Medietatis: Studien zur Geiste- und Literaturgeschichte des 19. Jahrhundert.* Munich, 1947.

Rheinfelder, Hans. "Leopardi und Pascal," in *Hochland,* 32, 2 (1935), 237–45.

Wasmuth, Ewald. *Blaise Pascal: Die Kunst zu überzeugen und die anderen kleinen philosophischen Schriften.* Heidelberg, 1950.

―――. *Blaise Pascal. Werke I, über die Religion und über einige andere Gegenstände (Pensées).* Heidelberg, 1963.

―――. *Der unbekannte Pascal: Versuch und Deutung seines Lebens und seiner Lehre.* Regensburg, 1962.

ANDREAS GRYPHIUS

Barner, Wilfried. *Barockrhetorik. Untersuchungen zu ihren geschichtlichen Grundlagen.* Tübingen, 1970.

Boockmann, Hartmut, Heinz Schilling, Hagen Schulze, and Michael Stürmer: *Mitten in Europa: Deutsche Geschichte.* Berlin, 1984.

Conrady, Carl Otto. *Lateinische Dichtungstradition und deutsche Lyrik des 17. Jahrhunderts.* Bonn, 1962.

Faber du Faur, Curt von. "Andreas Gryphius, der Rebell," in *Publications of the Modern Language Association of America,* vol. 74 (1959).

Flemming, Willi. *Andreas Gryphius: Eine Monographie.* Stuttgart, 1965.

Fricke, Gerhard. *Die Bildlichkeit in der Dichtung des Andreas Gryphius: Materialien und Studien zum Formproblem des deutschen Literaturbarock.* Reprint, Darmstadt, 1967.

Gerling, Renate. *Schriftwort und Lyrisches Wort: Die Umsetzung biblischer Texte in der Lyrik des 17. Jahrhunderts.* Meisenheim am Glan, 1969.

Jöns, Dietrich Walter. *Das "Sinnen-Bild": Studien zur allegorischen Bildlichkeit bei Andreas Gryphius.* Stuttgart, 1966.

Krummacher, Hans-Henrik. *Der junge Gryphius und die Tradition: Studien zu den Perikopensonetten und Passionsliedern.* Munich, 1976.

Mauser, Wolfram. *Dichtung, Religion und Gesellschaft im 17. Jahrhundert: Die "Sonette" des Andreas Gryphius.* Munich, 1976.

Schings, Hans-Jürgen. *Die patristische und stoische Tradition bei Andreas Gryphius: Untersuchungen zu den Dissertationes funebres und Trauerspielen.* Cologne-Graz, 1966.

Schöffler, Herbert. *Deutsches Geistesleben zwischen Reformation und Aufklärung: Von Martin Opitz zu Christian Wolff.* Frankfurt/M., 1956.

Schneppen, Heinz. *Niederländische Universitäten und Deutsches Geis-*

tesleben: Von der Gründung der Universität Leiden bis ins späte 18. Jahrhundert. Münster/Westfalen, 1960.

Steinhagen, Harald. *Didaktische Lyrik: "Über einige Gedichte des Andreas Gryphius,"* in *Festschrift für Friedrich Beissner, herausgegeben von Ulrich Gaier und Werner Volke* (Bebenhausen 1974), 406–35.

Szyrocki, Marian. *Andreas Gryphius: Sein Leben und Werk.* Tübingen, 1964.

———. *Der junge Gryphius.* Berlin (DDR), 1959.

van Ingen, Ferdinand. *Vanitas und Memento Mori in der deutschen Barocklyrik.* Groningen, 1966.

Vosskamp, Wilhelm. *Untersuchungen zur Zeit- und Geschichtsauffassung im 17. Jahrhundert bei Gryphius und Lohenstein.* Bonn, 1967.

Weithase, Irmgard. *Die Darstellung von Krieg und Frieden in der deutschen Barockdichtung.* Weimar, 1953.

Wentzlaff-Eggebert, Friedrich-Wilhelm. *Der triumphierende und der besiegte Tod in der Wort- und Bildkunst des Barock.* Berlin/New York, 1975.

Weydt, Günter. *Sonettkunst des Barock: "Zum Problem der Umarbeitung bei Andreas Gryphius,"* in *Jahrbuch der deutschen Schillergesellschaft,* 9 (1965), 1–32.

GOTTHOLD EPHRAIM LESSING

Barner, Wilfried, Gunter Grimm, Helmuth Keisel, and Martin Kramer: *Lessing: Epoche, Werk, Wirkung.* 4th ed. Munich, 1981.

Barth, Karl. *Die protestantische Theologie im 19. Jahrhundert: Ihre Vorgeschichte und ihre Geschichte.* Zollikon-Zürich 1947 (#6 Lessing).

Bohnen, Klaus. *Nathan der Weise. "Über das 'Gegenbild einer Gesellschaft' bei Lessing,"* in *Deutsche Vierteljahresschrift für Literaturwissenschaft und Geistesgeschichte,* 53, 1979, 394–416.

Bollacher, Martin. *Lessing-Vernunft und Geschichte: Untersuchungen zum Problem religiöser Aufklärung in den Spätschriften.* Tübingen, 1978.

Borchardt, Rudolf. "Lessing," in *R.B., Ges. Werke, Prosa III.* Stuttgart, 1960, 291–306.

Bothe, Bernd. *Glauben und Erkennen: Studie zur Religionsphilosophie Lessings.* Meisenheim/Glan, 1972.

Demetz, Peter. *Gotthold Ephraim Lessing—Nathan der Weise.* Frankfurt/M.-Berlin, 1966.

Fuhrmann, Helmut. "Lessings *Nathan der Weise* und das Wahrheitsproblem," in *Lessing-Yearbook 15* (1983), 63–94.

Göbel, Helmut. *Bild und Sprache bei Lessing.* Munich, 1971.

————. "Nicht die Kinder bloß, speist man / Mit Märchen ab. Zur Toleranzbegründung in Lessings Spätwerk," in *Lessing-Yearbook 14* (1982), 119–32.

Hazard, Paul. *Die Krise des europäischen Geistes 1680–1715.* Hamburg, 1939.

————. *La pensée européenne au XVIIIe siècle de Montesquieu à Lessing.* Paris, 1963.

Heydemann, Klaus. "Gesinnung und Tat: Zu Lessings *Nathan der Weise*," in *Lessing-Yearbook 7* (1975), 69–104.

Hirsch, Emanuel. *Geschichte der neueren evangelischen Theologie im Zusammenhang mit den allgemeinen Bewegungen des europäischen Denkens.* Vol. 4. Gütersloh, 1949 (7th Book: Semler und Lessing).

Hoensbroech, Marion Gräfin. *Die List der Kritik: Lessings kritische Schriften und Dramen.* Munich, 1976.

Höhle, Thomas, ed. *Lessing und Spinoza.* Halle/Wittemberg, 1981.

Kant, Immanuel. "Beantwortung der Frage: Was ist Aufklärung?" (1783), in *Werke*, W. Weischedel, ed. Vol. 6, 53–61.

König, Dominik von. *Natürlichkeit und Wirklichkeit: Studien zu Lessings* Nathan der Weise. Bonn, 1976.

Koselleck, Reinhart. *Kritik und Krise: Ein Beitrag zur Pathogenese der bürgerlichen Welt.* Freiburg/Munich, 1959.

Müller, Joachim. "Zur Dialogstruktur und Sprachfiguration in Lessings Nathan-Drama," in *Sprachkunst, Beiträge zur Literaturwissenschaft*, 1 (1970), 42–69.

Neumann, Peter Horst. *Der Preis der Mündigkeit: Über Lessings Dramen.* Stuttgart, 1977.

Pfaff, Peter. *Theaterlogik.* "Zum Begriff einer poetischen Weisheit in Lessings *Nathan der Weise*," in *Lessing-Yearbook 15* (1983), 95–109.

Politzer, Heinz. "Lessings Parabel von den drei Ringen," in *Gotthold Ephraim Lessing*, Gerhard and Sibylle Bauer, eds. Darmstadt, 1968, 343–61.

Pons, Georges. *Gotthold Ephraim Lessing et le Christianisme.* Paris, 1964.

Schilson, Arno. *Geschichte im Horizont der Vorsehung: G. E. Lessings Beitrag zu einer Theologie der Geschichte.* Mainz, 1974.

————. *Lessings Christentum.* Göttingen, 1980.

Schlütter, Hans-Jürgen. ". . . als ob die Wahrheit Münze wäre: Zu *Nathan der Weise* III, 6," in *Lessing-Yearbook 10* (1978), 65–74.

Schmölders, Claudia, ed. *Die Kunst des Gesprächs.* Munich, 1979.

Schröder, Jürgen. *Gotthold Ephraim Lessing: Sprache und Drama.* Munich, 1972.

Thielicke, Helmut. *Glauben und Denken in der Neuzeit: Die grossen*

Systeme der Theologie und Religionsphilosophie. Tübingen, 1983 (Chapter 5: Lessing).

―――. *Offenbarung, Vernunft und Existenz: Studien zur Religionsphilosophie Lessings.* 3rd ed. Gütersloh, 1957.

Wessels, Hans-Friedrich. *Lessings "Nathan der Weise": Seine Wirkungsgeschichte bis zum Ende der Goethezeit.* Königstein/Ts., 1979.

FRIEDRICH HÖLDERLIN

Bertaux, Pierre. *Friedrich Hölderlin.* Frankfurt/M., 1978.

Binder, Wolfgang. "Hölderlins 'Friedensfeier,' " in *W.B., Hölderlin-Aufsätze.* Frankfurt/Main, 1970, 294–326.

―――. "Hölderlins Patmos-Hymne," in *W.B., Hölderlin-Aufsätze.* Frankfurt/Main, 1970, 362–402.

Böckmann, Paul. *Hölderlin und seine Götter.* Munich, 1935.

―――. "Hölderlins mythische Welt," in *Hölderlin: Gedenkschrift zu seinem 100. Todestag,* P. Kluckhohn, ed. Tübingen, 1944, 11–49.

Buhr, Heinrich. *Hölderlin und Jesus von Nazareth,* E. Reichle, ed. Pfullingen, 1977.

Guardini, Romano. *Hölderlin: Weltbild und Frömmigkeit.* Munich, 1955.

Häussermann, Ulrich. *Friedensfeier: Eine Einführung in Hölderlins Christus-Hymnen.* Munich, 1959.

Heidegger, Martin. *Erläuterungen zu Hölderlins Dichtung.* Frankfurt, 1944.

Hötzer, Ulrich. *Gestalt des Herakles in Hölderlins Dichtung.* Diss., Tübingen, 1950.

Lachmann, Eduard. *Hölderlins Christus-Hymnen: Text und Auslegung.* Vienna, 1951.

Leube, Martin. *Das Tübinger Stift 1770–1950: Geschichte des Tübinger Stifts.* Stuttgart, 1954.

Müller, Ernst. *Hölderlin: Studien zur Geschichte seines Geistes.* Stuttgart and Berlin, 1944.

Prang, Helmut. "Hölderlins Götter- und Christus-Bild," in *Hölderlin ohne Mythos,* Ingrid Riedel, ed. Göttingen, 1973.

Prignitz, Christoph. *Friedrich Hölderlin: Die Entwicklung seines politischen Denkens unter dem Einfluß der Französischen Revolution.* Hamburg, 1976.

Rehm, Walther. *Griechentum und Goethezeit.* 3rd ed. Munich, 1952.

―――. *Orpheus: Der Dichter und die Toten.* 3rd ed. Düsseldorf, 1950.

Rumpf, Horst. *Die Deutung der Christus-Gestalt bei dem späten Hölderlin.* Diss., Frankfurt, 1958.

Schillemeit, Jost. " '. . . dich zum Fürsten des Festes': Zum Problem der Auslegung von Hölderlins 'Friedensfeier,' " in *Deutsche Vierteljahrsschift für Literaturwissenschaft und Geistesgeschichte*, 51 (1977), 607–27.

Schmidt, Jochen. "Die innere Einheit von Hölderlins 'Friedensfeier,' " in *Hölderlin-Jahrbuch*, Vol. 14 (1965–1966), 125–75.

―――. *Hölderlins Elegie "Brod und Wein": Die Entwicklung des hymnischen Stils in der elegischen Dichtung*. Berlin, 1968.

Schöne, Albrecht. *Säkularisation als sprachbildende Kraft: Studien zur Dichtung deutscher Pfarrersöhne*. 2nd ed. Göttingen, 1968.

Stoll, Robert Thomas. *Hölderlins Christushymnen: Grundlagen und Deutung*. Basel, 1952.

Szondi, Peter. *Einführung in die literarische Hermeneutik*, J. Bollack and H. Stierlin, eds. Frankfurt/M., 1975, 193–427.

Winkler, Eugen Gottlob. "Der späte Hölderlin," in *E. G. W., Dichtungen, Gestalten und Probleme*. Nachlass. Pfullingen, 1956, 314–37.

Wocke, Helmut. *Hölderlins christliches Erbe*. Munich, 1948.

NOVALIS

Behrens, Klaus. *Friedrich Schlegels Geschichtsphilosophie (1794–1808): Ein Beitrag zur politischen Romantik*. Tübingen, 1984.

Benz, Richard. *Die deutsche Romantik: Geschichte einer geistigen Bewegung*. Leipzig, 1937.

Dischner, Gisela, and Richard Faber, eds. *Romantische Utopie, utopische Romantik*. Hildesheim, 1979.

Faber, Richard. *Novalis—Die Phantasie an die Macht*. Stuttgart, 1970.

Haering, Theodor. *Novalis der Philosoph*. Stuttgart, 1954.

Heftrich, Eckhard. *Novalis: Vom Logos der Poesie*. Frankfurt/M., 1969.

Hiebel, Friedrich. *Novalis: Deutscher Dichter, europäischer Denker, christlicher Seher*. 2nd ed. Bern and Munich, 1972.

Kluckhohn, Paul. *Das Ideengut der deutschen Romantik*. Tübingen, 1953, esp. 131–56.

Kommerell, Max. "Hymnen an die Nacht," in *Gedicht und Gedanke, Auslegungen deutscher Gedichte*, Heinz Otto Burger, ed. Halle/Saale 1942, 202–36.

Kuhn, Hans Wolfgang. *Der Apokalyptiker und die Politik: Studien zur Staatsphilosophie des Novalis*. Freiburg i. Br., 1961.

Kurzke, Hermann. *Romantik und Konservatismus: Das "politische" Werk Friedrich von Hardenbergs (Novalis) im Horizont seiner Wirkungsgeschichte*. Munich, 1983.

Lindemann, Klaus. *Geistlicher Stand und religiöses Mittlertum: Ein Bei-*

trag zur Religionsauffassung der Frühromantik in Dichtung und Philosophie. Frankfurt/M., 1971.

Mähl, Hans-Joachim. *Die Idee des goldenen Zeitalters bei Novalis: Studien zur Wesensbestimmung der frühromantischen Utopie und zu ihren ideengeschichtlichen Voraussetzungen*. Heidelberg, 1965.

Malsch, Wilfried. *"Europa"—Poetische Rede des Novalis: Deutung der Französischen Revolution und Reflexion auf die Poesie in der Geschichte*. Stuttgart, 1965.

Minnigerode, Irmtrud von. *Die Christusanschauung des Novalis*. Diss., Tübingen, 1941.

Oberbeck, Helene. *Die religiöse Weltanschauung des Novalis*. Diss., Berlin, 1928.

Peschken, Bernd. *Versuch einer germanistischen Ideologiekritik: Goethe, Lessing, Novalis, Tieck, Hölderlin, Heine in Wilhelm Diltheys und Julian Schmidts Vorstellungen*. Stuttgart, 1972.

Peter, Klaus. *Stadien der Aufklärung: Moral und Politik bei Lessing, Novalis und Friedrich Schlegel*. Wiesbaden, 1980.

Rasch, Wolfdietrich. "Zum Verhältnis der Romantik zur Aufklärung," in *Romantik: Ein literaturwissenschaftliches Studienbuch*, Ernest Ribbat, ed. Königstein/Ts., 1979, 7–21.

Rehm, Walther. *Griechentum und Goethezeit: Geschichte eines Glaubens*. 3rd ed. Munich, 1952, esp. 255–70.

Ribbat, Ernst. (Ed.). *Romantik: Ein literaturwissenschaftliches Studienbuch*. Königstein/Taunus, 1979.

Ritter, Heinz. *Novalis Hymnen an die Nacht*. 2nd ed. Heidelberg, 1974.

Samuel, Richard. "Der Stil des Aufsatzes 'Die Christenheit oder Europa' von Novalis," in *Stoffe, Formen und Strukturen: Hans Heinrich Borcherdt zum 75. Geburtstag*, A. Fuchs and H. Motekat, eds. Munich, 1962, 284–302.

―――. *Die poetische Staats- und Geschichtsauffassung Friedrich von Hardenbergs (Novalis): Studien zur romantischen Geschichtsphilosophie*. Frankfurt/M., 1925.

Schanze, Helmut. *Romantik und Aufklärung: Untersuchungen zu Friedrich Schlegel und Novalis*. Nuremberg, 1966.

Schulz, Gerhard. *Novalis in Selbstzeugnissen und Bilddokumenten*. Reinbek bei Hamburg, 1969.

Seidel, Margot. *Die geistlichen Lieder des Novalis und ihre Stellung zum Kirchenlied*. Diss., Bonn, 1973.

Steinhäuser-Carvill, Barbara. "Die Christenheit oder Europa—eine Predigt," in *Seminar: A Journal of Germanic Studies*, 12 (1976), 73–88.

Strack, Friedrich. *Im Schatten der Neugier: Christliche Tradition und kritische Philosophie im Werk Friedrichs von Hardenberg.* Tübingen, 1982.

Timm, Hermann. *Die heilige Revolution: Das religiöse Totalitätskonzept der Frühromantik: Schleiermacher—Novalis—Friedrich Schlegel.* Frankfurt/M., 1978.

Träger, Claus. "Novalis und die ideologische Restauration," in *Sinn und Form*, 13 (1961), 618–60.

SØREN KIERKEGAARD

Adorno, Theodor W. "Kierkegaard: Konstruktion des Ästhetischen," in *Gesammelte Schriften*, Vol. 2, Frankfurt/Main, 1979.

Anz, Heinrich, Peter Kemp, and Friedrich Schmöe, eds. *Kierkegaard und die deutsche Philosophie seiner Zeit.* Copenhagen/Munich, 1980.

Anz, Heinrich, Poul Lübcke, and Friedrich Schmöe, eds. *Die Rezeption Søren Kierkegaards in der deutschen und dänischen Philosophie und Theologie.* Copenhagen/Munich, 1983.

Bahr, Hans-Eckehard. "Der Widerspruch zwischen Christlichem und Ästhetischem als Konstruktion Kierkegaards," in *Kerygma und Dogma: Zeitschrift für theologische Forschung und kirchliche Lehre*, 6 (1960), 86–103.

——. *Poiesis, Theologische Untersuchung der Kunst.* Stuttgart, (1960).

Elrod, John W. *Kierkegaard and Christendom.* Princeton, 1981.

Fahrenbach, Helmut. "Die gegenwärtige Kierkegaard-Auslegung in der deutschsprachigen Literatur von 1948 bis 1962," in *Philosophische Rundschau*, supplement 3, Tübingen, 1962.

Fischer, Hermann. *Die Christologie des Paradoxes: Zur Herkunft und Bedeutung des Christusverständnisses Søren Kierkegaards.* Göttingen, 1960.

Gerdes, Hayo. *Das Christubild Søren Kierkegaards: Verglichen mit der Christologie Hegels und Schleiermachers.* Düsseldorf/Cologne, 1960.

——. *Das Christusverständnis des jungen Kierkegaard: Ein Beitrag zur Erläuterung des Paradox-Gedankens.* Itzehoe, 1962.

——. *Søren Kierkegaards "Einübung im Christentum": Einführung und Erläuterung.* Darmstadt, 1982.

Hirsch, Emanuel. *Kierkegaard: Studien.* Vol. 1, Reprint. Vaduz/Liechtenst, 1978.

Lowrie, Walter. *Das Leben Søren Kierkegaards.* Düsseldorf/Cologne, 1955.

Patrick, Denzil G. M. *Pascal and Kierkegaard: A Study in the Strategy of Evangelism.* Vols. 1 and 2. London and Redhill, 1947.

Paulsen, Anna. *Søren Kierkegaard: Deuter unserer Existenz.* Hamburg, 1955.

Perpeet, Willi. *Kierkegaard und die Frage nach der Ästhetik der Gegenwart.* Halle/Saale, 1940.

Rehm, Walter. *Kierkegaard und der Verführer.* Munich, 1949.

Rohde, Peter P. *Søren Kierkegaard in Selbstzeugnissen und Bilddokumenten.* Hamburg, 1959.

Schulz, Walter. *Søren Kierkegaard: Existenz und System.* Pfullingen, 1967.

Thielicke, Helmut. *Glauben und Denken in der Neuzeit: Die grossen Systeme der Theologie und Religionsphilosophie.* Tübingen, 1983.

Thulstrup, Marie Mikulová, ed. *The Sources and Depths of Faith in Kierkegaard.* Copenhagen, 1978.

Thulstrup, Niels. *Kierkegaards Verhältnis zu Hegel: Forschungsgeschichte.* Stuttgart, 1969.

————. *Kierkegaards Verhältnis zu Hegel und zum spekulativen Idealismus 1835–1846: Historisch-analytische Untersuchung.* Stuttgart, 1972.

Thulstrup, Niels and Marie Mikulová, eds. *Kierkegaard and Human Values.* Copenhagen, 1980.

————. *Kierkegaard's View of Christianity.* Copenhagen, 1978.

FYODOR MIKHAILOVICH DOSTOYEVSKY

Bachtin, Michail. *Probleme der Poetik Dostoevskijs.* Munich, 1971.

Belknap, Robert L. *The Structure of "The Brothers Karamazov."* Den Haag-Paris, 1967.

Benz, Ernst. "Der widerkehrende Christus," in *Zeitschrift für slavische Philologie,* 11 (1934), 277.

Berdayev, N. *Die Weltanschauung Dostojewskijs.* Munich, 1925.

Bohatec, Josef. *Der Imperialismusgedanke und die Lebensphilosophie Dostojewskijs.* Graz-Cologne, 1951.

Braun, Maximilian. *Dostojewskij, Das Gesamtwerk als Vielfalt und Einheit.* Göttingen, 1976.

Doerne, Martin. *Gott und Mensch in Dostojewskijs Werk.* Göttingen, 1957.

Evdokimov, Paul. *Dostoievsky et le problème du mal.* Paris, 1978.

Forster, E. M. *Aspects of the Novel.* New York, 1927.

Frank, Joseph. *Dostoevsky. Vol. 1: The Seeds of Revolt, 1821–1849; Vol. 2: The Years of Ordeal, 1850–1859.* Princeton, 1976; 1984.

Fülöp-Miller, René, and Friedrich Eckstein. *Der unbekannte Dostojewski.* Munich, 1926.

Gerigk, Horst-Jürgen. *Nachwort zu Dostojewski, Die Brüder Karamasoff.* Munich, 1978, 1031–52.

Gibson, A. Boyce. *The Religion of Dostoevsky.* Philadelphia, 1973.

Guardini, Romano. *Religiöse Gestalten in Dostojewskijs Werk: Studien über den Glauben.* Munich, 1951.

Imbach, Josef. *Dostojewski und die Gottesfrage in der heutigen Theologie.* Rome, 1973.

Jones, Malcolm V., and Garth M. Terry, eds. *New Essays on Dostoyevsky.* Cambridge, 1983.

Komarowitsch, W. *Dostojewski, Die Urgestalt der Brüder Karamasoff.* Munich, 1928.

Lauth, Reinhard. *Die Philosophie Dostojewskis.* Munich, 1950.

————. "Zur Genesis der Grossinquisitor-Erzählung," in *Zeitschrift für Religions- und Geistesgeschichte,* 6 (1954), 265–76.

Lavrin, Janko. *Fjodor M. Dostojevskij in Selbstzeugnissen und Bilddokumenten.* Reinbek b. Hamburg, 1963.

Lettenbauer, Wilhelm. "Zur Deutung der Legende vom 'Grossinquisitor' Dostoevskijs," in *Die Welt der Slaven,* 5 (1960), 329–33.

Linnér, Sven. *Starets Zossima in* The Brothers Karamazov: *A Study in the Mimesis of Virtue.* Stockholm, 1981.

Maceina, Antanas. *Der Großinquisitor: Geschichtsphilosophische Deutung der Legende Dostojewskijs.* Heidelberg, 1952.

Mann, Thomas. "Dostojewski—mit Massen," in *Gesammelte Werke 9,* Frankfurt/M., 1960, 565–74.

Meier-Graefe, Julius. *Dostojewski, der Dichter.* Berlin, 1926.

Minor, Jakob. *Goethes Fragmente vom ewigen Juden und vom wiederkehrenden Heiland.* Stuttgart and Berlin, 1904.

Müller, Ludolf, "Die Gestalt Christi in Leben und Werk Dostojewskijs," in *Quatember, Vierteljahrshefte für Erneuerung und Einheit der Kirche,* 45 (1981), 68–76.

————. *Dostojewskij: Sein Leben, sein Werk, sein Vermächtnis.* Munich, 1982.

Nigg, Walter. *Religiöse Denker: Kierkegaard, Dostojewski, Nietzsche, Van Gogh.* Bern, 1942, 109ff.

Onasch, Konrad. *Dostojewski als Verführer: Christentum und Kunst in der Dichtung Dostojewskis—Ein Versuch.* Zürich, 1961.

————. *Dostojewski-Biographie: Materialsammlung zur Beschäftigung mit religiösen und theologischen Fragen in der Dichtung F. M. Dostojewskis.* Zürich, 1960.

Rammelmeyer, Alfred. "Dostojevskij und Voltaire," in *Zeitschrift für slavische Philologie,* 26 (1958), 252–78.

Rehm, Walter. *Experimentum Medietatis: Studien zur Geistes- und Literaturgeschichte des 19. Jahrhunderts.* Munich, 1947. (See "Zur dichterischen Gestaltung des Unglaubens bei Jean Paul und Dostojewski," 7–95.)

Sperber, Manès. *Wir und Dostojewskij, Eine Debatte mit Heinrich Böll,*

Siegfried Lenz, André Malraux, Hans Erich Nossack. Hamburg, 1972.

Steinbüchel, Theodor. *F. M. Dostojewski: Sein Bild vom Menschen und vom Christen.* Düsseldorf, 1947.

Stephun, Fedor. *Dostojewskij und Tolstoi, Christentum und soziale Revolution.* Munich, 1961.

Sutherland, Stewart R. *Atheism and the Rejection of God: Contemporary Philosophy and* The Brothers Karamazov. Oxford, 1977.

Thurneysen, Eduard. *Dostojewski.* Munich, 1925.

Tschizewski, Dimitrij. "Schiller und die 'Brüder Karamazov,' " in *Zeitschrift für slavische Philologie,* 6 (1929), 1–42.

Wellek, René, ed. *Dostoevsky: A Collection of Critical Essays.* Englewood Cliffs, NJ, 1962.

FRANZ KAFKA

Anders, Günther. *Kafka: Pro und Contra: Die Prozessunterlagen.* Munich, 1951.

Beicken, Peter U. *Franz Kafka: Eine kritische Einführung in die Forschung.* Frankfurt, 1974.

Beissner, Friedrich. *Der Erzähler Franz Kafka.* Stuttgart, 1952.

————. *Kafka der Dichter.* Stuttgart, 1958.

————. *Kafkas Darstellung des "traumhaften inneren Lebens."* Tübingen, 1972.

————, ed. *Kafka-Handbuch in zwei Bänden.* Stuttgart, 1979.

————. *Kafka in neuer Sicht. Mimik, Gestik und Personengefüge als Darstellungsformen des Autobiographischen.* Stuttgart, 1976.

————. *Kafka Kommentar zu den Romanen, Rezensionen, Aphorismen und zum Brief an den Vater.* Munich, 1976.

Binder, Hartmut. *Kafka: Kommentar zu sämtlichen: Erzählungen.* Munich, 1975.

Brod, Max, ed. *Franz Kafka: Briefe 1902–1924.* New York, 1958 (ed. published under license from Frankfurt).

Buber, Martin. *Zwei Glaubensweisen.* Zürich, 1950.

Caputo-Mayr, Maria Luise, ed. *Franz Kafka: Eine Aufsatzsammlung nach einem Symposium in Philadelphia.* Berlin/Darmstadt, 1978.

David, Claude. *Zwischen Dorf und Schloss.* "Kafkas Schloss-Roman als theologische Fabel," in *Wissen aus Erfahrungen: Werkbegriff und Interpretation heute: Festschrift für Herman Meyer zum 65. Geburtstag,* Alexander von Bormann, ed. Tübingen, 1976, 694–711.

Emrich, Wilhelm. *Franz Kafka.* Wiesbaden, 1975.

Fietz, Lothar. Möglichkeiten und Grenzen einer Deutung von Kafkas Schloss-Roman," in *DVjs,* 37 (1963), 71–77.

Flores, Angel, ed. *The Kafka Debate: New Perspectives for Our Time.* New York, 1977.

Göhler, Hulda. *Franz Kafka: Das Schloss.* Bonn, 1982.

Heller, Erich. "Die Welt Franz Kafkas," in *Heller, Enterbter Geist: Essays.* Frankfurt, 1954, 281–329.

———. *Franz Kafka.* Munich, 1976.

Henel, Ingeborg. "Die Türhüterlegende und ihre Bedeutung für Kafkas 'Prozess,' " in *DVjs*, 37 (1963), 50–70.

Höntzsch, Fred. "Gericht und Gnade in der Dichtung Franz Kafkas," in *Hochland*, 31, 2 (1933–1934), 160–67.

Isermann, Gerhard. *Unser Leben—unser Prozeß: Theologische Fragen bei Franz Kafka.* Wuppertal, 1969 (Das Gespräch, no. 83).

Kienlechner, Sabina. *Negativität der Erkenntnis im Werk Franz Kafkas.* Tübingen, 1981.

Kraft, Herbert. *Mondheimat: Kafka.* Pfullingen, 1983, 189–210.

Kurz, Paul Konrad. "Standorte der Kafka-Deutung," in *Kurz, Über moderne Literatur.* Frankfurt, 1967, 38–71.

Nicolai, Ralf R. *Ende oder Anfang: Zur Einheit der Gegensätze in Kafkas "Schloss."* Munich, 1977.

Philippi, Klaus-Peter. *Reflexion und Wirklichkeit: Untersuchungen zu Kafkas Roman "Das Schloss."* Tübingen, 1966.

Politzer, Heinz. *Franz Kafka, der Künstler.* Frankfurt, 1965.

Ries, Wiebrecht. *Transzendenz als Terror: Eine religionsphilosophische Studie über Franz Kafka.* Heidelberg, 1977.

Rochefort, Robert. *Kafka oder die unzerstörbare Hoffnung.* Vienna/ Munich, 1955.

Schoeps, Hans-Joachim. "Franz Kafka und der Mensch unserer Tage," in *Universitas*, 16, 2 (1961), 163–71.

Sokel, Walter H. *Franz Kafka–Tragik und Ironie: Zur Struktur seiner Kunst.* Munich, Vienna, 1964.

Stern, J. P., ed. *The World of Franz Kafka.* London, 1980.

Swander, Homer. "Zu Kafkas 'Schloss,' " in *Interpretationen 3, Deutsche Romane von Grimmelshausen bis Musil,* Jost Schillemeit, ed. Frankfurt, 1966, 269–89.

Wagenbach, Klaus. *Franz Kafka: In Selbstzeugnissen und Bilddokumenten dargestellt.* Reinbek, 1964.

———. "Wo liegt Kafkas Schloss?" in *Born, Dietz, Pasley, Raabe, Wagenbach: Kafka-Symposion.* Berlin, 1965, 161–80.

Weltsch, Felix. *Religion und Humor im Leben und Werk Franz Kafkas.* Berlin, 1957.

Wilhelm, Rigobert. "Das Religiöse in der Dichtung Franz Kafkas," in *Hochland*, 57 (1965–1965), 335–49.